THE POET KAO CH'I

THE POET KAO CH'I

1336-1374

BY F. W. MOTE

PRINCETON, NEW JERSEY

PRINCETON UNIVERSITY PRESS

1962

*

Publication of this book has been aided by
a grant from the Research Fund of Princeton University
and by the Ford Foundation Program to support publication, through university presses, of works
in the humanities and social sciences

*

Printed in the United States of America
by Princeton University Press, Princeton, New Jersey

TO THE MEMORY OF

WANG CH'UNG-WU

TEACHER · SCHOLAR · FRIEND

PREFACE

THE ONLY MODERN SCHOLAR who, to my knowledge, has written importantly about Kao Ch'i is Wang Ch'ung-wu, a leading specialist in Ming history of the Institute of History and Philology of the Academia Sinica, and subsequently of the Academy of Sciences until his recent death in Peking. Professor Wang's suggestive article, *"Tu Kao Ch'ing-ch'iu 'Wei Ai Lun,' "* written in 1942 (CYYY No. 12, 1947, pp. 273-82), was the starting point of my interest in and study of Kao Chi's life. His help in my study of the fourteenth century leaves me perpetually indebted to him. I must also acknowledge the assistance of Professor Cheng Ch'ien of the Department of Chinese Literature of National Taiwan University. In my study of Chinese poetry I have benefitted much from his instruction. He has read and criticized several of the translations included here, particularly the "Song of the Man of the Green Hill." However, Professor Cheng has not read this biography of Kao Ch'i, nor has he read most of the translations; hence the responsibility for errors and shortcomings is entirely my own. Portions of Chapters Two, Three, and Four of this book were presented before the Fifth Conference on Chinese Thought, held at Suffern, New York, in September 1960. To Arthur F. Wright, the chairman and organizer of that conference, and to its dozen participants who read and criticized those portions of the book at that time, I must record a debt of gratitude. I hope that they will note errors corrected, concepts clarified, and arguments strengthened as a result of their helpful and penetrating discussions. I must also acknowledge with gratitude the help given by P. J. Conkwright of the Princeton University Press, in aiding with the maps. Ch'en Hsiao-lan too worked on the maps, and contributed in innumerable other ways to the work of transforming an idea into a book.

CONTENTS

CONTENTS

ILLUSTRATIONS

THE POET KAO CH'I

INTRODUCTION

THE CHINESE POET Kao Ch'i is usually regarded as the best of his century, and many critics throughout the succeeding centuries have ranked him as the best the Ming dynasty (1368-1644) produced. He lived only into the seventh year of that dynasty, when he was executed by its founding emperor, ostensibly on suspicion of sedition —actually, perhaps, for other reasons. He died at the age of thirty-eight before, as the critics have agreed, his immense powers reached their fruition. Even though he merits a high position in China's literary history, he is little known in China today, and virtually unknown in the West. In the traditional view of Chinese scholars, the Ming dynasty was not a great age for poetry, and in this as in other cases Westerners have developed a traditional Chinese view into an extreme prejudice. Few of the great poets of the last two or three dynasties are known in the West; none perhaps rewards the effort to know him more richly than Kao Ch'i.

Yet to know him requires some effort, for despite the greatness of his poetry, to have been the best poet of his age has won him little fame, and the circumstances of his death caused his poetry to be somewhat unnaturally obscured during the remaining two and a half centuries of the Ming dynasty. To a certain extent, men of that age were prevented from writing about him, and from praising him highly. Thus even the facts of his life were recorded in less detail than otherwise would have been the case. This contributed further to his undeserved obscurity.

But our interest in Kao Ch'i is not alone in his poetry. In this effort to re-create his life, the poetry is looked upon primarily as a source for the historian and not as art in its own right. Our purpose is not to restore to him the fame which he merits as a poet. Rather it is to see him as a man of his time, remarkable by reason of his artistic genius, but also a man whose life represents for us something of the significance of the age in which he lived. Through him we are enabled to see much of his time and his place, his society and his civilization. In his poetry we find a marvelously sensitive record of what the great and small affairs of his daily life, as well as some of the larger issues of his time, meant to a man like him. This discovery may bring us closer to the meaning of his life, and of his times. As the work of an historian, this is the effort toward which this biography strives.

Kao Ch'i's life illustrates several things of possible interest and importance in the study of Chinese history. His biography in the official dynastic history of the period (the *Ming Shih*, ch. 285, *Po-na* edition, p. 21-b) is one page, less than 200 characters, in length. His funerary inscription, eulogies, and other early biographical materials were written at a time and under circumstances which prevented a full and objective account of his life from being written. Thus the materials of the kind on which the historian usually depends are negligible. Yet, as the leading poet of his age and as a man who played an important role in the affairs of his age, his life is of historical importance. Little of Kao Ch'i's life can be reconstructed from the few strictly biographical materials and historical documents. The present work is an attempt to reconstruct it more fully from existing materials of that kind, taken together with those which the historian usually does not use, at least not carefully and exhaustively. I refer primarily to his poetry, the poetry of his friends and associates, and their other belletristic writings. Such writings from Kao Ch'i and his circle serve here as a major source material for history, and illustrate the peculiarly close relationship of history and literature in China. *Wen shih pu fen chia*, "Literature and History do not divide their patrimony," says an old Chinese academic maxim, or more simply, literature and history are inseparable. The wisdom, indeed the necessity, of observing this is widely recognized but inadequately followed. This life of Kao Ch'i and study of his times is an attempt to observe it as fully as is possible, and at least part of its motivation is to exploit this method of historical study.

To the Chinese student of his traditional civilization, Kao Ch'i's importance lies chiefly in the field of literature. But only the Chinese student of literature has access to Kao Ch'i the poet, unless we too can read his poetry in the original, or in those rare translations which stand as poetry in their own right. And even the great translators can do no more than open a small door on the realm of Chinese literary values. Although a fascinating source for the historian, Kao Ch'i's poetry strongly tempts him to forget history and read it simply as art. Ideally in this case, the historian himself should be an Arthur Waley,[1] an Ezra Pound, or a Kenneth Rexroth. Many of the poems so stiffly translated here deserve the services of a poet-translator of that high caliber; the versions presented here as historical documents are indeed a disservice to Kao Ch'i the artist. But poet-translators inevitably would have chosen in many cases other poems to translate. The historian-translator or biographer-translator must select for content of a particular kind; the poem which reveals the most interesting facts is not always the poem which embodies the greatest artistic achievement, or which can be translated the most effectively. Yet I think there are few poems in Kao Ch'i's extensive collection that do not, in the original Chinese, reveal his stature as a poet. Should this study of Kao Ch'i's life serve to call him to the attention of a

[1] Waley, of course, uniquely possesses the qualifications of historian, poet, and sinologue.

poet-translator, the disservice to Kao Ch'i the artist may yet be remedied, and Kao Ch'i's importance in the field of literature may also someday come to be appreciated in the West.

Here our interest is in Kao Ch'i the man, revealed to us primarily by Kao Ch'i the poet. In reconstructing the civilization of China's fourteenth century, the career and the thought of a man like Kao Ch'i are important. While he did not have a long or glorious official career, the career to which he was drawn and to which he had access, and his reasons for making the choices he made, are of greatest interest. Likewise, while he is not a philosopher of original achievement, he is a good example of an important kind of scholar-intellectual-artist in early modern China. And, insofar as we can reconstruct his life, he is a man whose attitudes toward life interest and inform us. In particular, he exemplifies a peculiarly Chinese concept of and urge toward "heroism," a kind of Confucian heroic virtue that differs greatly from expressions of heroism more common in the West. This heroism reflects the Chinese cosmology and embodies the humanistic values of its cultural tradition. Thus while they are superficially relevant, Carlyle's "Hero as Poet" or "Hero as Man of Letters," for example, are misleading comparisons. Kao Ch'i's concept of heroism is implicit in his life and his writings, and it may be of some interest to attempt to draw forth a definition and an understanding of it. Of central importance here are the concepts of the good society, the individual's responsibility to work for its realization, and the role of poetry in expressing the heroic individual's sensitiveness to these values and in evidencing his capacities for their realization. Moreover, an understanding of these things illuminates aspects of the role of poetry in China's traditional civilization that might not be visible from easy analogy to our own civilization. For Kao Ch'i, although the greatest poet of his age, was not a professional poet in the sense that we think of the poet in the West. Being a poet was not an eccentric form of behavior, although being a great poet was as rare and valuable a thing then as ever. It was not his life in poetry which identified Kao Ch'i in the minds of his contemporaries, even though it was his startling achievement in poetry that displayed to them his potentiality for human greatness. Ideally, poetry was not an end in itself, although in the less-than-ideal circumstances in which his career worked itself out, it may well have come to substitute for the larger ideal. Thus the failure, intentional and unavoidable, of this work to become a literary biography of Kao Ch'i, and the effort to use his poetry as no more than a mirror in which to see the man, may not do too great violence to the values by which he would have wanted to be judged.

CHAPTER ONE

PROLOGUE: THE SMUGGLERS, THE CLERK,

AND THE MONK

ABOUT THE MIDDLE of the fourteenth century a strange collection of men became the leading figures on the stage of Chinese history. They were in almost no way characteristic of the actors who usually dominated that stage. It was as if the proper drama had paused for a long intermission, during which a whole arena of character players and minor stars were allowed to occupy stage front and center. These proved to be a motley assortment of thieves and villains, ruffians and rascals, clowns and bit players. The main drama gave way temporarily to what seemed to be a talent show for amateurs, a chaos of smaller acts.

And yet, as it turned out, this confusing interlude was no intermission, for out of it developed a new variation on the classic theme. Before it was over, the proper drama had emerged again from its midst. The welter of simultaneous performances gradually gave way to one unifying series of episodes, expanding in scope until finally the whole stage was held by it. Before the end of the third quarter of the century, a new episode, which proclaimed itself the Great Ming dynasty, had taken over the theater of Chinese history. It held unchallenged sway for 276 years. The transition out of long decades of chaos through a sudden and dramatic climax of events in the 1360's appeared as if from the sidelines. No one seemed to notice its beginnings, and no one would have predicted that this odd actor, a tall, lean-faced, and strikingly ugly youth dressed in the ragged robes of a mendicant Buddhist monk, would be transformed into the new hero. But such was the case. For this talented and untypical amateur in the monk's robes was Chu Yuan-chang, founder and first emperor of the Great Ming dynasty.

The Great Ming dynasty's predecessor was the Great Yuan dynasty, the dynasty of the Mongols. Under Genghis Khan the Mongols had started out to conquer China merely for raid and plunder, and under Genghis' successors they managed to gain military control of the northern third of China proper. Finally under Genghis' grandson, Kubilai Khan, the Mongols completed their conquest of China in the years 1275-1279. Gradually they changed their objectives from sudden plunder by raid to prolonged plunder through rule. To Kubilai, being emperor of China came to be more important than being the Great Khan of the Mongol Hordes. But neither Kubilai nor his much less competent successors could see very far beyond plunder and exploitation, to the underlying problems of government. Kubilai may have tried to fulfill the responsibilities of rule, and without much success, but his successors were lesser men, most of whom died violent deaths after brief reigns marked by excesses, viciousness, and callous disregard. The Great Yuan dynasty was an age of suffering for the Chinese people, a century in which their livelihood, their government, and their ancient civilization suffered grave decline.

Rebellion against the Mongol rulers had smoldered since their invasion of the country in the early part of the thirteenth century, but so overwhelming was Mongol military strength then that no real rebellion came to pass. Later in the century, during Kubilai's reign (1260-1294), there were several "Chinese" attempts to throw off the oppressive and discriminatory alien rule. Throughout the fourteenth century Kubilai's heirs, who scarcely seemed concerned, relinquished more and more of the effective control of the empire. By the 1350's, rebellions openly challenged the imperial rule in all parts of the country, but particularly in the region lying on the southeast edge of the Central Plain—the northern parts of modern Anhwei and Kiangsu, and the western part of Shantung. This region along the Huai River, between the lower reaches of the Yellow and Yangtze rivers, was relatively poor. It had been devastated by the invasions and subsequent harsh rule of the Chin Tartars in the early part of the twelfth century, and again by the Mongol conquest of North China in the early part of the thirteenth. The population was greatly reduced even before the disasters of the fourteenth century, in the first half of which famine, plague, drought, and locusts struck year after year. At the same time, the poverty and distress produced disorders with which the local government found itself increasingly unable to deal. Deteriorating conditions gradually brought about general chaos. Finally in 1351 there was a great flood of the Yellow River, which broke its dykes and inundated the Huai region, leaving further misery in its path. The following year an ambitious high official, anxious to make his reputation, obtained permission from the unconcerned Mongol court to repair the dykes and restore the river to its old channel. Although the official's notions of hydraulic engineering command our respect, his methods in mobilizing the people of the region to perform the labor aroused further hatred of the government, and provided an explosive situation conducive to rebellion. Hundreds of thousands of people were mobilized and forced to provide their own rations while slaving under armed guard on the labor of dredging and dyking. It was unwise to bring masses of disgruntled and hungry peasants together, where any inflammatory leadership could turn them into an army of desperation. The opportunity to do this was not missed.

Rebellious leadership came from several quarters, but all of it had certain features in common. It all came from the lower levels of society, from the poor, and in many cases the illiterate or nearly illiterate peasants. Moreover, much of it came from semiclandestine religious movements, movements combining a potent magical doctrine with fanciful and impractical social and political objectives. The Huai region had long been a stronghold of the White Lotus religion. This was a vulgarized form of Buddhism with strong additions of the superstitious folk religions. Throughout the almost one thousand years that it had existed in China, from its inception as a highly philosophical sect in the early part of the fifth century, it had evolved to the point of becoming the antithesis of the original White Lotus Society. Eventually a secret sect, preaching that the Pure Land would be achieved on earth with the coming of the Buddha Maitreya, it promised a millennium that implied the destruction of the present world order, and hence was dangerously rebellious. Successive dynasties had suppressed it, but it remained strong among the common people in some regions. The Huai region was one of these in the late Mongol period. In its vulgarized forms, however, this sect worshipping Maitreya became indistinct from other vulgarized forms of the worship of Maitreya, some of which had absorbed Manichean doctrines in the T'ang period. In these sects, Maitreya, whose symbolic color was white, came to stand for the forces of light which would triumph over the forces of darkness. This too was a rebellious doctrine, for it preached dissatisfaction with the present world; the worse conditions became, the surer were its believers that the forces of light would soon conquer the world. Thus desperation fed hope, and the more desperate the common people became, the more willing they were to risk their lives for movements whose leaders claimed to be the agents or the personifications of Maitreya, or of the

Prince of Radiance (*Ming Wang*). In fact, these two doctrines and their leading deities became hopelessly merged and jumbled, and in the popular conception they were one. By the middle of the fourteenth century, leaders of the sect were secretly gathering the people to burn incense and listen to the prophecies of the end of this world of suffering. Their color symbolism had changed—perhaps under Manichean influence—so that red instead of white now represented to them fire and light and conquering radiance. From their conspiratorial religious convocations at which the burning of incense was the principal rite, they became known as the Incense Army. From their use of red banners and headcloths, they became known as the Red Army, or the Red Turbans. They had acquired a political objective—the restoration of the revered Sung dynasty, which had fallen to the Mongols in 1279. A child called Han Lin-erh, of a family that for generations had been active in the White Lotus religion, now was said to be the descendant of the old Sung imperial line, and at the same time bore the title of Prince of Radiance. Han Lin-erh's father was among those who saw the possibilities in the vast Yellow River dyking project. He circulated the jingle predicting: "A stone man with one eye; disturb the Yellow River and the whole world will revolt." He had a stone figure with one eye buried in the path of the river project where the conscript peasant laborers were sure to find it. When they did, proving his prophecy, the people were greatly stirred. Unrest swept across the region, and several Red Turban leaders rose up to establish local regimes acknowledging the restored "Sung" dynasty and defying the authority of the Yuan. The Mongols badgered them intermittently, but could not mobilize enough military force to deal decisively with all of them. It was the beginning of the end for the hated Mongol regime.

The Red Turban movement, unified by loose agreement

on certain aspects of their doctrine, lacked centralized leadership. The area throughout which it was spread was very great, and historians customarily have referred to it as having two main wings. The one was the north or the east wing, centered on the Huai region, but spreading to neighboring portions of modern Kiangsu, Shantung, Hopei, and Honan. The other was the west or south wing, centered on the middle Yangtze valley, with its main strength in modern Hupei. Originally the whole movement may have sprung directly from the activities of one man, a Buddhist monk at a monastery in Yuan-chou (in what would be modern Kiangsi) called P'eng Ying-yü, who appears to have been a fervent and inspiring organizer. As early as 1338 an ill-organized peasant mob of five thousand had revolted under leadership inspired by his preaching. Like the Boxers in 1901, they put the word *fu*, meaning Buddha, on front and back of their jackets, thinking thereby to gain protection against spear or sword. This premature effort was easily crushed by local government forces, and P'eng fled into the Huai region, where he continued his undercover agitation. He is the one prominent organizer who was active in both the eastern and western wings, and he remained the chief leader of the latter.

But the doctrines of the sect did not command disciplined adherence, and the organization was of the loosest kind. No one leader ever succeeded in mobilizing all the latent strength in this vast movement. Generally speaking, the eastern wing acknowledged the pretensions of Han Lin-erh, who was manipulated by a wily organizer called Liu Fu-t'ung, and adhered to the fiction of the restoration of the Sung dynasty. After 1355 they used the new reign-title *lung-feng*. The western wing, calling itself the T'ien-wan dynasty, was led by a man called Hsü Shou-hui. He had been selected by P'eng Ying-yü to proclaim himself emperor in 1351. When conflicts of interest developed eventually between adherents of the two wings, they fought each other as readily as they fought other enemies. But in 1351, the year of their general uprising, they represented together a loosely knit movement that stretched from Shantung southwest to the Yangtze and beyond in Hupei and Hunan, cutting the Mongol empire of China in two. It was never reunited until the Mongols were driven out and the new Ming dynasty established to succeed them.

These Red Turban rebellions were not actually the first successfully to defy the Yuan government in the last decades of its rule, but once the widespread disorders of the incense burners broke out, it became clear to all that the Mongols could no longer maintain any pretense of local authority in well over half the empire. The Mongol court itself was torn by bloody factionalism. It feared the Chinese, and would not trust Chinese officials with positions of power. Its military arm, on which its rule had always rested, was now weakened and divided. But as the military was the only source of power, leaders of the different court factions fought bitterly to control it. The strongest military force which the court could now use was not its regular Mongol armies, which had disintegrated and no longer served to garrison much of China proper. Rather, it was the local forces recruited and led by certain officials loyal to the throne. One such official was Chagan Timur, a Mongol whose family had settled in what would be modern Honan and had intermarried with local Chinese. Chagan Timur was a man of great military ability, and when nearby areas of the Great Central Plain fell to rebels in 1352, he organized an army led by kinsmen and associates to restore order and the authority of the Mongol throne. His initial successes were rewarded by the throne with high office. He pacified much of North China, and in 1359 defeated the Red Turbans at K'ai-feng, where Liu Fu-t'ung had established his "Sung" emperor, Han Lin-erh. But he had already come into conflict with a jealous rival Mongol leader Bolo Timur, and in 1360 the two used their armies against each other instead of fighting the rebels. The Mongol court was unable to make peace between the two. Still a third Mongol leader, the Chancellor Toqto, also combined strong military power with political ambitions; in addition, he held office at the central court, which gave him decisive control of political maneuvering there. It was he who in 1352 suppressed the Red Turban uprising that had seized Hsü-chou the previous year, killing the peasant leader "Sesame-seed Li" and forcing the other local leaders to flee to the Huai region headquarters. In 1354 Toqto followed this up with decisive victories over Chang Shih-ch'eng at Kao-yu, in northern Kiangsu, and it was generally expected that he would continue westward into the Huai region and clear it of all rebellious activity. But the court became jealous of his waxing powers, and ordered him to the far west, where he was murdered before the year was over. His death deprived the court of its most vigorous high official. It also caused many previously loyal officials to recognize the futility of struggling further for the Mongol cause, and emboldened would-be insurgents to defy the Mongol government. The factions of Bolo Timur and Chagan Timur tended to splinter and quarrel among themselves, greatly reducing their effectiveness as defenders of the Mongol cause. In 1362 Chagan Timur was assassinated by a turncoat insurgent whom he had pardoned. His adopted son—actually his nephew, born into the Chinese family of his wife and thus not even a Mongol, but given the Mongol name of Koqko Timur—inherited Chagan's military forces and government positions, and soon emerged as the most formidable figure in the pro-Mongol camp. But Koqko, too, was deeply involved in revenge of his foster-father's death, in other factional struggles, and in empire-building activities of his own. Known in history both as Koqko Timur and by his Chinese name Wang Pao-pao, he was undoubtedly one of the most capable men of his age. The Ming founder later called him the best and most admirable of his enemies. But although his career extended well into the 1370's and included brilliant military achievements, Koqko Timur was too heavily involved in damaging factional struggles to produce any lasting accomplishments. And thus throughout the 1350's and 1360's the Mongol power dwindled and disappeared, and the whole of China, but particularly the Great Central Plain and the northern provinces, descended into disorder and chaos. Not only the Red Turbans, but ambitious rebels of all kinds, set out to win for themselves bandit strongholds, then self-styled princedoms, and finally to contest for the Mandate of Heaven.

This story concerns the "Southeast" corner of China, a term which is not geographically accurate, but which historically designates the lower Yangtze delta region. In Chinese history the region is also known as Chiang-yu or the right bank of the Yangtze, and as Che-hsi or the west bank of the Che River. Both names are fixed in history, having served in earlier times as the names of administrative subdivisions of the empire. The region is known historically and poetically as Wu, from the dialect spoken there, and from early kingdoms that bore the name in that general area in late Chou times (before 221 B.C.) and in the third century A.D. Wu, however, is an ambiguous geographical designation, sometimes meaning the whole lower Yangtze region, sometimes the prefecture of Soochow, and sometimes other groupings of prefectures in the triangle between the modern cities of Nanking, Shanghai, and Hangchow. It is this triangle lying just south of the Yangtze and bordering the sea that concerns us, and we shall call it the Southeast. In the Southern Sung period it had held the capital of the empire (Hangchow, then called Lin-an), and its other great city was Soochow. It was the richest and most populous part of China.

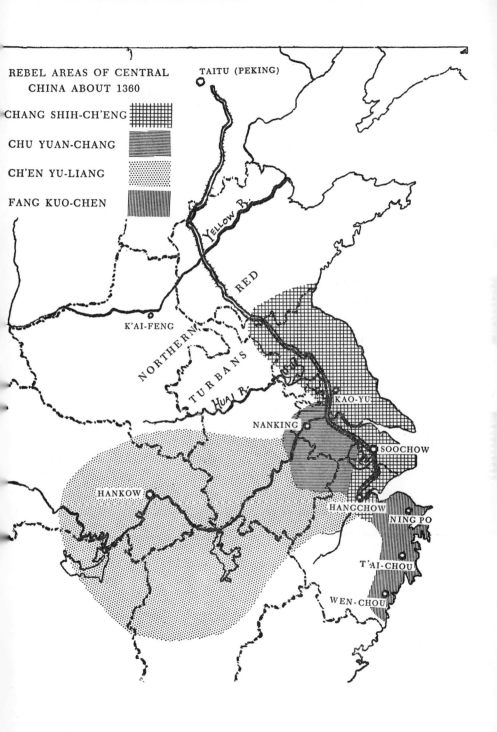

REBEL AREAS OF CENTRAL
CHINA ABOUT 1360

CHANG SHIH-CH'ENG

CHU YUAN-CHANG

CH'EN YU-LIANG

FANG KUO-CHEN

TAITU (PEKING)

YELLOW R.

RED

K'AI-FENG

NORTHERN

TURBANS

HUAI R.

KAO-YU

NANKING

SOOCHOW

HANKOW

HANGCHOW

NING PO

T'AI-CHOU

WEN-CHOU

In the Mongol period it remained the cultural and commercial center of the nation, although the political capital was in the north, at modern Peking. For example, the census of 1393 (early in the Ming period and the first census after the late Yuan period) shows that the single prefecture of Soochow had a registered population of two and a half million persons, while the entire province of Shantung, the most populous in the north, had only five and a quarter million persons. And in the Yuan period, the memorials of officials frequently refer to the wealth of the region, saying that Soochow and four neighboring prefectures customarily supplied seventy per cent of the revenues of the entire realm. While this is something of an exaggeration, it is true that the Southeast supplied the grain which was transported to the capital at Peking each year by the canal or by sea, and thus was of crucial economic importance to the Yuan government.

The Huai region adjoined the Southeast on the north, just across the Yangtze. The Huai belonged to "North China"; it was an arid region of marginal agriculture and wheat farming. The Southeast, however, was "South China," a lush and verdant rice-growing region of much more abundant life. The Southeast managed to remain somewhat more placid than the areas surrounding it on all sides. Perhaps because economic pressures were less severe and distress afflicted fewer of its people, it maintained far greater political and social stability throughout the whole Mongol period. Yet it was the prize sought by ambitious rebellious leaders and Yuan loyalists alike, for control of its resources was crucial to the success of both. Thus our story, centered on the Southeast, inevitably concerns the rebellious movements in the immediately adjacent regions. Most important were those of the two smuggler rebels, the clerk who became a rebel leader, and the monk who became bandit, rebel prince, and finally emperor. These were the four leading figures in the chaotic drama of the Southeast in the 1350's and 1360's.

FANG KUO-CHEN

The first of the smugglers was Fang Kuo-chen. The histories describe him as a tall man of impressive appearance and great physical strength, with a dark and ferocious countenance. He was not a very ambitious man, nor did he possess any special talents or unusual qualities. Fang was clearly no contestant for the Mandate of Heaven. He was a troublemaker, a typical bandit chief, out for profit and little else. He was a native of T'ai-chou (modern Lin-hai) on the central Chekiang coast, from a family that engaged in sea transport of salt. Salt was an important government monopoly, and as a source of income to the state, second in importance only to the agrarian taxes. Its production and distribution were closely regulated. Profits to be made from illicit distribution and sale were enormous; hence those legally engaged in such activity often used their legal connection with the trade as a cover for smuggling.

In 1348 an enemy of the Fang family reported Fang Kuo-chen to the authorities for having illicit dealings of this kind with a notorious pirate of the Chekiang coastal waters. Government forces were dispatched to seize Fang. He got wind of the matter, murdered the informer and his entire family, and then with his three brothers and their families took to the sea to engage in open piracy. In the following years he attacked and sacked coastal cities such as Wen-chou and T'ai-chou. He repeatedly defeated government forces sent against him, and after 1351, when the Red Turban uprising in the Huai region threatened the Grand Canal, cutting the capital off from its grain shipments from the Southeast, the court was forced to make peace with Fang. They offered him an official position if he would use his naval forces to defend the lower Yangtze, and, if need be, to ship grain to the north by the coastal sea route. He refused appointments to prefectural governorships in interior locations, realizing full well that the source of his unlimited bargaining power with the Yuan court was his naval force, said to have numbered over a thousand ships of all sizes and kinds. He accepted official appointment from the Yuan court in order to remove that pressure and to give himself greater freedom of movement, but he did little or nothing for the government that did not also profit himself directly. Moreover he was a treacherous collaborator, on several occasions renouncing his association with the government, slaughtering Yuan officials and plundering government strongholds, and turning again to piracy. In ordinary times a man like Fang Kuo-chen would have been unable to lead such a career; the government would have marshalled forces sufficient to eradicate him. But in this age the government was beset by uprisings on all sides, and was forced to try to win over rebels by offering them legitimacy and the opportunity for proper careers in officialdom. Fang, however, was interested only in loot, and he flaunted the government, alternately taking up and putting aside the proffered legitimacy as it suited his whim and his immediate interests. This is a game that local and regional military leaders have always been able to play with weakened central governments—some men have built great careers on the possibilities inherent in this situation. But Fang lacked such vision. He never became more than a robber baron, and although a real threat to safety and stability in the region, none of the more ambitious regional leaders who were his rivals in the Southeast at this time took him seriously. They all recognized, as did the Mongol court, that he was merely treacherous, not really dangerous.

Fang Kuo-chen ultimately acquired a land base as well as his naval forces. In 1356 the desperate Yuan court made another effort to recruit his help, both in suppressing other nearby rebels and in shipping grain to Peking by the sea route. They offered him the local administrative control of Wen-chou, T'ai-chou, and Ningpo, three coastal prefectures of Chekiang. This he accepted, and actually supplied the ships for some token deliveries of grain to the capital. As governor of three prefectures with a population of about two million people, he had a strong base from which he might have expanded inland, and in the next few years he made some moves in this direction. But he seems to have been incapable of converting naval strength to land-based military strength, and was similarly incompetent as an administrator. Although his forces made occasional pirate-like raids on rich cities farther inland, the territory under his control remained more or less static, and for ten years he held his three prefectures, neither expanding nor shrinking, until forced to acknowledge the new Ming dynasty late in 1367. Fang ended his days some years later. Although the bearer of a nominal title awarded him by the Ming founder for having played a relatively neutral role throughout the 1360's, and for having accepted surrender without further resistance in 1367, he was a virtual prisoner in the new Ming capital at Nanking.

So much for the southern edge of the Southeast triangle in the last years of the Yuan.

CHANG SHIH-CH'ENG

Chang Shih-ch'eng also began as a salt smuggler. He was a native of another T'ai-chou, a prefectural city just north of the Yangtze in Kiangsu, somewhat east of Yangchow, and on the southern edge of the Huai region salt-producing area. Like Fang Kuo-chen, he was aided by his three brothers; and his family, too, was in the business of distributing and selling salt. However, Chang's salt transportation was done by barge and small boat on the inland waterways, and not at sea. But the illicit profits were no less, and the Chang brothers gained many adherents by distributing these large sums among their friends and followers. Writing shortly before 1366, T'ao Tsung-i, a man of the Southeast region, explains that Chang and his friends had vast plans, for which this formation of a band of loyal followers was but the preliminary step. He also notes that it was the general breakdown of law and order, the economic distress of the people, and especially the widespread uprisings of the Red Turbans and others after 1351 which emboldened men like Chang to harbor seditious thoughts.

In 1352 an uprising was apparently planned by a rich friend of Chang, but local officials learned of it and imprisoned the friend. This led Chang and his cohorts to plot another uprising in 1353, but before the time set for its outbreak, followers of Chang became involved in murders of revenge against some local officials and members of prominent families, and this forced Chang's hand. He assumed leadership of his own friends and personal following plus that of his imprisoned friend, recruited more followers from among the severely oppressed salt field workers, and plundered and looted the city of T'ai-chou and surrounding towns. His movement spread, and in 1354 he seized three prefectural cities: T'ung-chou on the north bank of the Yangtze, T'ai-chou to the north, and Kao-yu still farther north. Chang's ambitions were greater than those of Fang Kuo-chen; he immediately displayed this by proclaiming himself Prince Ch'eng, announcing a new dynasty called the Great Chou, and by establishing a new calendar and a reign-title, *t'ien-yu*, or "Heaven-supported." Then he besieged and captured Yangchow, the great city of the region, thereby severing the Grand Canal. At this point Chancellor Toqto came into the Huai region with an immense army, determined to put down the rebellions there. He administered crushing defeats to Chang's forces at Kao-yu, and was about to annihilate him when the emperor, acting on the slanderous advice of courtiers jealous of Toqto's great powers, cashiered him. Chang seized the opportunity to withdraw temporarily from Kao-yu and during the next year regrouped his army farther south. This was the turning-point in Chang's career. One of his followers, a man from the Southeast triangle farther south across the Yangtze, told Chang of the wealth to be had there merely for the taking, and succeeded in convincing him that his future lay south of the river. Chang cautiously sent one of his brothers with a portion of his army to cross the river and investigate. Early in 1356 he followed with the rest of his forces, capturing Soochow, which became his capital, and all the neighboring prefectures. Chang thus became the master of the richest prefectures in the empire. Besides Soochow, it included the neighboring prefectures of Sung-chiang and Ch'ang-chou in modern Kiangsu, and Chia-hsing, Hu-chou, Shao-hsing, and Hai-yen in northern Chekiang. After 1358 he also held Hangchow, so that all of the Southeast triangle from Lake T'ai east to the coast—by far the richest two-thirds of it—was in his hands. In addition, he continued to hold the still larger areas north of the Yangtze, which, while far less populous and productive, nonetheless included the rich salt fields, full of potential revenue.

By the late 1350's Chang appeared in many ways the strongest of all the rebels in China. He controlled a small but compact area with about twelve million people, probably one-fifth of the total population of the empire, and an area that produced almost one-third of the agrarian tax revenues of the realm and over half of the salt revenues. He had great cities, important commercial centers, and trade routes, the Yangtze delta and the lower Grand Canal, a vast rice surplus, and a dense population from which soldiers could be recruited and trained. But Chang did not develop an aggressive military machine on the basis of these geopolitical assets. Late in 1357 he was hard-pressed by a fierce army of central Chinese aborigines which had been brought into the area by the Mongols to fight rebels for them, and Chang made peace with the Mongol court, sur-rendering his dynastic titles and aspirations to accept an ap-pointment from the court as T'ai-wei, or Grand Marshal. He kept his territories, his wealth, and his armies; his only obli-gation was to send one hundred and ten thousand *piculs* of rice annually to the capital in ships provided by Fang Kuo-chen, who likewise had surrendered to the government. The officials of his Great Chou dynasty had to take other titles as officials of the Yuan empire, but these superficial changes made little difference. Now that the aboriginal armies in Hangchow were his allies, he could use this alliance to am-bush their chieftain and bring about his destruction, and thereby take Hangchow without a fight. The Yuan govern-ment gained little by this alliance with Chang. By 1363 Chang, too, found it no longer profitable, and again pro-claimed himself independent. This time he called himself Prince of Wu, built palaces, and established a court on the traditional imperial pattern. He now had armies numbering in the tens of thousands, and territories stretching from the Shantung border south to Hangchow and beyond, west to the Anhwei boundary north of the river, and to Lake T'ai south of the river. He had several capable military command-ers, and a number of eminent literary figures to head his civilian bureaucracy and decorate his court. He lived in great style on his immense revenues, patronized the arts and let-ters, and appeared to be the most successful of contenders for the throne that the Mongols through their incompetence were rapidly losing. Yet by 1367 Chang's dynasty had collapsed, and he committed suicide while a prisoner of his rival to the west, Chu Yuan-chang.

The histories say that Chang Shih-ch'eng was a man slow of movement and of few words; though likely to give the appearance of having much ability, he was actually muddle-headed and weak of will. They note that his wealth was his undoing. He gradually grew extravagant, undisciplined, and inattentive to government. His brother and some of his lead-ing lieutenants in particular were avaricious in accumulating things of value. Gold and jewels and other valuables, works of art and ancient books were collected in great quantities, and their homes and palaces became scenes of unending song and dance and feasting. His generals fell victim to the same influences; they became so addicted to these pleasures that they ignored his commands to go into battle, claiming illness or making other excuses. Even the defending forces on the various boundaries of his territories regaled themselves day and night with similar luxuries and pleasures. In 1353 and 1354, when with only eighteen followers he seized the city of Kao-yu, Chang Shih-ch'eng was a dashing hero. Twelve or thirteen years later he was so subverted by the pleasures of being a rich rebel prince that he never had a chance of becoming an emperor. Historians have judged that he de-feated himself. We shall have an opportunity to examine that judgment in closer perspective.

CH'EN YU-LIANG

Ch'en Yu-liang was the son of a poor fisherman of Mien-yang in Hupei, near Hankow in the central portion of the Yangtze valley. As a boy he acquired the beginnings of an education, becoming at least literate enough to serve in the local government office as a minor clerk. By temperament, however, he was more drawn to violence. A fortune teller is said to have predicted to him that he would know fame and riches, and throughout his whole career he appears as a violent man in restless, impatient pursuit of both. He joined the western Red Turban uprisings in the early 1350's, and his climb to eminence is marked by successive murders of his superiors in order to supplant them. But his story must begin with that of his lord and victim, Hsü Shou-hui.

Hsü Shou-hui is one of the clowns of history in the mid-fourteenth century. He too was a man of central Hupei, a man so simple-minded that it is said he became a cloth peddler because he was incapable of any other occupation. He should have remained a peddler, but an accident of history intervened. In 1351 P'eng Ying-yü, who for fifteen years had been preaching the imminent descent of the Buddha Maitreya and secretly organizing his Red Turban underground, felt that the time had come for new uprisings. Leaders groomed by him had been captured and executed in earlier failures, and he needed a man of prepossessing appearance who could serve as a puppet leader for his movement. He happened across Hsü Shou-hui and was struck by his tall frame and handsome appearance, as well as by his simple-minded pliability. P'eng made Hsü the leader of a new Red Turban uprising which late in 1351 seized several prefectures in central Hupei. This time the Red Turbans possessed the advantage of having in their ranks one able general, Ni Wen-chün, who beat off the Mongol government's counterattacks and assured the success of the uprising. Near the end of 1351 Hsü was proclaimed emperor of a new Red Turban dynasty, and he used the reign-title "T'ienwan." The capital was at Ch'i-shui, a small county seat east of Hankow.

The widespread uprisings of 1351 so disorganized the Mongol government that most of the rebellions prospered. This rebellion of the western wing of the Red Turbans was spectacularly successful from the beginning. In 1352 it seized

Hankow, to which its capital was moved, then Wuchang, and much of the area comprising the modern provinces of Hupei, Hunan, and Kiangsi. Its generals ranged far and wide, taking every city they besieged, but often abandoning them as they passed on. One of its armies came eastward to Kiangsu and Chekiang, and in 1352 took Hangchow, which it held briefly. But P'eng Ying-yü disappeared from the scene and Hsü Shou-hui was incapable of providing any kind of real leadership. He became a puppet of his leading general, Ni Wen-chün, who in 1356 proclaimed himself prime minister. The T'ien-wan territories were broad and its armies large, but it lacked effective administration and governmental principles. It did not hold firmly to any set boundaries, and did not govern continuously in any but a few central prefectures. It did not effectively exploit the potential of the region it could have controlled. Ni Wen-chün, who was also the son of a poor fisherman's family, grew ever more arrogant and tyrannical, alienating important fellow rebels. The most important of these, Ming Yü-chen, split off from the movement and established himself as an independent war lord in Szechwan. Finally in 1356 Ni attempted to assassinate the useless figurehead Hsü Shou-hui, but failed. He fled to a stronghold of his own forces, where one of his lieutenants, an ambitious young man who believed in the Red Turban doctrines no more than Ni himself, but who had been drawn to the uprising by the hope of personal rewards, assassinated him. This man was Ch'en Yu-liang.

After murdering his chief, Ch'en Yu-liang took his place as the number-two man in the T'ien-wan dynasty. He immediately injected a new effectiveness and energy into the sagging movement, and for three or four years served it vigorously and ruthlessly. In 1360 he tired of serving the useless Hsü Shou-hui. Ch'en was campaigning in the Anhwei section of the Yangtze, moving eastward toward the Kiangsu border, when Hsü decided to move his capital downstream. Ch'en permitted this, seeing in it his opportunity. When Hsü and his court arrived, Ch'en took them all within his walled camp at Chiang-chou (modern Kiukiang) and murdered the entire entourage. He kept Hsü alive for a short time longer, but soon, following his successful siege of the firm little Yangtze bastion of Ts'ai-shih-chi (on the Anhwei-Kiangsu border), he had Hsü clubbed to death by bodyguard soldiers armed with iron maces, aboard one of the high fighting ships that had been used to approach and storm the walls of the city. Then in frantic haste, without waiting for the selection of an appropriate day or the preparation of proper ceremonies, he rushed to take possession of a local temple, and in the middle of a stormy night, by the light of flickering torches, proclaimed himself the emperor of a new "Han" dynasty. He ordered all the old T'ien-wan officials who had survived the liquidation of Hsü Shou-hui's court to serve his new dynasty in the same capacities, and they were forced to don court robes and greet him on the sandy beach the next day at dawn, to offer their felicitations on the transfer of the Mandate of Heaven. It was a windy, rainy day, and the weather so upset the ceremonies that none could take it as an auspicious omen. Ch'en's unseemly haste made him the laughingstock of later historians, but at the time his great military force and his unrestrained ferocity as a leader made all the lower Yangtze area dread his next step.

Ch'en's military forces included both formidable land armies and immense inland waterway naval forces. It is customary to forget that naval forces on the Yangtze and the vast network of connected rivers and lakes played a major role in the military history of China. All the rebellions of the area as well as the defending government forces made great use of naval forces. Ch'en's next move was to come farther east to try to seize Nanking (then called Chi-ch'ing), the base of Chu Yuan-chang, who represented the southern-most outpost of the eastern Red Turbans. Here Ch'en was tricked into an ambush and defeated, whereupon he returned to his ships and sailed back up the river. The next few years saw a continuing duel between Ch'en and Chu. Chu might have been trapped between Ch'en on the west and Chang Shih-ch'eng on the east. Ch'en tried to arrange a joint squeeze action against Chu, but Chang was too busy having a good time, and also somewhat fearful that Ch'en would not make a good neighbor. Chu relied on Chang's indecision to turn his whole naval strength against Ch'en, forcing him upstream and seizing some of his major strongholds there.

Finally in 1363 the two met on the Po-yang lake in Kiangsi, in one of the great naval battles of Chinese history. Ch'en's force had been long in preparation, and consisted of an imposing array of more than one hundred great battleships moved by sail and oar, with high battlements from which archers could fire down on smaller ships. The largest of these were protected by iron plate armor, and on them he carried his family and all the officials of his court. Chu's smaller ships and lesser forces battled Ch'en indecisively for three days and nights. At last, Chu took advantage of a change in the wind and of the greater maneuverability of his smallest ships to move burning rafts into the solid front of Ch'en's navy, setting his ships on fire. Panic ensued. Ch'en himself was struck by an arrow and killed, and his court and most of his soldiers were drowned or burned to death. This quickly ended Ch'en's dynasty and the rebellion of the western Red Turbans.

Historians of the time, including those partisan to Chu Yuan-chang, saw the downfall of Ch'en as the result of a series of lucky accidents. But it is also true that his rash temper led him into ill-considered actions, and his administration was both harsh and short-sighted. His movement possessed awesome power, but it lacked resilience and showed no constructive efforts or thoughtful planning. The end of this short Han dynasty was perhaps predictable from the moment of its hectic beginnings at Ts'ai-shih-chi, the night that old Hsü Shou-hui was clubbed to death.

CHU YUAN-CHANG

Of any man in his troubled times, Chu Yuan-chang, the monk, might well have appeared the least likely to ascend the stage of history. He was born in 1328 into a destitute peasant's family in the poorest part of the Huai region. Forty years later he proclaimed a new dynasty, the Great Ming, and he is known in history as Ming T'ai-tsu, its founder. As a boy he received no education, except for the lore his maternal grandfather spun for his boyish ears. This old man was a geomancer and fortuneteller by trade. He remembered the fall of the Sung dynasty in 1279, when he had been a soldier in the last Sung resistance forces that had been driven all the way to Kwangtung Province. He had wandered far and performed many strange, even miraculous, deeds. His conversation, full of superstition and peasant wisdom, made a deep impression on the boy.

To add to his family's livelihood, Chu was hired out as a cowherd to a richer neighbor, forced to spend his earliest years in productive work. The family moved about cultivating idle land on a sharecropping basis in the north Anhwei plain, which was repeatedly ravaged by drought, famine, pests, and plague during Chu's young years. In 1344, when he was sixteen years old, an epidemic carried off his father and mother and two older brothers all within a few days. As an infant Chu had been very sickly, and his parents had offered him to the Buddha if his life were spared. Now he was a helpless orphan, and it seemed best to fulfill this promise, for there was no other way to guarantee food and lodgings for him.

His one remaining older brother talked it over with the boy, and they agreed this was best. He went off to a poor little temple nearby and became a lay novice. This meant in fact that he became a young servant, who tended the incense, swept floors, and worked in the temple garden, in return for a straw mat to sleep on and two scant vegetarian meals a day.

But his temple, too, was suffering from the economic distress of the time, and could not even provide this slim care for another person. So within a month of his arrival Chu was given a patched robe and bowl, and sent out to wander and beg, as a part of his training for the monastic profession. For three or four years he wandered in the region to the west of the Huai River, in what would be modern Anhwei and Honan. We know very little about these years, but it seems certain that at this time he became associated with the Red Turban movement which was strongly entrenched there, that he kept up association with several of his boyhood friends who had become soldiers of fortune, and that he developed other connections that were to be of importance to him later on. Late in 1348, at the age of twenty, he returned to his temple, where he spent the next three years. Once again we know little about his activities, but he appears to have begun to learn to read and write in preparation for becoming a regular monk. These were stirring years, however. Rebellions fomented on all sides; the great Yellow River flooded, necessitating repairs on the dykes in 1351; Red Turban agitation was going on secretly throughout the region at all times; and in 1352 there was a successful Red Turban uprising at nearby Hao-chou, under the leadership of a man called Kuo Tzu-hsing. It is likely that young Chu Yuan-chang was much more concerned about these events than with his monkish studies and temple duties.

At the beginning of 1353 he felt his position at the temple to be precarious, because a Mongol army had moved into the region to stem the spread of the Hao-chou rebellion. While the army was afraid to make a direct attack on the Red Turban rebels there, it was scouring the countryside for likely collaborators. Monks were particularly suspicious, because the Red Turban doctrine, which taught that Maitreya would come and drive out the Mongol oppressors, was spread by monks. It was often monks who gathered the simple country people together to burn incense and stir them up with these teachings. Moreover, it was well known that Chu Yuan-chang had spent years in the Huai region, where these teachings were rampant. Twenty years later, Chu wrote a description of this period of his life, telling that he received a letter from a friend in Hao-chou, urging him to come and join the rebellion there. At the same time his own temple was one of those burned by the Mongol army in its efforts to intimidate the monks and prevent the people from being swayed by their seditious teachings. On the one hand, Chu was drawn to the more active life of the rebel; on the other, he was afraid to remain where the government could apprehend him and make a scapegoat of him. After much hesitation and after repeatedly consulting the wisdom of the Buddha through divination, he gave up his monk's robe and bowl and fled to Hao-chou, to become a soldier in the forces of Kuo Tzu-hsing.

Chu was a tall man. He had a long face with a prominent ridge on his skull, and an underslung, protruding jaw, wide slanting eyes, and a large flat nose. He was ugly in a manner that impressed rather than repulsed people. Even as a young man there was an intensity, almost a ferocity, about him that made people respect him. He was a natural leader, intellectually quick and resourceful, physically vigorous and courageous. He rose rapidly in the service of Kuo Tzu-hsing, becoming first his personal orderly, then a trusted lieutenant, then the husband of Kuo's adopted daughter. Kuo himself was the son of a famous fortuneteller who had married a

rich wife; he had used his inherited wealth to cultivate a following among the restless and ambitious young men of his
town, giving money away and spending it freely on entertainment and hospitality. He was early attracted to the Red
Turban doctrines, and supported the incense-burning and the
underground agitation. In the early part of 1352, when successful Red Turban rebellions had appeared in so many
places nearby and far away, Kuo felt the time had come. He
was able to call forth a following of more than a thousand
men, with whom he attacked and seized Hao-chou. As men
came willingly to serve a successful leader, his forces quickly
expanded. He divided his army into five commands and appointed five commanders-in-chief, who were free to attack on
any front where success and plunder seemed likely.

But Kuo was not a commanding personality, and his five
commanders-in-chief became jealous of one another, insubordinate, and uncooperative. In victory they were arrogant,
and in defeat they became unreliable. In the fall of 1354 the
Mongol Chancellor Toqto moved south into the rebel territory with a vast army of thirty thousand. He first attacked
the Red Turban stronghold at Hsü-chou, a hundred miles
northwest of Hao-chou, where "Sesame-seed Li" had his
base. Toqto captured Hsü-chou, killed Li, and scattered his
forces. Two leaders of the Hsü-chou rebellion fled to Hao-
chou to join Kuo Tzu-hsing, and although they came empty-
handed, they expected commands and high honors. This put
a further strain on Kuo's leadership. Chu found the atmosphere oppressive, for, although he had come to stand high
in Kuo's favor and had received a military command from
him, he felt that the factional bickering and Kuo's inability
to supply decisive leadership promised little for the future.
Therefore, in 1354 he received permission to take an independent unit, recruited by himself, and campaign to the
south on his own. Many recruits came quickly to his stand-

ard—still the red standard of the Red Turbans, bearing the symbols of the spurious "Sung" dynasty of the pretender Han Lin-erh. Among the recruits were some boyhood friends from his old village, uneducated ruffians like himself, but men of proved fighting ability. There were also two or three men of learning, who knew something of history and advised Chu about principles of government. They instructed him in ways of administering the government of counties that came under his control, and filled his head with the thought of emulating the founder of the great Han dynasty of fifteen hundred years before, who had risen from the peasantry to establish one of the longest and most glorious dynasties of Chinese history.

Chu spent that year and the next tasting the flavor of independent leadership, successfully holding a small area just north of the Yangtze across from Nanking. Late in 1355 he crossed the river, and early in 1356 took Nanking, which by this time was isolated from other centers of the Mongol government's dwindling authority by the Red Turban rebellions, by Chang Shih-ch'eng to the east, and by Fang Kuo-chen and others farther south. Chu continued to hold a small area north of the Yangtze, but he expanded his territories significantly to the south, until he held one-third of the Southeast triangle—the portion lying west of Lake T'ai—as well as some small areas in southern Anhwei and eastern Kiangsi. This little base around Nanking was half a province in size. Its population in 1360 was perhaps eight or nine million, and it was distinctly poorer in agricultural production and other resources than Chang Shih-ch'eng's area to the east. From this base Chu expanded slowly and carefully. His watchwords were economy, discipline, and system. For six or seven years he did little but work and build the foundations of solid government and military strength. In 1363 he was forced into the life-or-death struggle with Ch'en Yu-liang, his fellow Red Turban leader to the west, and when he emerged victorious he felt that his time was now at hand. Kuo Tzu-hsing's base north of the Yangtze had long since disintegrated, and Kuo himself had been forced to flee to Chu for protection, dying in 1355, before Chu had crossed the Yangtze.

Chu's relations with the Sung pretender, Han Lin-erh, had undergone a similar transformation. As the Red Turban empire in the Huai region also disintegrated under internal and external pressures, Han Lin-erh came every year to depend more on Chu, his most successful adherent. This increasing dependence was marked by annual promotions in rank and title. In 1361 Chu was appointed Duke of Wu. In 1363 Han Lin-erh, too, was forced to flee to Chu for protection, establishing his temporary capital in the territory held by Chu just north of the Yangtze. The following year Chu named himself Prince of Wu, one year after his rival to the east, Chang Shih-ch'eng, had promoted himself to the same rank. Han Lin-erh and his "Sung" dynasty had become a nuisance, and Chu Yuan-chang increasingly ignored him, acting in his own interests. It was not until 1366, however, that he arranged a convenient accident to dispose of Han and the Sung allegiance. In that year he sent a trusted follower to escort the pretender across the Yangtze to Nanking; during the crossing the boat overturned, drowning Han. The comedy of the Sung restoration came to an end.

Chu now struck out to end the long decades of disorder and to restore unity to China. His last remaining obstacle was the other Wu princedom, that of Chang Shih-ch'eng. This occupied him for a year. Then in 1368 he was able to launch the final mopping-up campaigns to the north against the Mongol remnants, and to the south against other rebels. Simultaneously, he proclaimed himself the new emperor of China. This was not to be another false dynasty, prematurely proclaimed by an overeager rebel chieftain. Chu Yuan-chang, the destitute and illiterate monk from the Huai, clearly and unequivocally inherited the Mandate of Heaven in 1368. As might have been predicted, his thirty-one year reign was vigorous and systematic. That he was to become the cruelest and most vicious tyrant of all Chinese history was not, perhaps, to be foreseen by those who had known him as a poor wandering monk. But of that there is much more to be told in the story which follows.

By the middle of the fourteenth century, life was difficult and unpredictable for everyone in China, from the Mongol rulers to the poorest peasant. Those who rose most quickly and reaped the greatest rewards were men of violence, of great strength, and of daring. They were not, as would have been more usual in that civilization, the men of great learning and of cultivation. This was now a free-for-all world in which cultivated men were handicapped by their learning. Their traditional Chinese civilization made them cautious and thoughtful, as it made them shrink from violence and, normally, deficient in the martial virtues. Yet among the men of learning there were also those who both harbored high ambitions and felt deep concern for the state of the world. What could they do? Their Confucian morality put them on the side of legitimacy, but the legitimate Mongol emperors clearly did not deserve the Mandate of Heaven; they were abusing it, making a mockery of legitimacy itself by their desperate willingness to extend it to bandits like Fang Kuo-chen and Chang Shih-ch'eng. Their humanistic philosophy had instilled in many of them a serious concern for the well-being of the society, yet how could they serve it in an age when their civilian skills could not be employed, and when only the military path offered a way to effective action? Their learning had given them a sense of history, and

張吳王遺像

Chang Shih-ch'eng, as Prince of Wu

A modern portrait, from Chih Wei-ch'eng, *Wu-wang Chang Shih-ch'eng tsai-chi*

Scenery of the Wu Region
A late Ming period woodblock illustration of the San Mao lakes

ochow (see map, page 58). From *Ming Shan T'u*, illustrations
pended to the *T'ien-hsia Ming Shan Chi*, of Wu Ch'iu-shih.

they thought deeply about the courses followed by great men of earlier troubled times. This also gave them a sense of tragedy, an awareness of the futility of any course of action in an age fated to be under the domination of evil forces. But their learning also cultivated in them a sense of the beauty and the power of the word. To some, the creative life in poetry and literature could give meaning even to an age such as this. In a world where men like the smugglers, the clerk, the monk, and all their often disreputable and unworthy cohorts assumed the leading roles, what course was left for the man of learning or the poet? By all the reason inherent in their civilization, this should be their world, but clearly there was no hope of realizing their claim to it.

Kao Ch'i was such a man—a scholar, a poet. His life is a classic tragedy of China, of a civilized man in an age fated to be dominated by force.

Chu Yuan-chang, the Ming Founder, OPPOSITE

Official portraits of the emperor show him as a handsome, benevolent, sage-like person. The tradition behind this unflattering portrait is none the less of long standing, and it is supported by literary evidence. Many modern scholars accept it as the embodiment of an authentic tradition about Chu's appearance. (Photo courtesy of the National Central Museum, Taiwan.)

CHAPTER TWO

THE YOUNG POET OF SOOCHOW

THE KAO FAMILY had lived in the city of Soochow for some generations, and by the mid-fourteenth
century they considered themselves natives of Ch'ang-chou,
one of the two counties (*hsien*) whose county seats were within the walls of Soochow. Ch'ang-chou County lay to the east
of the city, and Ch'ang-chou therefore claimed the eastern
half of the area within the city walls. Wu County lay to the
west and shared the city walls with Ch'ang-chou. Wu County
had a much longer history; Ch'ang-chou County had been
created by subdividing Wu only in the T'ang dynasty, and in
common speech Wu continued to stand for the whole city,
both counties, and indeed the whole area of the prefecture,
whose seat was also within the city walls of Soochow. Kao
Ch'i is sometimes called a "man of Wu." But the family
home was just inside the northeast corner of the city wall,[1]
and the family owned rural property on the Wu-sung River,
also to the east of the city and in Ch'ang-chou County. As
citizens of the Great Yuan dynasty, under which the poet
was born in 1336, they clearly belonged on the registry for
Ch'ang-chou County.

But the family had not always been citizens of Wu, nor
even of the lower Yangtze delta area (known historically as
"the South"). They had come south to the temporary Sung

[1] Kao Ch'i lived at the *pei kuo* quarter of Soochow. This would seem
to indicate that he lived just outside the city wall to the north of the
city, and we know that this was true of some of his friends of the *pei
kuo*. But internal evidence in his poetry indicates that his home was
just inside the city wall.

capital at Lin-an, or "Temporary Peace," as the Sung re-
named the city of Hangchow when the invading Chin Tartars forced the Sung emperors out of their capital at K'ai-
feng in 1126. This temporary capital became in fact their
permanent one, for the Sung were never able to regain the
North. Most of the refugees who fled there in the early
twelfth century, such as the Kao family, eventually resigned
themselves to being citizens of the South, and when in 1279
the Mongols reunited the empire under one rule, none of
them went back to the North. Even when the Ming dynasty
restored the North and all of China to native Chinese rule
again in 1368, virtually none of these descendants of refugee
gentry families returned to the North. They had become
men of the South, and preferred its rich green fields laced
with waterways and its soft verdant hills to the starker scenery and the harder life of the North. They spoke now only
the mellow, fluid dialects of Wu. They ate its foods, drank
its golden rice-wine, wore its silks, and lived its leisurely, elegant life. Yet they did not forget their Northern ancestry,
for the North was antiquity. Until this time China's long
history had been played out mostly in the Great Central
Plain of the North. Many of these new Southerners could
trace their ancestry to places and persons that had figured
in that long history. The Kao family traced its line to Kao
Huan, known in history as Shen-wu, the founder of the
Northern Ch'i dynasty, which ruled most of North China
from A.D. 550 to 577. The Ch'i dynasty capital was at Yeh
(modern Lin-chang) in the northeast corner of Honan. On
meeting a military man from "the Bronze Terrace," a poetic
allusion to the old Ch'i capital at Yeh, Kao Ch'i wrote a
poem in which he referred to his ancestry:

> In the past my ancestors made Yeh their capital;
> Shen-wu was the hero of his age.

Still today at the Bronze Terrace
The young men continue to emulate him.[2]

The poem continues with many historical allusions, expressing admiration of the heroic virtues of the man of the
North, with whom he sought to establish some identification of himself. Occasionally in his prose writings, as in his
poetry, he signed himself "Kao Ch'i of Po-hai." Po-hai, located on the north Shantung coast, was the area from which
the founder of the Ch'i dynasty is supposed to have come;
Kao Huan had been enfeoffed Prince of Po-hai before he
usurped the Eastern Wei throne and established his own
family as emperors of Ch'i. Elsewhere he signed himself
"Kao Ch'i of Ch'i." This Ch'i is also a name for Shantung,
and one which the Ch'i dynasty, founded by his ancestors,
had taken its name. (However, the Ch'i in his personal name
is another character.) Thus the memory of an illustrious past
was strong in the Kao family, and was a source of pride to the
young poet. But it had little or no practical meaning, for the
family no longer had any connections in the North. The
family records state that for generations after the Ch'i dynasty they had dwelt in K'ai-feng, the Northern Sung capital, from which they had fled with the Sung court to Hangchow after the debacle of 1126.[3] They had probably always
been a family in the officialdom, but not a particularly distinguished one. No other prominent ancestors are pointed
out, neither from the centuries of residence at K'ai-feng, nor
from Hangchow. Apparently none of this Kao family, from
the fall of the brief Ch'i dynasty in 577 to Kao Ch'i himself,

[2] CCSC 4/16a-b
[3] There is a poem "Sung Kao Erh-wen-hsüeh yu Ch'ien-t'ang" (CCSC
8/106) in which he mentions meeting a man named Kao from K'ai-feng
who is travelling via Soochow to Hangchow and who also claims descent
from the Po-hai Kao clan. The poem makes it clear that until this chance
meeting, Kao Ch'i had not known that there still was a branch of the
clan living in K'ai-feng.

had ever merited a biography in any of the dynastic histories or had achieved any other distinction. From Hangchow, the head of the family probably came to Soochow in some minor official capacity, and settled down there to stay. But whether this was in the Southern Sung period or in the early part of the Mongol Yuan dynasty, we do not know.

We know the names of Kao Ch'i's father and grandfather, but there is no other information about them. We know from an allusion in one of his poems that he lost both of his parents while he was still very young.[4] He had an older brother, Kao Tzu, whose two sons were close to Kao Ch'i's own age. These nephews, along with some cousins and other more distant clansmen, are mentioned; but his was a small family, and except for his attachment to his older brother, his family seems to have played a small part in his life until he was married and had a family of his own. We do not know the names of his teachers, but he obviously received the best kind of traditional education in the Confucian classics and their commentaries, in history, and in the later belles-lettres. It was the kind of education designed to prepare a man for public life, and more specifically for the civil service examinations which in normal times were the gateway to public life. In this respect as in most others, the Yuan dynasty does not qualify as "normal times," because the examination system functioned only in a very limited fashion and was riddled with corruption; as a result, many qualified persons refused to take the examinations. More convenient routes to office were open to Mongols and other aliens who had come in with them. These groups dominated the higher offices, making the usual official career for Chinese much less attractive. But by the late Yuan, many Chinese did hold subsidiary offices, some of enough dignity and importance to satisfy their holders and to make the official career seem

4 ccsc 2/17b, "Feng shu ts'ao"

worthwhile. Throughout the dynasty, the Chinese kept on preparing for the examinations as if they were still operating as before. Thus the life of preparation was still normal for a young man in those families which could afford it and in which it was the tradition, even though the life of service after that preparation was not in most cases possible or highly desirable. Kao Ch'i's youth must have been heavily involved in this life of preparation. There is ample evidence of it in the man it produced, but there is no direct evidence about it in the sources for his life.

The city of Soochow in which he grew up in the 1340's and 1350's was a great city. Only Hangchow, the former capital and still the greatest city of the realm, about eighty miles to the southeast, was a greater city in the Southeast triangle. Our best information about Soochow at this time comes from the 1379 gazetteer of the prefecture of which it was the seat. By the census of 1374, according to the gazetteer, the registered population of the two counties was over six hundred thousand; and the whole prefecture, which also included four other counties with their seats in nearby cities, had a population of two million. Mid-Yuan dynasty figures, which may be less reliable, put the prefecture's population at half a million higher, while the prefecture in which Hangchow was located was slightly under two million at the same time. Although the figures may be either too high or too low (probably the latter), they are a reliable indication that Soochow was in the most populous region of China at that time, for the single prefecture boasted a larger registered population than some entire provinces in the North. The population within the walls and in the closer suburbs may have been about one-quarter of a million. There was no sharp demarcation between the life of the city and that of the country roundabout; the city walls were not a bastion of light against dark and crude ways of the rural countryside, in the way that they may have been in medieval Europe or in other parts of the Orient. Although this was the middle period of China's two-thousand-year history as an empire, it was actually much later than that in her overall development as a civilization; in most ways it is not analogous to the corresponding middle period of European history. Although the Mongol invasion marked a low point in the whole imperial history, especially in the level of governmental efficiency and in some aspects of cultural development, it was in no sense comparable to Europe's dark ages. The level of the economy, the sophistication of life, the depth of cultural and intellectual activity, even in this low point, all seem more analogous to the Renaissance or to early modern Europe. And to Marco Polo and other European travelers who came to China in the Mongol period, the most advanced cities of Europe at that time were crude villages compared to the splendid cities of China. Soochow was among the most splendid of these, and the countryside all around it partook of the life of the city in a way that has no parallel in pre-modern times in the West.

The very appearance of the city gave evidence of this. Its city wall was large in compass and of irregular shape, bulging out here and there in graceful curves to enclose an area or to avoid another. The new wall built in the late Yuan period was forty-seven *li*, or about sixteen miles in circumference. It was low in comparison with the walls of the cities of the North, only about twenty feet high; it was made of grayish material, part brick and part stone, topped with crenellations, to be sure, and there were fortified gates and moats both within and without the wall. But not even this could succeed in giving it the appearance of a fortress. It sat low and broad and open on the soft green countryside. Its wall did not shield the view of the many imposing roofs, high and broad with gently upsweeping curves at the corners, of temples and government buildings. And the wall was dwarfed into insignificance by the many soaring temple pagodas within and without. Six great gates opened to travel by land, and five to travel by water. Out from each of these extended fingers of busy city life, ordinarily needing no protection of the wall. These were built-up areas of houses and shops, markets and inns, boat docks and warehouses, temples and fairs. It was a bustling city life overflowing into the surrounding countryside, blending into the life of the market towns and the country villages beyond. A great volume of travel entered and left the city every day by land and by boat on the innumerable canals and rivers. Much of it was that of the city dwellers themselves, going to visit their farms or their country residences, paying visits to temples and scenic spots, or coming into the city from their gardens and estates to buy things or to conduct the leisurely affairs of government or of private life in the metropolitan center.

The city was famous for certain articles of manufacture, and its markets and shops offered the products of distant places. It was also a center of cosmopolitan entertainment, having both its local theater and music, as well as those of Hangchow and of the North. It was above all a center of learning and of literary and artistic pursuits. Here flocked many of the great writers and scholars and painters of the day, drawn to this comparatively peaceful and undisturbed region, and supported by its great wealth. The 1379 gazetteer says of it: "Soochow from early times has been known as a populous and flourishing place; the suburbs lying about the city on all sides contain no empty land. Among the people there are no distinctions of aristocratic and lowly, so frequently it is true that all the people have property. As a result their customs are much given to extravagance, and little to the virtue of frugality." The gazetteer goes on to describe the many festivals of the year, and the extravagance with which these lighthearted people celebrated them: "At the New Year they all gather at great festival fairs in the temples for joyous celebrations, showing off their new clothing and tasting the many kinds of foods and sweets. In each family the relatives all gather from far and wide, and in every home there is drinking and feasting. On all the doors are pasted strips of colored paper bearing the New Year's couplets. . . . On the 13th day of the New Year everyone pops rice in the kitchen cooking pans, playfully foretelling by the way the rice bursts into 'flowers' whether it will be an auspicious or an ominous year for him. On the 15th day the shadow lanterns are displayed. They are made in intricate and beautiful patterns, far excelling those of any other region." The record continues through the year, detailing the Soochow people's love of pleasure and beauty, and the annual cycle of their fortunate life.

The Yangtze River lay about fifty miles to the north; the mouth of the river at the seacoast was about seventy-five miles to the east. About twenty-five miles to the west lay Lake T'ai, the great drainage basin of the Southeast triangle, out of which flowed innumerable streams north to the Yangtze or east to the sea. The region around Lake T'ai was the richest rice-growing bottomland in all of China. It is also a region of great scenic beauty, with mountains and hills and thousands of islands. On its shores were temples and country villas, fishing villages and farming villages in thick profusion. It provided water routes connecting to all the important cities of the triangle, as well as to the Grand Canal and Yangtze arteries, and thus was of great strategic importance to the defense of the region. Moreover, its innumerable bays and inlets could be hiding places for bandits, and provided places of concealment for others who wanted to flee the bustling life all around.

Beyond Lake T'ai to the west, the character of the region

gradually changes. The western point of the Southeast triangle is hillier and poorer, and more sparsely settled. It is still the green South, but it cannot compare in its natural wealth, the wealth of its soil, to the eastern two-thirds. Its great city is Nanking, a hundred miles directly west-north-west of Soochow, but, according to the old gazetteers, by the water route seven stages away, at a distance of five hundred and eighty-eight *li*, or almost two hundred miles. Nanking, called Chi-ch'ing in the Yuan period, had been the capital of successive Southern dynasties in the period of the division of North and South, from the third through the sixth centuries A.D. Its historical importance derived not from the wealth of the immediately adjacent counties, nor from command of natural routes of commerce, but from its strategic importance as a military stronghold. Over it, according to tradition, hovered the atmosphere of rulership; it was meant to be the seat of political power. And it was a natural bastion, with the Yangtze curving around its northern and western sides, and the Purple Mountain and other hills protecting it on the south and east, like "a coiling dragon and a crouching tiger." But in the later Sung and Yuan periods it was not a great city like Soochow and Hangchow. In the mid-Yuan period the entire prefecture had a population of only one million, less than half that of Soochow's prefecture, and when Chu Yuan-chang took the prefecture in 1356, the *Ming Veritable Record* tells us that he seized there "over half a million civilian and military population," showing that it had declined still more. In the 1340's Hangchow also declined somewhat, as the result of two great fires in successive years (1341 and 1342), which burned three-quarters of it, and the misfortunes of warfare that were particularly severe in the early 1350's. Increasingly throughout Kao Ch'i's early life, his city of Soochow and the surrounding region became the richest and most fortunate in the whole Southeast, hold-

* 46 *

ing on to its traditionally flourishing condition better than any other region amidst the general breakdown of order and decline of well-being that marked the late Yuan period.

Of this period of Kao Ch'i's life, however, we have no records in his own poetry. He wrote poetry seriously from his early teens, but probably destroyed many of the earlier poems in 1362, at the age of twenty-six, when he first went through his accumulated works to prepare a collection of them. There are references to his growing reputation as a young poet in his late teens, but there is no poem that can be dated with certainty before the twentieth year. Of his life in these years we can surmise much, however. Beyond study, which of all his activities must have been the most demanding in time and energy, there were friends, and there was travel to and from the family farm east of the city, to supervise its operation, to manage the collection of rent and payment of taxes, and to enjoy the simpler life of the countryside.

Of his friends of this period of his youth we know of only one: Wang Hsing, the boy who lived next door, a very remarkable person in his own right. He was five years older than Kao Ch'i. His father was a poor seller of medicinal herbs, a shop clerk employed by an old man named Hsü. As a child Wang Hsing had attracted the attention of old Hsü and his wife by his intelligence and his amazing memory. The boy entertained the old lady by telling her romances based on the histories, and she urged her husband to give this bright lad some proper education, in the classics. Old Hsü started him on the *Analects*, and was amazed that each night the boy committed to memory what he had been taught that day.[5] Thus begins one of those classical tales of the poor but bright Chinese boy who acquired a Confucian education and rose to high position, fame, and wealth. Wang

---

[5] One of several recognizable clichés in the account of Wang Hsing's life.

Hsing became a famous child prodigy, and attracted considerable attention from the wealthy and the prominent by his amazing displays of memory, and by the learning he acquired so easily. But he refused the patronage of the Maecenas of the region, and of government officials of the Yuan dynasty and then of the government established in Soochow by Chang Shih-ch'eng. He preferred to earn his own living by teaching, a profession which he took up before his twentieth year.

Kao Ch'i at that time was in his early teens, and their friendship must have dated from this time. The two young scholars matched wits and learning for their own amusement. Kao Ch'i wrote, for example, a long and amusing poem to Wang Hsing, begging for the gift of a cat to free his house of troublesome rats. But the poem is so laden with allusions as to be untranslatable; it has all the earmarks of a humor burdened with learning, the kind in which young friends, each confident in his erudition, might have indulged. But it is also immature and meaningless as poetry. Every line is an obscure allusion to some anecdote in one of the histories or to a line by one of the T'ang poets. Kao Ch'i early outgrew this childish delight in pedantry for its own sake. (This poem is not dated, but it must be among the earliest.)[6]

There certainly were other friends as well, but Wang Hsing is the one who remained an important friend on into Kao's later life, and who is recorded by name in his poetry and other writings. In Kao Ch'i's extant works there are a dozen poems mentioning Wang Hsing, or addressed to him, and several prose writings as well, but most or all of them appear to date from a slightly later period in his life.

All of the extant poems mentioning visits to the rural property on the Wu-sung River east of the city, on which the family undoubtedly was financially dependent, probably also date

[6] ccsc 6/3b-4b

from slightly later in his life, but from them we can gather something of the flavor and meaning of this experience of visiting the place and of his assumption of some responsibility toward its management. A biographical sketch written shortly after his death states that the family had been considered wealthy in his father's youth, and had owned "more than one hundred *mou*" (over seventeen acres) of rice paddy land, where the Wu-sung River crossed the Sandy Lake at the Village of Tall Trees.[7] His father, it continues, had often taken up temporary residence there in order to supervise the farming operations. Perhaps this property was divided or had decreased in size before Kao Ch'i and his older brother inherited it, when Kao Ch'i was a young child, for the family was considered to be in financial decline in the poet's youth.

The usual means of travel to the farm was by boat, out of the east gate of the city, along the river, and perhaps at the last passing through meandering canals and lakes in order to approach directly to the property itself. There is a remarkable poem—probably a later one, for it displays a maturity and command of subtle mood that the earliest poems lack— which describes leaving the east gate of the city at dawn, probably to travel to the Eastern Cottage, the name by which they referred to the farm. The poem is called, "On Hearing the Sound of Oars, When Leaving the East Gate of the City at Dawn."

The city gate opens at sunrise; the road lies at the water's edge.
Through the mist come human voices; a fish market is nearby.

[7] The *Soochow Prefectural Gazetteer* of the *T'ung-chih* period, ch. 8, pp. 17b-18a, states "The Sandy Lake [Sha-hu] is east of the prefectural city 20 *li*; another name for it is the Golden Sands Lake. . . . The Green Hill [Ch'ing-ch'iu] and the Mound of Tai [Tai-hsü] and the two P'u villages are located here." Some other sources put it as far as 40 *li* to the east.

Whose oars, unseen in the fog's expanse, move with such
  flying speed?
Still half in a dream a startled duck flies up from the
  water's edge willows.
At the crossing point, chill waves lap against the sand.
From the distance I hear the creaking of wheels, and
  again the splash of oars.
A traveller's cart winds along the twisting hillside road.
Looms whir where women work, in houses behind the
  bamboo.
I am but a wanderer from the wilds;
Is it not by chance that I was dropped here into the
  Yellow Dust, to set forth on my travels at dawn?
These sounds, I am vaguely reminded, I have heard
  somewhere before.
Was it in a boat, on waking after drinking, just as the
  east grew light?[8]

The original is full of the mysterious feeling of one who
hears sounds, vaguely familiar, through the heavy mists of
morning, and is startled to wonder who and where he is.

Another poem, more prosaic but not without charm, tells
of arriving at the Eastern Cottage at evening, after travelling
from the city. It is called, "In a Boat on the Lake on a Cold
Night, Arriving at the Eastern Cottage."

A new moon rises over the harbor of a fishing village.
The ducks and geese are still out, calling *cah-ti cah-ti.*
Across the lake comes the faraway sound of bells, from
  a temple lost in the mists.
All the people living here have already reached home; I
  alone am still on the way.
The chill wind rustles, the chill waves rise;
And I forgot to bring a pot of wine along in the boat.

[8] ccsc 10/1b

At the eastern home they still have not gone to bed,
   as though waiting for me—
Pale lamp light there among the yellow leaves, and the
   whirring shuttles in the looms.[9]

In other poems written about the "Village of Tall Trees"
he says that on returning there he feels like a fish returned
to his own deep pool; he speaks of his warm feeling for his
tenant who worked the property for him, and the joys which
the rustic life brought him.[10] The region about Soochow at
that time was noted for the vast accumulation of landholdings in the hands of some great landlords, but the Kao family
was not among them. They may well have been wealthier in
the days of Kao Ch'i's father and grandfather, but in Kao
Ch'i's youth they were probably still comfortably, if not
lavishly, provided for by this bit of ancestral land. Moreover,
their feeling about it was intimate and warm, not impersonal
and businesslike. It was not merely the source of their income, or part of vast landholdings. It represented their ancestors' beneficence to them, as well as the rustic pleasures
and the virtues of simple living. Kao Ch'i was very sensitive
to these values; they were no poet's affectation with him. Perhaps he derived much of this from his visits to the rural village which in one sense was his real home.

Of his early youth there is little else that can be said. Some
of the elements of this beginning are standard for his civilization and his age, and some are unique with this man. From
these beginnings developed one of the great poets of China's
long history.

[9] CCSC 10/12a

[10] A set of five of these poems is translated in full below, end of
Chapter 8, pp. 231ff. Although dating from later in his life, they illustrate the importance to Kao Ch'i of the country home.

CHAPTER THREE

THE MAN OF THE GREEN HILL

AS KAO CH'I approached early manhood, his fame as a young poet was already spreading. One of the eulogies written on his death by a friend and fellow townsman recalls: "In his grandfather's and father's generations the family was not prominent, but possessed wealth; coming to Kao Ch'i's time, his family's fortunes declined but became distinguished by talent. Before he was twenty, Kao Ch'i was already well-known for his outstanding brilliance. . . . He was particularly devoted to writing poetry. . . . At that time even older scholars and established men of learning all valued him very highly, and considered themselves incapable of equalling him." If the family could produce genius, its fortunes were as secure as if it had great wealth.[1]

A young man of such widely recognized talent should have been able to spend these years hopefully preparing for an official career, confident that he would achieve fame and fortune early in life. Normally he might have taken the first of the three examinations as early as his mid-teens, and it was not unheard-of for such a youthful genius to pass the third

[1] Although in many cases these elements from the brief eulogistic biographies are clearly *topoi*, expressed in familiar clichés, they no doubt indicate something more than merely a later stereotyped idealization of the man. Biographical writing in China, and in particular the stereotyped elements of biographies, were the subject of the Fifth Conference on Chinese Thought chaired by Professor Arthur F. Wright, at Suffern, N.Y., in September 1960. The early life of Kao Ch'i was discussed at that conference, the proceedings of which have been published in a volume edited by Professor Wright and Edwin G. Pulleyblank, entitled *Confucian Personalities*, Stanford, 1962.

and final examination by his twentieth year. Then he would be appointed to a junior compiler's post at the Han-lin Academy, the highest organ of literary affairs of government, or to a junior secretarial position in some ministry or bureau at the capital, where he could display his talents and form associations that would lead to his employment in positions of responsibility, and to his further advancement. Normally this is what the young Kao Ch'i would have been thinking, and what his friends would have been predicting for him. But the Yuan dynasty was not normal in this respect; the official career did not hold such promise or beckon such talent. And by the time Kao Ch'i reached his mid-teens, that alien dynasty was beset by such troubles that it clearly was being shaken to its foundations. An ambitious man of talent might well hesitate to build his career on service to it. Kao Ch'i did not even take the examinations, even though his education had been precisely the kind that would have prepared him for them.

He was fifteen the year the Yellow River burst its dykes, causing the great flood of the Central Plain, and leading to the repair project that served to incite the peasant masses of North China to revolt. In the summer of that year, Liu Fu-t'ung announced that Han Lin-erh was a descendant of the imperial line of the former Sung dynasty. He proclaimed his Red Turban movement to be the restoration of that dynasty, with Han Lin-erh as its emperor. Other Red Turban uprisings had led to the seizure of much of Shantung and adjoining areas. And in the fall of the same year Hsü Shou-hui, the cloth peddler of Hupei, established his T'ien-wan dynasty in the central Yangtze basin, representing the western wing of the Red Turbans. Fang Kuo-chen had rebelled three years earlier and was pillaging the Chekiang coast immediately south of Soochow with his pirate forces. When Kao Ch'i was sixteen all these rebellions spread and came closer to the

Southeast triangle; that was the year Kuo Tzu-hsing staged his uprising at Hao-chou and Hsü Shou-hui's far-ranging forces captured and sacked Hangchow. In the following year Chang Shih-ch'eng launched his independent uprising just north of Soochow, across the Yangtze, and proclaimed himself Prince Ch'eng of the Great Chou dynasty. The Southeast triangle was threatened on all sides. The atmosphere grew tense with alarm. People discussed military matters, and planned means of local self-defense against marauding rebels and bandits. But the Yuan government's local officials in this region took no positive steps to prepare defenses; indeed, they appeared more anxious to surrender their responsibilities and protect their own skin.

These were times that might well discourage a man whose abilities were useful only in times of peace. The older men were dispirited, and tended to withdraw and wait out the storm. But among younger men, active and ambitious like the young Kao Ch'i, these times were a spur to action. The scholar educated in the Confucian tradition—could he not also envisage himself a hero? Did not that tradition sometimes demand action, and physical courage, and the defense of its principles? If the Mandate of Heaven were about to be transferred to some great new dynastic founder who would conquer the world and restore peace and good government, was it not better for a young man—who had assumed no duty of loyalty to the crumbling old order by becoming an official in its government—to hold himself free to serve a just, new cause? Theoretically, the demands of Confucian loyalty were somewhat ambiguous in a case like this; practically, the incompetent Mongol government had done little to earn the devoted support of its subjects, and there were even those who seriously doubted the legitimacy of the Yuan's claim to be the rightful rulers of the Chinese. So a young man of Kao Ch'i's generation might well have been uncertain and undecided about what he should do, and how he should prepare for his unpredictable future.

But certain elements of his future were predictable. Life went on, even in times like these. As he approached adulthood, the matter of marriage faced him and presented certain difficulties. Earlier, a betrothal had been arranged with the daughter of a rich man of Ch'ing-ch'iu, the "Green Hill," in a village northeast of Soochow on the Lou River.[2] Like Kao Ch'i's father and grandfather, the girl's father, Chou Chung-ta, probably lived off the income of rural property, while leading a life of leisure and cultivation of poetry and the arts.

One of Kao Ch'i's students, who wrote his master's biography shortly after the poet's death, tells the amusing story of his wedding arrangements. The poet was quite mature when about seventeen years of age, although he had not yet reached the age of the formal recognition of adulthood, the capping ceremony, which traditionally was performed at the age of nineteen. Because his family had suffered financial decline, they had not been able to carry out the prescribed Six Ceremonies of preparation for marriage, which included hiring a go-between to arrange the ceremonies, exchanging gifts, exchanging names, fixing an auspicious date, entertaining the bride's parents, and the like. These were costly activities that had to be carried out with fitting pomp and dignity in order to maintain the prestige of the families involved. At this time old Mr. Chou fell ill. A friend of Kao Ch'i, who must have been well acquainted with the Chou family, jokingly suggested that if Kao's future father-in-law were ill, he (the unnamed friend) should pay a courtesy call. Kao Ch'i might well have been sensitive about this, since his inability to carry out the marriage preparations must have been embarrassing

[2] The Chou family home at the Green Hill evidently was very close to the Kao family's rural property at Sandy Lake, for Green Hill was on the shores of that lake.

to him. But he agreed that it was a good idea, and even said he was willing to go along with the friend. So they arrived together at the Chou family mansion.

The old man was well enough to receive Kao's friend at his bedside, while Kao, who must not have met the old man previously, waited outside in a parlor. Old Mr. Chou said: "My illness has taken a turn for the better, but I am still not well enough to go out with you to meet this new guest you have brought with you. However, I hear that he is an accomplished poet. There in the parlor hangs a painting of geese in the reeds which unfortunately lacks a poem colophon." This message was conveyed to Kao, who took the hint, and as quickly took a brush and dashed off a four-line poem. The poem read:

> The west wind tears at the blossoming water reeds.
> The good birds come flying past; a wing feather falls.
> The sandy beach is broad, and the water cold; no fish is to be seen.
> I am covered with the frosty dew, so long have I been standing here waiting.[3]

Old Mr. Chou laughed when the poem was taken to him, for while it reads very well as a description of a fall scene at a river's edge with the wild geese flying, it is full of obvious allusions to Kao's own situation vis-à-vis the marriage. In the standardized symbolism, geese are the symbol of the marriage go-between, falling feathers are messages sent, the cold is the Kao family's declining fortunes, the fish is the bride who has not yet been seen, and the long waiting can be taken as a reference to Kao's own impatience with the delays forced upon him by circumstances. Old Chou said to Kao's friend:

[3] Cited in the biography by Lü Mien, prefaced to ccscc, vol. 1, section "Pen chuan," p. 2a-b.

"If he really is so anxious to marry, please then do me the favor of telling him to go home and select a proper day, and they shall be wed."[4]

This marriage, begun so informally, was most successful. Kao became an intimate friend of his father-in-law and of his wife's six or seven brothers; they had many interests in common, and he was much respected by them. His talent and his growing reputation served in place of family fortune to secure him widespread respect. He spent a great deal of time visiting at Ch'ing-ch'iu, the Green Hill, often staying in his father-in-law's home for long periods. We can imagine that the family life in this great household meant much to him, and compensated for the lack of it in his own home. His parents, of course, had long been dead, and the only immediate family we know about was his older brother Kao Tzu, who seems to have been away from home in official service "with the garrison forces in the eastern Huai region" throughout these years.

Kao Ch'i's wife also wrote poetry, a fact which indicates that she had acquired more than the minimal education of women of her social class; yet it was not uncommon in families with strong literary interests for the women to receive good educations. There is one poem Kao Ch'i wrote to her from Nanking, in reply to one she sent him there, but hers is no longer in existence. There is another poem written for her in the last years of his life. Both are filled with a fond and tender regard for her, and both contain allusions which show she must have known history and literature in order to be able to understand them. Both poems seem to evidence that they profoundly understood one another. But there are only two or three such extant poems, referring directly to her. She bore him four children, and she outlived him. We know

4 *Ibid.*

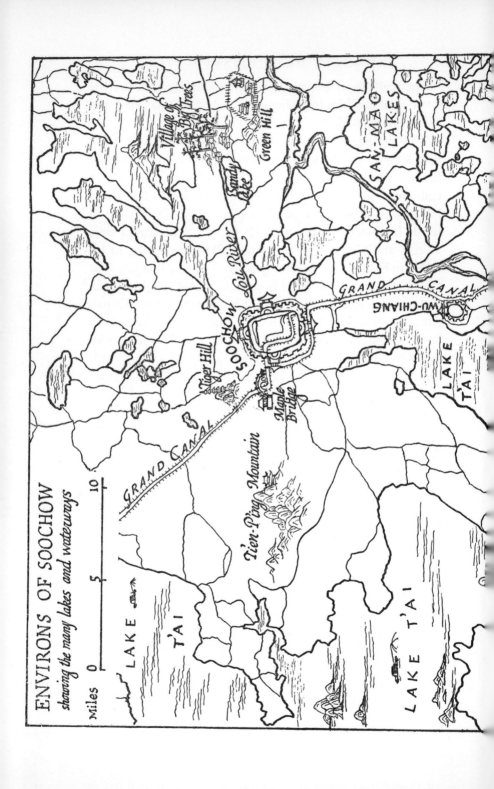

ENVIRONS OF SOOCHOW
showing the many lakes and waterways

miles 0   5   10

LAKE

T'AI

GRAND CANAL

Tien-P'ing Mountain

LAKE T'AI

Tiger Hill

SOOCHOW

Lou River

Maple Bridge

Village of Big Trees

Small Lake

Green Hill

SAN-MAO LAKES

GRAND CANAL

WU-CHIANG

LAKE T'AI

nothing more about her. This meager evidence leaves us wondering what she was like, and wishing we knew more.[5]

The marriage took place in 1353. Throughout 1354 and 1355 Kao Ch'i spent his time partly at the home inside the north wall of the city, partly at Green Hill or at his family's rural property nearby. These were tense years, years in which the spreading disorders encircled the Southeast triangle. The year 1356 abruptly and dramatically brought the rebellions to them. In March of that year, Chang Shih-ch'eng's forces crossed the Yangtze and took Soochow, and in the following month Chu Yuan-chang, who in the winter before had crossed the Yangtze farther west, near Nanking, now besieged and captured Nanking. These two cities now became bases of rebellions which defied not only the legitimate Yuan government but also each other as they expanded their territories south of the river. Chang Shih-ch'eng followed up the capture of Soochow by quickly taking the surrounding prefectures—Sung-chiang and Ch'ang-chou in what would be modern Kiangsu, and Hu-chou, Chia-hsing, and parts of other prefectures in Chekiang, along the southern shore of Lake T'ai. The battle line between Chang and Chu cut from north to south on a line running through Lake T'ai. In these years the most contested point on this line was the city of Ch'ang-chou, just halfway between Soochow and Nanking. The capital of a rebel state, maintaining itself by military force, Soochow was threatened from the west by a dangerous enemy, and by strong government forces based at Chia-hsing, near Hangchow. These government forces were not regular Mongol or conscript Chinese armies, for the Yuan government no longer had any strong regular forces in this part of China.

---

[5] Kao Ch'i's poetry contains very few poems alluding to other romances or even brief romantic encounters with courtesans or other women. As far as we can discern from his poetry, such affairs, rather common for men in his society, played a very small part in his life.

They were an army of aboriginal tribesmen specially brought into the Southeast triangle from Central China, modern Hunan. They were ferocious and undisciplined forces, out for plunder and unwilling to cooperate with or take orders from local government officials. They were a scourge to the local populations, and as much of a threat as a help to the government which nominally employed them. They proved to be no great help or comfort to the Yuan government, but they were a potential threat to rebel movements like those of Chang and Chu, and they were a source of the greatest danger to the well-being of the suffering civilian population. Fortunately they did not raid Soochow.

But Soochow was undergoing its own sufferings at this time. Chang Shih-ch'eng's entry into the rich region south of the Yangtze was accompanied by violence. An account of this incident tells us much about the conditions of the time. The leader of a small bandit gang from the county of Chiang-yin on the south bank of the Yangtze fled north to Chang Shih-ch'eng's camp in 1354 or 1355 to seek his help in putting down a rival. He was the man who gave Chang the idea of invading the Southeast triangle. Chang had already proclaimed himself Prince Ch'eng, and had set up a kind of mock government in the eastern Huai region, where he was in familiar home territory. At first he was unreceptive to the idea that he expand into the unfamiliar region south of the river, but after the serious reverses he suffered in 1354, when he was even driven out temporarily from his important bastion at Kao-yu, he was desperate. The prospects for his rebellion in the Huai region were somewhat dimmed, and he was in the mood to look about for other prospects.

Late in 1355, in the face of famine in the Huai region, Chang made the decision to send his younger brother Chang Shih-te, in command of several thousand remnant forces, to attempt a crossing and explore the possibilities. It was the promise of "the broad fertile lands, the abundance of money and of grain, and the riches in sons and daughters, jewels and silks" which moved him to look to the south. Chang Shih-te was probably the most capable member of the Chang family, a military commander of ability. He forced his way across the Yangtze early in 1356, meeting almost no opposition, and seized the subprefecture (*chou*) of Ch'ang-shu, north of Soochow on the river. The government of the Chiang-che Province was located at Hangchow. The responsible official there was an ineffective Mongol military man with no regular government forces to rely on. He issued instructions to the *daruhaci*, the chief Mongol official of each prefecture, to organize whatever regular troops and civilian militia he could bring together to resist the "bandit invasion." But the *daruhaci* of Soochow, an old man, died at this moment, and a new one had to be transferred from the neighboring Sung-chiang prefecture. He hastily organized a small force to take the field and meet the invaders, leaving a Chinese official, his civilian second-in-command, to defend the city, with a minor Mongol official responsible for whatever military action would be needed. This field force disintegrated through desertion of the unwilling, totally untrained, hastily impressed peasant component, which had constituted its major strength. Commanders in nearby county seats, which Chang Shih-te encountered on his march toward Soochow, were defeated after halfhearted battles, and surrendered. Finally, Shih-te and three or four thousand bandit troops arrived at Soochow, and deployed themselves around the city wall for one night. The Chinese official who was responsible for the city's defense was an elderly man of literary ability but little else. There was no attempt to defend the city.

The following morning the gates were opened, and Chang Shih-te walked in, without having had to fire an arrow or unsheath a sword. There followed a wild few days of pillaging and destruction, and for the first time in centuries, Soochow tasted the fearful violence of warfare.[6] The Mongol garrison commander hid in a Chinese home, but was discovered. He slit his own throat, but failed to die; Chang's bandit troops discovered him and murdered him. The newly appointed *daruhaci*, still in the field with a handful of soldiers, heard that the city had fallen, and committed suicide. The Chinese chief official hid out in his study and wrote poetry. Neighboring cities voluntarily surrendered, hoping to avoid similar slaughter and destruction. Within a few days order was restored, and Chang Shih-te commenced to build a civilian government to replace that which had existed. He took over one of the largest Buddhist temples and converted its spacious buildings into a palace for his brother, self-proclaimed Prince Ch'eng. His chief lieutenants competed madly among themselves to find the most imposing buildings, confiscating temples, former government offices, and the homes of the rich, which they converted into their official residences. About a month later Chang Shih-ch'eng arrived and moved into his new palace. He established ministries and bureaus and all the paraphernalia of a government in imitation of an imperial regime. Soochow became Lung-p'ing, the capital of his Great Chou dynasty. But it is doubtful if many of the residents ceased to call it by its old name.

While Chang Shih-ch'eng settled down to the enjoyment of the pleasures of being a prince in Soochow, his three brothers moved on to new fields of conquest farther south, in the service of his rebel dynasty. In 1357 the most able of them, Shih-te, attempted to take Hangchow, while another of Chang's lieutenants engaged the fierce Miao army at nearby Chia-hsing. The Miao forces gave Chang's armies their first severe defeat since crossing the Yangtze, but this campaign, which kept

[6] I.e., since the sacking of the city by the Chin Tartar army in 1130, the one time that Chin forces, pressuring the Sung, had crossed the Yangtze.

the Miao army tied down through the summer of 1357, gave Chang Shih-te the opportunity to enter the lightly defended Hangchow. Hangchow suffered the same fate as Soochow: it was pillaged, sacked, and plundered, with great loss of life and property, while the light government force that should have defended it retreated and hid in the nearby mountains. Then the Miao armies, which had just inflicted a severe defeat to Chang's forces sent against them at Chia-hsing, came on to "liberate" Hangchow. The unfortunate city again suffered street fighting and looting, as the Miao forces fought their way in, and Chang Shih-te retreated in defeat. Chang's southward expansion thus faced two severe setbacks in the latter part of 1357, and the whole Southeast triangle was plunged briefly into bloodshed and suffering.

Chang Shih-ch'eng faced other threats as well in the year following his seizure of Soochow. Fang Kuo-chen's pirate raids were now being extended to cities well up into the Yangtze estuary. Chu Yuan-chang's forces were pushing eastward both by land and water, and in a severe battle at Ch'ang-chou early in 1358 they took this outpost city and captured Chang's brother Chang Shih-te, who was defending it. Shih-te was taken to Nanking, where he was forced to write letters to persuade his brother to surrender to Chu. Intellectually and physically he was the ablest and most energetic of the Chang brothers, and his mother put great pressure on Chang Shih-ch'eng to come to terms that would free him. Shih-ch'eng received the letters, pondered them, discussed them with his officials, and took no action. Shih-te was enticed and intimidated to surrender to Chu and serve him, but stubbornly refused. Eventually he was put to death.[7]

This blow to Chang Shih-ch'eng's movement had grave re-

[7] *Ming Shih* (hereafter *MS*), ch. 123, pp. 7b-8a says he starved himself to death in prison, after secretly sending word to his brother to surrender to the Yuan government, and continue to resist Chu Yuan-chang. This may be the correct version.

sults, both in practical terms and in its effect on morale. Under all of these military pressures, including new aggressive action from the Miao armies, now anxious to move northward from Hangchow, and the psychological consequences of the serious reverses following the first easy victories, Chang decided to play another game. There was resistance to him because he was a "bandit" in the eyes of the Chinese upper segment of society whose view of legitimacy made them bulk rebels and bandits together and scorn both. Then, there was fearful military pressure against him from the Miao forces, nominally acting for the Yuan government, but actually lawless and undisciplined looters and plunderers of the civilian population. There was the increasing threat from Chu Yuanchang's strong military force, successfully encroaching on his western boundary. And there was the necessity of keeping up defenses against raids from Fang Kuo-chen's pirate forces. For all these reasons it seemed wisest to Chang to surrender to the Yuan government, and become legitimate. The Yuan government was so pressed by rebel uprisings, and so desperate for grain shipments which were now cut off via the Grand Canal, that they were quite willing to accept Chang's surrender virtually on his own terms. They recognized his control of the larger portion of the Southeast triangle, and allowed him to keep control of it as Grand Marshal ("T'ai-wei"), a special kind of local military governor. He could keep all his Great Chou dynasty officialdom as members of his staff, could retain his armies as the military command of his new position, and could manage local fiscal control as he wished. The only charges put upon him were to acknowledge the suzerainty of the Mongol government and use its calendar, to fight off other rebel enemies of the Yuan government, and, most important of all, to supply grain to be shipped to the capital. This occurred in the early fall of 1358.[8]

[8] Wu K'uan's late fifteenth century *P'ing Wu Lu* makes it appear that

Later that same fall Fang Kuo-chen also surrendered to the Yuan and received a position in the provincial government, which made it possible for him, too, to retain all of his real power; however, it put upon him the responsibility for supplying the ships to send Chang's grain offering to the capital via the coastal sea route. The sum sent was small, only about one hundred thousand piculs a year, in contrast to the three or four million piculs normally sent before the beginning of these troubles. Chang could easily afford this—the cost was small in return for what he received. For while Fang Kuo-chen and Chang remained jealous and suspicious of each other, they ceased open attacks on each other. Moreover, Chang was now on the side of the government, so the pressure from the fierce aboriginal Miao troops was relieved. So hated were the Miao troops and their commander Yang-wan-che that local Yuan officials in Hangchow immediately entered into a plot with Chang to get rid of him. They sent word to Chang to dispatch an army secretly against Yang-wan-che, who, unprepared and surprised, was unable to defend himself. His forces demolished, he hanged himself late in 1358. Although this freed the region of the terror of the bloodthirsty and unmanageable aborigines, it put the whole region of northern Chekiang, except for Fang Kuo-chen's three coastal prefectures, into Chang's hands without a fight. Chang Shih-ch'eng was left with only one enemy close at hand: Chu Yuan-chang and the Nanking-based branch of the Red Turban movement. Now he could concentrate his military power against this single enemy.

This move worked greatly to Chang's immediate practical advantage. Most important of all, perhaps, it raised his

---

this occurred in 1357, and many other sources for Ming history, apparently following this, say the same. T'ao Tsung-i's *Cho Keng Lu*, a contemporary account, states that this occurred in the eighth month of 1358, and other evidence supports this.

prestige in the eyes of his own new subjects. Although clearly a bandit who had manipulated himself into a kind of legitimacy, and for reasons that could not commend him greatly in their eyes, still, it was now no longer treason to serve him. Superficially at least he was on the side of right. He had been offered chances to surrender to Chu Yuan-chang and the Red Turbans, and had refused, and this was even more important in the eyes of the scholar-officialdom class in society. In their eyes the Red Turbans were the most reprehensible kind of scum imaginable—superstitious rabble-rousers, worthless dregs of society, enemies of the cultural tradition, bandits of the most feared and hated kind. In comparison, Chang Shih-ch'eng was a man who at least pretended to honor the traditional values. He was crude and violent and lacked education, but he aspired to become a true gentleman, a patron of talent, a sponsor of literary endeavors. He had established bureaus of government for the purpose of encouraging literature, and had appointed men of scholarly interests and literary taste to his staff. Although a salt smuggler turned rebel, he was a man who seemed to be susceptible to influences from the cultured upper classes. Might he not prove to be a man with whom the locally influential could collaborate to create some measure of regional stability, to protect their common interests? By putting himself on the side of the government and firmly against the Red Turban rebels at Nanking (who were still known by the reputation of the whole Red Turban movement more than by the individual character which Chu Yuan-chang's local government gradually acquired), Chang Shih-ch'eng strengthened himself immeasurably. It is against this background that we follow the young Kao Ch'i's activities in these years.

Kao Ch'i was twenty the year that Chang Shih-ch'eng crossed the Yangtze and moved into his palace, converted from Soochow's largest and most splendid Buddhist temple.

There was a short period of disorder in which the city suffered greatly from the invaders' lawless actions, but after Chang Shih-ch'eng himself arrived, and a kind of government was put together and public safety was again maintained, many of the people came to find some good in Chang's regime. Kao Ch'i soon came very close to becoming involved in it, due to his reputation as a budding poet. Chang appointed to high office as many noted men of education as he could persuade to accept it. Among those who did accept was a man by the name of Jao Chieh, a proud and impressive figure who had seen years of service in the Yuan government and fancied himself a poet and a patron of talent. He was living in Soochow when Chang's troops captured the city. At first he refused to have anything to do with the new regime, but Chang called on him in person, flattered him, and offered him high office with no grave responsibilities. He could spend his days lavishly entertaining his friends, feasting, and holding poetry competitions. Kao Ch'i may well have known Jao before he became an official under the rebel regime, and Jao almost certainly had known about Kao Ch'i. One story is that Jao had first tested him as a poet when Kao was only fifteen, but it is more likely that this occurred in 1356 or 1357, when Kao was twenty, and during the first year of Chang's government in Soochow. The story goes that Jao managed to have Kao brought to him, and gave him a topic and a rhyme pattern in which he was to compose a poem spontaneously. The young man's poem was so excellent and displayed such maturity of learning and of literary style that Jao and all of the old scholars present were amazed. They applauded him as a rare new genius of literature, and sought to patronize him and bring him into the rebel regime as an ornament to its government.

Kao Ch'i's own attitudes toward the rebel regime at this time are difficult to determine. Among his prose writings is a

"Biography of the Chaste Madame Mei," a short account of
the noble death of a young woman who lived near him. She
was seized by the soldiers of Chang Shih-te in the first days
following the fall of Soochow, and died defending herself
against dishonor at the hands of the soldiers. In the biography Kao explains the background of the disorders that led to
her death: "In the spring of the sixteenth year of *chih-cheng*
[1356] when the Huai army [of Chang Shih-ch'eng] moved
southward, the officials responsible for defending the city
failed to maintain vigilant guard, thus the city was lost. . . ."
Apart from this, any criticism of the invaders is implicit
rather than explicit. And in none of Kao's other writings is
there any direct evidence of how he felt about the invaders
in this first year of their possession of his city. Writing in the
early years of the Ming dynasty shortly after his death, his
biographers say that although many persons of the time were
eager to ingratiate themselves with the new conquerors and
rushed to accept office and rank from them, Kao alone remained aloof. They may be correct. To be sure, he was not
alone in his aloofness; the majority of the scholar-gentry
would have nothing to do with Chang Shih-ch'eng in an
official way, even though a larger number must have felt
some sympathy for him, preferring him to the Mongols, the
Miao armies, and other rebels like Fang Kuo-chen and the
various Red Turban leaders. But Kao Ch'i appears to have
been most reluctant to become identified with Chang's government at this time. Involvement was difficult to escape, for
Chang himself and many of his leading officials made the
pursuit of literature their chief activity, and they would not
be satisfied until so outstanding a talent participated in their
poetry contests, attended their parties, and appeared to be
their "guest," that is, a virtual member of their official en-
tourages.

It was probably to escape the pressures put upon him by

the admiring officialdom of the Chang regime that Kao Ch'i moved in 1358 to Ch'ing-ch'iu, the Green Hill, where his father-in-law's estate was located. He was twenty-two this year, and he took upon himself the name "Ch'ing-ch'iu-tzu," which may be translated "the man of the Green Hill." This self-chosen name became the poet's informal nickname. His formal name, Ch'i, and his courtesy name, Chi-ti, continued to be used as custom and etiquette demanded, but to most people he now became best known as Kao Ch'ing-ch'iu. In this year he wrote a poem called the "Song of the Man of the Green Hill," characterizing himself as a man driven to writing poetry by an overpowering inner compulsion. This poem became very famous, and served both to spread his fame and fix his new name. It is not a great poem, for it still indulges in a kind of youthful display. And in all likelihood it derived much of its meaning from allusions to contemporary affairs, allusions that are no longer comprehensible. Thus in reading it today one is forced to take it rather literally, whereas other levels of meaning probably made it more interesting to Kao's contemporaries. But it is still valuable for its evidence of the young poet's spirit, his conception of himself as poet, and his lively imagination. He himself supplied the introductory preface, in which he shifts from the first to the third person, in setting the mood for his fanciful poem about himself.

The Song of the Man of the Green Hill

AUTHOR'S PREFACE: *By the Yangtze's edge there is the Green Hill [Ch'ing-ch'iu]. I've moved my home to the south of it, and so have adopted the cognomen, "the man of Ch'ing-ch'iu." This man lives there in idleness, with nothing to do. All day long he works earnestly at making poems, and while there he happened to write this "Song of the Man of Ch'ing-*

ch'iu" in which he sets forth his mind, in the hope of dispelling the ridicule of him for his addiction to poetry.

The man of Ch'ing-ch'iu, he is thin and unsullied—
Originally he was a genie-courtier at the Pavilion of
  Five-colored Clouds
What year was he banished to this lower world?
He tells no one his real name.
He wears rope sandals, but he has wearied of distant
  roaming.
He shoulders a hoe, but he is too lazy to till his own
  fields.
He has a sword, but he lets it gather rust.
He has books, but he leaves them piled in disorder.
He is unwilling to bend his back for five catties of rice.
He is unwilling to loosen his tongue to bring about the
  fall of seventy cities.
But, he is addicted to the search for poetic lines.
He hums them to himself, he sings them for his own
  pleasure.
He wanders through the fields, dragging his cane, wear-
  ing a rope-belt.
Bystanders, not understanding him, laugh and ridicule,
Calling him a "muddleheaded scholar of Lu," a verita-
  ble "madman of Ch'u."
The man of Ch'ing-ch'iu hears it but cares not at all,—
Still the sound of poetry-chanting comes in unbroken
  gurgle from his lips.
He chants poetry in the morning 'till he forgets to eat;
He chants poetry in the evening 'till he has dispersed
  all ill-feelings.
When intent on his poetizing
He groans like a man sick from too much drinking;
He finds no time to comb his hair,
And has no time to attend to family affairs.

His children cry, and he knows not to pity them.
Guests call, and he shows them no hospitality.
He is not concerned that shortly he will be destitute;
He envies not at all the way Mr. Yi[9] prospered.
It grieves him not to wear rough uncut homespun;
He longs not at all for the colored tassels of an official's
    hat.
He pays no attention to the bitterly fought duel of
    dragon and tiger,
Nor gives he notice to the frightened scurryings of the
    golden crow and the jade rabbit.
Instead, he sits alone, facing the shore.
He walks alone, in the grove.
He sharpens his native powers, he conserves his native
    energies.
None of creation's myriad creatures can conceal their
    nature from him.
Through the vast, misty realm of the eight farthest
    limits he wanders in his imagination.
Sitting there, he makes the formless become real.
He has acquired the sensitivity of the one who could
    shoot an arrow through a suspended flea,
The strength of one who could behead a great whale.
He becomes pure as one who drinks the nourishing dew,
Lofty as the ranks of soaring crags and cliffs.
Towering above, the bright clouds open to him;
Luxuriantly the frozen plants again grow.
He ascends to clutch at the roots of Heaven, seeking
    out the caves of the moon.
With rhinoceros horn magic lens he scans the Oxen
    Ford, seeing the myriad wonders in its depths.

[9] An allusion to a man of antiquity who became very wealthy through
thrift and industry.

Wonderful, suddenly, to be in the company of gods
    and spirits!
Grand spectacle, vaster than the expanse of rivers and
    mountains!
The stars and the rainbows lend him their radiance;
The mists and the dews nourish his heroic spirit.
The sounds he hears are divine harmonies,
The tastes, the flavors of the unearthly broth.
"In this world below there is no object which delights
    me;
Even instruments of bronze and jade emit harsh clank-
    ing sounds.
In my thatched hut, by the river's edge, the storm clears;
Behind my barred gate, now I've slept out my sleep,
    and I've just finished a poem.
So I strum the wine pot and sing a joyous song,
Giving no thought to startled mundane ears.
I want to call to the old man of Mount Chün, to bring
    out the long flute of magic powers
And accompany this song of mine, under the bright
    moon.
But then I think sadly how the waves would suddenly
    rise,
Birds and beasts would shriek in fright, the very hills
    shake and crumble.
The Lord of Heaven would hear it and be angered,
Would send a white heron to fetch me back.
He would let me go on no longer with these tricks of
    this world;
I would don again my jewelled waist pendants, and go
    back to the City of Jade."[10]

[10] CCSC 11/1a-2a

This long poem is in the form of a song, with long and short lines, a strong rhythm, and a recurring rhyme on the syllable *"ing"* in alternate lines. It is full of classical and literary allusions which need not be explained, for most of them would convey little meaning to the Western reader, even when fully explained. But the Western reader can grasp the attitude of the poet toward the day-to-day world, and can sense the scope of the poetic imagination which took Kao Ch'i out of that world and into a vast and unlimited realm of excitement and delight. And yet, though he claims to scorn the things it can offer him, we see also that he does not want to forego the day-to-day world. He will not "bend his waist" for the sake of the trifling emolument of office (ever, or just in times like these?); he will not use his superior talents of mind and of skillful speech "to bring about the fall of seventy cities" (in the service of any ruler, or merely those on the scene at this time?). But he does implicitly affirm his confidence in his own powers and abilities by the comparisons these allusions bring to himself. He ignores the "duel of dragon and tiger," meaning the struggle for the mastery of the world, in which Chang Shih-ch'eng and Chu Yuan-chang and the Yuan court are embroiled. He gives no notice to the "scurryings of the golden crow and the jade rabbit": these designate the sun and the moon, or the passage of time, but in this context they might also be intended to refer to the scurryings of the lesser animals, the hangers-on at the courts of the powerful. He will withdraw from the ways of the world and refine his senses, improve his powers, and conserve his strength. This is all stated in traditional metaphor, mostly Taoist in flavor, and with exuberant imaginative force. But it could also refer clearly to his decision to withdraw from the contemporary struggle until the air has cleared and the scene shifted, until the future is more certain and a person can see which way to turn. In the meantime, he proclaims, the poet's life brings him the only rewards he desires, and it is a life of freedom and independence from the world about him. People may ridicule him for eccentricity, but he does not care; he will not be moved by such ridicule to abandon these ideals. Thus the proud young poet, at the age of twenty-two, proclaims himself to the world.

There are other poems written this year, telling of the life at P'u-li, the village at the Green Hill where the Chou family estate was located. He was very sensitive to the charms of the pleasant countryside. In a set of four poems he describes the daily life at P'u-li; the first of these is typical:

> Long bridges and short bridges, amidst willow trees;
> Ponds in front and ponds in back, with lotus blooming.
> People look where the pennons rise, above the wine
>   shops;
> Gulls escort a boat returning to the fisherman's home.
> A breeze seems about to stir up little waves, but doesn't.
> A hazy sun is on the point of setting, but still has not.
> How beautiful, the water reeds among the winding
>   streams!
> Not bad, this minced fish, served with kumquats![11]

Even in these troubled times the simple pleasures of the rural village, enjoyment of scenery and of local delicacies, were still possible. The Green Hill itself, nearby, was a pleasant climb, and afforded a beautiful view of the surrounding fields and lakes. Friends came to drink with him, exchange poems, and talk about the stirring events all around them. Farewell parties were given for departing friends; in a poem written in the autumn of this year to send off a friend going to the Yuan capital to seek a post in the government, Kao wrote:

[11] CCSC 14/6a-b

"I too have ambitions, but just now I cannot leave; raising my head to look into the 10,000 *li* journey ahead of you, I am overcome with vague and inexpressible thoughts."[12] These thoughts may well have been that the times offered him no hope of realizing his ambitions, hence it was better not to go. Perhaps it was in this same year that he wrote a poem about the shrine at P'u-li to a worthy of the T'ang dynasty who found the official career unsatisfactory, and retired to P'u-li to become a hermit there. In several poems written about the man in these years, Kao showed that he had thought deeply about the problem of whether he should seek a career, or should withdraw and wait. He praised the hermit who recognized that "the time was not right," and withdrew.

Kao and his wife probably had a small cottage of their own in the village of P'u-li. And their first child, a daughter, must have been born this year. Too, his wife's father and her brothers provided him with company, and shared many interests. He wrote a number of poems to be inscribed on paintings in the father-in-law's collection, as well as poems describing his house and garden and social gatherings in the Chou household. But in the early winter of this same year, for some reason that is not clear, he left this pleasant life to wander for two or three years in the region immediately to the south, in what would be northern Chekiang today. We can only speculate about his reasons for this. Perhaps it was because Ch'ing-ch'iu was not far enough from Soochow, and he still felt some embarrassing pressures to join Chang's rebel regime. Perhaps he felt that travel was part of a man's education, and he should see Hangchow and the famous scenic and historic places nearby. Perhaps he was seeking a career, and wanted to visit persons and explore

[12] The last two lines of the poem "Sung Chang Kung-shih Hsiang hui-shih ching-shih," ccsc 10/8b-9b

possibilities. Or perhaps he had some family business which is not explained. We know that some generations earlier the Kao family had lived at Shan-yin County (modern Shao-hsing, near Hangchow) before moving to Soochow; perhaps there remained some branch of the family at that place, and this occasioned his travel. In any event, he has left no explanation of the travel, nor has he told what it accomplished for him. In later years he wrote a preface to a collection of fifteen poems written during these journeys, and this, more than anything else he wrote, tells us about the two years and more of wandering:

"From the year *wu-hsü* [1358] to the year *keng-tzu* [1360] in the reign-period *chih-cheng*, I was travelling throughout the several prefectures of the Southeast. As I viewed those mountains and streams, the poems which I composed were extremely numerous, but with the passage of a long time they have become scattered and lost. In a moment of leisure, while putting my desk to order, I came across a number of these sheets, but most of them were spoiled and tattered and partially missing, so that many of the poems were incomplete. Hence I selected those which seemed worth preserving, and again set forth in poetry the mood of that time, where necessary to complete them, thus making fifteen poems. Although I was not able to go north to the Yellow River or west as far as Mounts Sung and Hua in order to make poems about their perilous routes and extraordinary appearance, nonetheless where I have written here of the conditions of travel and have recorded the famous places which I passed, a similar purpose of cherishing worthy men and reflecting on the past is often present. Therefore I have been unable to discard these poems, and thus have made a copy of them, for myself to read."[13]

[13] Quoted in Kao's *Nien-p'u*, under the year *chih-cheng* 18 (1358)

Assuming that Kao arranged these fifteen poems in chronological sequence, which seems likely from their content, we can piece together from them the outlines of his journey. Number One tells of leaving the south gate of Soochow one cold evening at the end of the year.[14] To quote from this poem: ". . . I say farewell to the pleasures of my home region, and set myself forth on the dangerous road ahead. Leaving the wine aside, I part from guests and family, and drive my cart through the crossroads of the suburbs. . . . I turn my head, to look back on the high city walls; the setting sun enlarges clouds and trees. In this time of disorder there is little safety; in the striving for livelihood there are many who go hungry. Along the road I meet many coming to and fro; who does not feel pressed by this to hurry? This far journey is my own desire; move on then, why worry oneself with sad thoughts?"

Number Two speaks of crossing the Che River a few days later, and finding lodgings for the night in a home there. The local people warn him not to stray too far as he walks about, for dangerous tigers come out at night. It is cold and he does not sleep well. He reminds himself with a start that a great river now separates him from his home. Number Three speaks of passing through Hsiao-shan County, and again complains of the cold, remarks on a beautiful view of the mountainous country, and regrets that the times are those of warfare and disorder. Number Four tells of the crossing of the Ch'ien-ch'ing River, approaching Shao-hsing, which seems to have been his first objective, since he passed by Hangchow. Undoubtedly this is also because Hangchow was under attack at the time. He speaks of being in a hurry to press on to the east, to Shao-hsing, and thus cannot stop to visit the shrine of a famous man of the Han dynasty. Number Five

[14] This and the following quotations are from the fifteen travel poems, ccsc 3/13a-18b

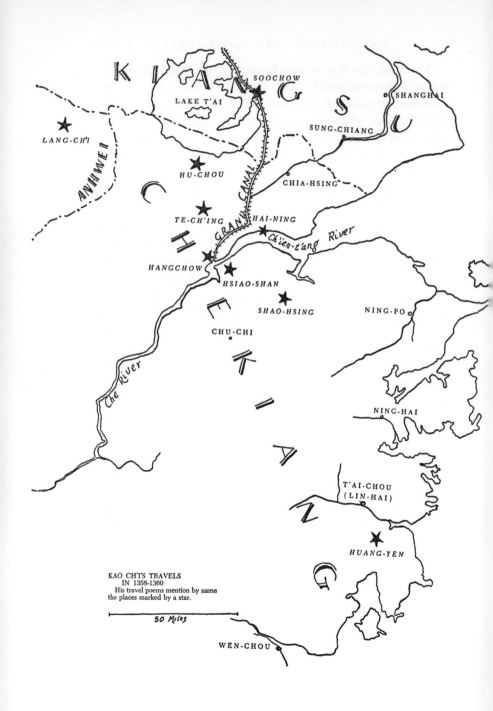

KIANGSU

ANHWEI

CHEKIANG

LANG-CH'I ★

SOOCHOW ★
LAKE T'AI
SHANGHAI
SUNG-CHIANG
HU-CHOU ★
CHIA-HSING
TE-CH'ING ★
HAI-NING ★
GRAND CANAL
Ch'ien-t'ang River
HANGCHOW ★
HSIAO-SHAN ★
Che River
SHAO-HSING ★
CHU-CHI
NING-PO

NING-HAI

T'AI-CHOU
(LIN-HAI)

HUANG-YEN ★

KAO CH'I'S TRAVELS
IN 1358-1360
His travel poems mention by name
the places marked by a star.

50 Miles

WEN-CHOU

finds him in the city of Shao-hsing (Shan-yin), but disappointingly says nothing of family there, or of other reasons for having come.

Number Six is entitled, "Hearing That the Long Spears Army Is Coming, I Leave the City of Shao-hsing and Spend the Night at Mount K'an." Bandits of the Huai region who had surrendered to Chu Yuan-chang, the Long Spears were feared for their ferocity and their violent treatment of the civilian population in cities they garrisoned. This attack on Shao-hsing is probably that recorded in the Ming *Veritable Record* in the fourth moon of 1359. Kao Ch'i found himself in the thick of fierce fighting between the forces of Chang Shih-ch'eng and Chu Yuan-chang, but he appears to have remained in areas held by Chang, who, since the eighth moon of the preceding year, had been a Grand Marshal in the Yuan government. This poem speaks of the forces of a Mongol prince based at Shao-hsing, and of his feud with another prominent Mongol official of the region. The poem says: "When I arrived, the disorders had just been settled, but the atmosphere in the city still was very somber." This undoubtedly refers to the murder of the prince, a man well-liked by the local population, and the bloody retaliation by his followers which ended the feud. Kao goes on: "But then I hear that there is an army approaching; I am thrown into confusion, how dare I remain here? So again I leave hastily by the west gate. The weather is so cold that it stops travel by boat. . . . Fields have been abandoned, and no one has harvested the rice. The dwellers of this region have all fled; where shall the traveller find rest?" Fortunately he escapes, though he must brave tigers and travel by night. His regret is that he has not had time to visit the famous scenic mountains of the region.

Number Seven finds him travelling westward and crossing the Che River at another point—farther west than when he first came into Hsiao-shan County, as described in poem Number Two. He speaks of waiting for the ferry, through the cold night with a group of fish merchants, and describes the sights and sounds of the crossing of the rapid stream, with mountains fading into the distance behind as new ranges appear through the mists before. In Number Eight he is in Hangchow at last, visiting the old Sung palace sites. This appears to be in the autumn, probably of 1359, and some months after Number Seven. "The traveller," he says, "mourns the surrendered ruler, and the old-timers still resent the treacherous prime minister." These are references to the last emperor of the southern Sung, and to his Prime Minister Chia Ssu-tao, who was blamed for the fall of the dynasty to the Mongols. He ends this poem: "How distant is vast Heaven. I cannot learn from it about the rise and fall of dynasties. Today the fate of the dynasty again is in decline; a chill comes over me as I turn again to gaze [on the old Sung ruins]." Number Nine describes the famous Ch'ien-t'ang tidal bore, the awesome sight and sound of the incoming tide. He evidently saw this famous sight under a full moon, the proper thing for the tourist to do even today. In Number Ten he is in Hu-chou (modern Wu-hsing) prefecture on the southern shore of Lake T'ai, near the city of Te-ch'ing, about halfway between Hangchow and Hu-chou. He passes a famous battlefield of earlier history, and makes the usual kinds of comments on the grim spectacle of unburied bones and his feeling that there are restless spirits of the slaughtered soldiers lingering about the place. This leads him quite naturally to comment on the times: "Of recent years warfare has gone on unceasingly, as the strong struggle to swallow the weak. Who in the end gains from it? The dead lie scattered from one end of the world to the other. How I regret that I have no way to end this chaos. I can only stand here uselessly feeling grieved by it all." Numbers Eleven and Twelve are also written in Hu-chou prefecture, at the county seat city of Te-ch'ing, where he is visiting famous local scenes. The last three are written from Hai-ning, farther east from Te-ch'ing, and on the northern shore of Hangchow Bay. They, too, are comments on famous places there, and on their historical associations, providing the poet with an opportunity to compare the disasters of the past with the present disorderly and difficult times. And so this series of fifteen poems ends, leaving Kao Ch'i still some sixty or seventy miles south of Soochow. Whether this was the homeward journey we cannot tell.

All fifteen poems are cast in a rather conventional mood of travel poems, calling for thoughtful and even noble reflections on the historical associations of places, and on comparisons and allusions which display the author's learning. At the same time they have a highly personal tone, and tell something of the author's own travel experiences. Fortunately there are other extant poems from this two-year period of travel. Some of them are much more intimate, revealing private thoughts more than noble sentiments. They tell of parties he attended, pleasures he encountered, and of lonely thoughts of home and family. They also indicate that he visited a number of places not included in the itinerary provided by the set of fifteen. Curiously, they contain only a few very indirect references to the fighting going on throughout the region at the time, to military preparations and the consequences of warfare, and to the personalities involved and the character of the movements they led. It is probable that such references were among the passages that Kao Ch'i removed from his poetry when he prepared collections of his writings in the following years—removed for reasons that will be clear as we consider the character of early Ming rule.

We know from these other poems that he went as far

south as Huang-yen, on the central Chekiang coast near T'ai-chou, hence well into the area dominated by Fang Kuo-chen. But this was in 1358 and 1359, at a time when Fang was temporarily serving the Yuan government as an official, and when it may not have been dangerous for a traveler from Chang Shih-ch'eng's region to cross the boundary into a rival leader's region. He also passed through Lang-ch'i County in what would be the easternmost portion of modern Anhwei, in the wild and mountainous region where the three provinces of Anhwei, Kiangsu, and Chekiang meet, south-west of Lake T'ai. Passing through this little mountain county seat town in the tea-growing region, he remarks: "Although this is only a small 'three-family' county [in an historical allusion to a small and remote region], the place is so remote that it has no need for military defenses."[15] We know that in 1359 he was in Hu-chou, the great city on the southern shore of Lake T'ai; during that year Hu-chou was the scene of furious fighting between armies of Chang Shih-ch'eng and Chu Yuan-chang, so it is possible that Kao Ch'i was forced to flee for temporary safety to the wild mountainous region which neither side felt was worth fighting for. There are also other poems from Hangchow, but they do not mention that in the summer of 1359 Chang Shih-ch'eng was expending a vast sum and employing a huge force of im-pressed laborers to rebuild the walls of Hangchow. The task was completed late in the year, and in that winter the new walls were put to the test, when an army of Chu Yuan-chang's came and attacked, unsuccessfully, the city. By the winter of 1359 Kao apparently had gone farther north, on the slow and indirect journey back to Soochow. Despite this ominous atmosphere, he enjoyed many of the usual tourist pleasures at Hangchow. He writes of boating on the famous West Lake by moonlight, drifting through miles of fragrant

[15] CCSC 12/1b

lotus flowers, and listening to the distant singing of girl entertainers. However, he says, his companions were in an
heroic rather than romantic mood, and carried nothing but
wine in their boat.[16] This was in the late summer of 1359,
with "autumn in the air." He also writes of the pupil of a
famous singing girl whom he heard singing in the manner
learned from a courtesan who had entertained the Yuan
emperor Wen-tsung (reigned 1328-1332) in splendid days
now gone. It is a poem in which allusions to T'ang history
speak all too clearly to the present, to cities overrun and
palaces, once filled with carefree pleasure, now fallen to ruin.
"The Son of Heaven now has many cares, and feastings
within the palaces are rare; now he knows that pleasure and
song give birth to sorrows and disaster."[17] This poem also
seems to refer directly to an event of that year: the visit to
Soochow of an imperial commissioner, bringing rewards and
high honors to Chang Shih-ch'eng, who since the previous
autumn had nominally given up his rebellious ambitions to
become an official of the Yuan government. But Kao sees
no end to the distressing chaos that has befallen the realm.

Other poems of these travel years indicate that he had a
strong interest in Taoism and Taoist adepts and recluses. He
speaks of visiting a famous Taoist adept at Hai-yen on the
north shore of Hangchow Bay. He wrote a poem at Huang-
yen, near T'ai-chou, "in the fall" (which can only be the fall
of 1359, indicating that he must have gone south from
Hangchow that year before returning north to Lang-ch'i and
Hu-chou and Hai-ning); this poem tells of a visit to a
mountain made famous by its Taoist associations, and he
speaks of these in the poem.[18] He also wrote a set of nine
poems celebrating a famous spot near Shao-hsing where
Taoists had congregated throughout history; several of these

[16] ccsc 15/19b [17] ccsc 8/11b-13a
[18] ccsc 4/7a-b

poems are in praise of famous Taoist recluses.[19] However, his interest in Taoist lore seems to have been simply that of the cultivated man, and there is no reason to believe that he visited these places as a serious student of Taoism.

Most interesting perhaps, even though not very informative about the poet's activities, are the very intimate poems written while he was away on these roamings. He must have been overcome frequently by feelings of loneliness and longing for home. There are three songs to the morning star which rises in the western sky just before dawn, and to which poets sing on lonely sleepless nights. These are not clearly dated from the years of travel, but their content makes it evident that they must have been written at this time. In the first of the three he says: "How would I willingly have left my parental homeland; over mountains and rivers my distant route has gone, nor has it all been pleasurable." And in the second he complains: "When away from home one has no old, true friends. I want to return, but still stay on, undecided about either course. In these old worn garments I am ashamed to meet my wife waiting at home."[20] The last line is an allusion to a man who spent the family's money to buy elegant clothing so that he could travel to famous places and make an impression on important people, thereby gaining a chance to display his abilities and secure a high position in government. After unsuccessful years of such travel, his money gone and his elegant clothing in tatters, he is ashamed to go home and admit his failure to his wife. These may be merely conventional sentiments of a traveler, but they seem to indicate that Kao Ch'i had some purpose in undertaking this long journey, and that he had not accomplished it.

Other poems also speak longingly of home. Two tell of returning there in a dream:

[19] ccsc 5/14b-15b   [20] ccsc 8/3a-b

Why is it that so often I go home in my dreams?
It can only be that I am not used to staying so far away.
When I awake and do not see the faces of my family
It seems just like that morning long past when I had just
    parted from them.

*   *   *

Suddenly I dreamed that I was going home; I had al-
    ready boarded the river boat.
The route along which I had come still looked just the
    same.
My family wouldn't know the passes and mountains of
    these distant places;
How is it then that in my dreams they appear here at
    my side?[21]

Others tell of writing and receiving letters from home.
One, "Sending a Letter Home," bears the poet's explanatory
comment, "While a traveller in Shao-hsing" (that is, Yueh-
ch'eng), hence must date from late 1358 or early 1359.

Why should I always be writing these letters home?
The way is long, and I fear their arrival is uncertain.
But also I worry that when they arrive they only increase
    my family's concern for me,
Hence I dare not write too much of the traveller's sor-
    rows.[22]

And there is another on the same subject, which, in the
original, is one of his best short poems. It is called, "Writing a Letter Home at Night":

Pale moon in the sycamores, sky clearing after rain.
Cicadas making a desolate sound,—I sit before my lamp
    in the night.

[21] ccsc 18/5b   [22] ccsc 17/14a

Who has any feelings here, in this ancient temple, for
    the traveller in his bare cell?
Solitary, I write a letter home, for I cannot go to sleep.[23]

The young poet, twenty-two or twenty-three years old,
away from home on his first extended journey, and spending
many lonely nights in the plain guest quarters of remote
temples, or in the livelier surroundings of wayside inns, must
have thought often of home. A number of fine poems record these moods, but none tells us what business kept him
there, preventing his return to his family. Another such is
called, "Late Spring in a Wayside Inn":

Awaking after drinking, I idly write a poem of farewell
    to spring.
Misty rain and fading flowers,—one branch of blossoms
    left.
Don't look there on the far horizon, where flowers
    bloom in the grass,—
The traveller's sorrows are still as many as last year at
    this time.[24]

Letters from home brought momentary gladness, but they
also increased the longing for home. There is a brief poem,
written in the five-word line form: "On Receiving a Family
Letter":

Before I have read the letter itself
I already feel my cares ease
For here by lamplight, looking at the envelope's seal
I have found the words "All is well."[25]

Another poem, very similar in content, is written in a
longer seven-word line, and adds a little to the scene; it is

[23] ccsc 18/26b   [24] ccsc 18/14b
[25] ccsc 16/14b

* 86 *

called, "On Receiving a Family Letter While Travelling in Yueh" (modern Chekiang):

> On receiving a letter from home my heart is
>   immediately gladdened
> For on the outside wrapper I've seen the words
>   "All is well."
> My home is a thousand miles away and letters do
>   not easily come.
> I don't dare rush hastily through it by the light
>   of the oil lamp.[26]

One letter brought word that his infant daughter was ill. It must have been in the winter of 1359, for it bears the author's comment that it was written at Hangchow. It is called, "Hearing of My Daughter's Illness, On a Night While Travelling":

> The year is at its end, but the time of my returning
>   still is unclear.
> Who else is there to pity you in your illness?
> Next door the neighbor's children laugh in the eve-
>   ning lamplight.
> In this wayside inn, I go to sleep, alone and in sad-
>   ness.[27]

No doubt his little daughter had enough pity from a fond mother and her family, but the lonely father, hearing the sad news, felt she must lack his tender attention as much as he lacked the warmth of the family circle.

There are other poems written in these years, but their content becomes repetitious. He meets an old friend, parts from him, and then feels all the more lonely, saying, "As I lie here in this lonely inn tomorrow, listening to the rain,

---

[26] ccsc 18/24a   [27] ccsc 17/10b

who could again come knocking to visit with me about old times?" Or again, "Dreading sadness, I dare not turn my mind to thoughts of home."

Without any more explanation than can be found for his having embarked on this journey, Kao Ch'i returned in 1360 to Soochow.

CHAPTER FOUR

THE POET AS HERO

A COMPILER of a biography of Kao Ch'i, in the early eighteenth century, wrote: "Discuss the times, and you can know the man."[1] The comment was intended to explain the lack of information about Kao's life; the circumstances of his death prevented the writing of obituary biographies and official necrologies, and those circumstances can be explained only in relation to the character of the first reign of the Ming dynasty, in the seventh year of which Kao Ch'i died. But the statement also suggests that Kao Ch'i's entire life assumes fuller meaning in relation to his times. The times explain the concealment and suppression of information about him, and knowledge of the times is our chief guide in reconstructing the missing pieces. In turn, Kao Ch'i's life enables us to see those times far more clearly.

This life, like most problems of history, presents us with certain incontrovertible facts and with a still larger area of relatively safe assumptions. From these we may or may not be able to fashion an account that satisfies our desire to know about Kao Ch'i. Perhaps if we were interested in him merely as Kao Ch'i the poet, this knowledge would suffice. But if we see him as a figure of some broader significance in the history of his era, the facts and the safe assumptions, however carefully worked out, may not satisfy. One can go further only by bringing the imagination to bear on the

[1] Chin T'an, preface to *Ch'ing-ch'iu Kao Chi-ti Hsien-sheng Nien-p'u,* dated 1728

problem—a disciplined and well-guided imagination, it is
hoped. Obviously the hazards are great in this kind of reconstruction of a whole picture from fragments, and yet they
are hazards which historians have often been willing to risk.
In the case of Kao Ch'i's life, "little risked, little gained."

When one comes to that portion of Kao Ch'i's life which
falls in the years after his return to Soochow in 1360, one
may well be struck by the feeling that some of the most telling facts must have been erased, leaving suspicious gaps that
beg to be filled in. Soochow in the 1360's was the scene of
events of such interest and importance, and Kao Ch'i was
so surely aware of and interested, even involved, in them,
that his silence about them is very disturbing. These gaps
cannot be accepted; they must be filled in. And when we examine the boundaries of these areas of uncertainty, we find
that the broken-off lines point consistently in one direction,
while the scattered and overlooked fragments fit harmonious-
ly into one pattern. Viewing these indicators, one is tempted
to feel certain that his reconstruction cannot have erred. The
life of Kao Ch'i now takes on more depth and meaning, and
the history of the era becomes illumined. Yet one cannot forget that this light is of different character from that cold,
hard light of proved fact; the reconstruction remains, for all
its satisfying consistency, somewhat hypothetical. Yet, one
must turn to such hypothesis for an understanding of Kao
Ch'i's brief life.

In a drinking song probably written in these years, Kao
Ch'i speaks of himself as a scholar of Wu, poor and without
accomplishment, who has been favored by the encouragement of friends. As a youth, he tells, he did not study with
the wholehearted devotion of a true scholar, but fell in with
the ways of young men with warrior ambitions. "Astride my
horse I betook myself off to distant places, hoping to achieve
glory by deeds of daring. But in the end my plans accom-

plished nothing, and I returned home, to take up the scholar's mode of life anew. Only then did I begin to penetrate
the *History* and the *Odes*, and became somewhat acquainted
with the Confucian works. I completely gave up the ways of
the martial heroes. . . ."[2] This appears to be a reference to
his travels to the south, where his plans to find a career as a
wandering hero produced no results. In exaggerated modesty
he speaks of his mean accomplishment as a scholar up to
that time, but this is mere convention. Of interest is his
point that his travels in search of adventure had brought him
no rewards, and that this failure had turned him to more
serious pursuits. While not foregoing the heroic ideal of the
warrior, he sought to supplement it with the accomplishments of the scholar. Thus indirectly we have an indication
of what the years of travel meant to him.

On returning to Soochow in 1360, Kao Ch'i almost certainly became involved in the affairs of Chang Shih-ch'eng's
regime. We have no evidence that he held any official position in this regime, and, if he did, it must have been some
insignificant advisory position, perhaps on the staff of one
of Chang's lieutenants. But his relations with important figures in that regime in the early years of the 1360's are very
clearly those of a close and important friend, of counselor
and advisor, drinking companion and fellow spirit. By 1358
Chang Shih-ch'eng had given up, in name at least, his pretensions as Prince Ch'eng, rebel leader of an insurrectionist
dynasty. In 1359, as Grand Marshal in Soochow, he had received the visit of the Mongol Chancellor of State, Prince
Bayan, who came bearing imperial gifts and honors; in return
he had promised to send annual shipments of grain to the
hard-pressed Mongol capital at Peking. In name, his rebel
cohorts were now imperial officials, but as members of his

[2] This is a rather loose translation of lines from the song "T'ing chün
pai yü chih," ccsc 4/4a-b

staff they bore the same relationship to him as they had before. His rebel movement became the government of the region, and the region under his domination quickly expanded as he moved forces still loyal to him personally into neighboring areas that previously had held out against his rebellion, but that now accepted his protection in the name of the Yuan state.

It was obvious to everyone that Chang was serving himself, and that the new loyalty to the Yuan had little real meaning. And yet it brought to his movement some measure of that valuable commodity, legitimacy. A man could serve him now without having the degrading appellation "bandit" attached to his name. Moreover, in most realistic terms, Chang was in fact the protector of the rich Southeast against the scorned and feared Red Turban rabble movement to the west. A clear-headed man would realize that if he accepted actual appointment from the newly legitimate Chang, Chang could again turn rebel and thereby compromise his followers, making rebels of them too or forcing them to denounce him. But if a man so compromised were to denounce Chang, he must either bear the brunt of Chang's anger, or flee. And where could a man flee? To Chu Yuan-chang and his Red Turbans, who were equally illegitimate and even less congenial? To the defunct Yuan government, regions that could be reached only by traversing other rebel-held areas? To wild mountain fastnesses beyond the reach of any government? Serving Chang was hazardous to be sure, but there was no one else to serve. Most men of Kao Ch'i's class and education saw these issues clearly, and most of them evaded the hazards. The writings of the period show that men often pondered the wisdom of the classics, seeking analogies to their own times. Turning to the *Book of Changes* for guidance, they would refer most often to the twelfth hexagram, "P'i" or "Standstill," and to the eighteenth, "Ku" or "Decay."

Under "Standstill" it is advised: "Evil people of the time of Standstill do not further the perseverance of the superior man. The great departs; the small approaches. . . . Thus the superior man falls back on his inner worth in order to escape the difficulties. He does not permit himself to be honored with revenue." And under "Decay" one is told: "He does not serve kings and princes; he sets himself higher goals."[3] These clearly were times of standstill and decline, of decay and disorder. The wise man withdrew, "did not permit himself to be honored with revenue" of office, took no part in the current mismanagement of the world, and devoted himself to the cultivation of the self.

Yet a young and vigorous man, particularly one who lacked the discouraging experience of years of devotion to a failing cause, and who was confident of his powers to help set the world aright with his learning and his zeal, and to achieve fame and fortune in the process, might not accept this passive wisdom. Even the *Book of Changes* could give men different advice. Under the same hexagram "Standstill" one reads: "Perseverance brings good fortune and success," and "The standstill comes to an end. First standstill, then good fortune." And under "Decay" one sees that the conditions of stagnation and decay embody a demand for removal of the cause. The meaning of "Decay" is not merely "what has been spoiled," but "*Work on* what has been spoiled." The hexagram reads:

> The wind blows low on the mountain:
> The image of Decay.
> Thus the superior man stirs up the people
> And strengthens their spirit.

[3] The wording here and in subsequent quotations is altered slightly from the Willhelm-Baynes translation of the *I Ching*, Bollingen Series xix, New York, 1950, vol. ii, pp. 83ff., and pp. 114ff.

The message of "Standstill" is that fate has been against man and the times are wrong; but fate is changing, and from the nadir of the present moment, change must bring improvement. The message of "Decay" is that man has erred, but that he can work to bring about a correction of the evil times. In both cases, the activist finds encouragement while the defeatist finds a rationalization of his passive course.

Kao Ch'i, returning to Soochow in 1360, was a self-confident young man of twenty-four. He was beginning to enjoy wide acclaim as a man of genius, and he had been stirred by the things he had seen in his travels and the knowledge he had gained of the world. Whereas three years earlier he had been willing to avoid entanglement in politics by becoming the Man of the Green Hill, the poet who cared nothing for the superficial values of this world, now he returned to cultivate the rousing company of men who talked of this world and its workings. He probably continued to live at his father-in-law's home at the Green Hill, but he spent much time in the city, too. In these years he became known as the leader of the "Ten Friends of the North Wall" (also known as the "Ten Talented Ones"), a group of young poets and men of literary interests. This circle of friends was a remarkable group of able young men. Most were roughly his own age, and all were residents of that northeast quarter of the city just inside and just outside the city wall, where Kao Ch'i's own family home was located. They gathered for recreation of all kinds—visiting famous places, climbing hills to write poetry on the scenes viewed from their summits, drinking and feasting, traveling on horseback or by boat to nearby places, visiting old temples to discuss philosophy with famous monks and Taoists, and sharing each other's family celebrations. Some, like Kao Ch'i, were natives of Soochow; some were sons of families that had come there only in those

troubled years, fleeing disorder and unrest in their home regions. Later in life when Kao wrote a set of ten poems,
"Reminiscing about Ten Friends on a Spring Day," he included eight of the "Ten Talented Ones of the North City
Wall." Throughout his life the number of poems he wrote to
them and about them and in their company was very large.
These youthful companions remained among the important
associates of his life.

The unusual conditions of the times—the region cut off
and surrounded by hostile forces, and normal careers for
ambitious young men now out of the question—undoubtedly
fostered this association of the Ten Friends. In a short essay
addressed to one of them, Kao Ch'i wrote:

"For generations we have lived here by the north city wall
of Wu [Soochow]. Of scholars in that same quarter of the
city who pursued literature and with whom I was a close
friend, there was (at first) only Wang Chih-chung [Wang
Hsing]. But in the past ten years or more there have come to
live in Soochow, for various reasons, Hsü Yu-wen [Hsü Pen]
from P'i-ling, Kao Shih-min [Kao Hsün-chih] from Ho-nan,
T'ang Ch'u-ching [T'ang Su] from K'uai-chi, Yü T'ang-ch'ing
[Yü Yao-ch'en] from Yung-chia, and Chang Lai-yi [Chang
Yü] from Hsün-yang, and all of them have found temporary
homes here as neighbors of mine. In consequence of their
coming, the literary character of the northern wall quarter
has come to flourish indeed! With nothing to do, I spend
day and night with these several gentlemen, sometimes argu-
ing philosophical points and refining definitions for the sake
of improving our learning, perhaps responding to each other
in song and replying to each other's poems in order to set
forth our ambitions, sometimes strumming lutes and lyres
to express our innermost feelings, or perhaps just sitting together at the banquet table, joining in the pleasures of the
feast. Although it is a time of chaos and disorder, and we

have long been forced to withdraw into seclusion, yet together we have found pleasure and lighthearted joys, so that
there is none of us who has not benefited from our association."[4]

This essay introduces the names of five of the Ten Friends,
and describes well their activities and the value of the friendship to all of them. It emphasizes that the "time of chaos
and disorder" has "forced them to withdraw into seclusion."
This cliché, properly interpreted in the context of those
times, means that the disorders had forced them to give up
hopes of following the traditional course of seeking public
careers through the civil service examinations. It explains
why they were all still young "commoners" despite their education, talents, and interests, why they were not officials,
expectant or actual. It does not mean that they were solitary
hermits, cut off from the world and human company. But
forced upon them was a way of life that fell far short of
satisfying their high-spirited ambitions. How should one seek
fame and fortune in the world that surrounded them? Educated in a tradition which both called them to service and
urged them to pit their wits against the world and master it,
how should they create for themselves the opportunity to do
so? Of these things they talked as they sat through the night,
drinking the mild wine of the region and debating the rele-
vance of various historical parallels. Answers to these problems they sought in the lore of the past, and in the wisdom
of men about them.

Above all, in the manner of men of talent and cultivation,
it was in poetry that they set forth their feelings and urged
each other on. Poetry could express soaring thoughts that
must otherwise remain locked within a man. Poetry could
display the real nature of a man. It could make apparent to
another of equal vastness of spirit what a man was truly

[4] FTC 2/3a

worth. To be sure, poets could also be men of fanciful temperament, vague and unreal men of mere sentiment. But poetry at its best went beyond that; it was also the medium of heroes. It was the voice in which the resolute man of action and of profound thought expressed himself. And this circle of young poets included no dreamy troubadors, no dilly-dallying escapists. These were men of strong mind and vast purpose, men at once realistic in their view of the world's problems and romantic in their conception of the hero's role that they might assume. Kao Ch'i, although one of the youngest, found himself the acknowledged leader—as a poet, and in other ways as well.

All of the Ten Friends were, of course, at least reasonably good poets, and all practiced the art assiduously. In addition to Kao Ch'i, two others achieved lasting fame as first-class poets: Hsü Pen and Chang Yü. Hsü's family came originally from Szechwan, but having been brought to eastern China by government service, they had taken refuge in Soochow from the disorders of the time, and had settled there. Hsü Pen too was a young man of genius, known both as a painter of landscapes and as a poet. Chang Yü similarly was of a family from another province that had settled only recently in Soochow; like Hsü, he was noted as a painter and as a litterateur. Chang was three years older than Kao and Hsü was only one year older. These two, with Kao Ch'i's long-time neighbor Wang Hsing, were Kao's closest friends. There are many poems mentioning Hsü and Chang and Wang, telling of excursions they made together, visits to each other's homes, and poems written in response to each other. There are a dozen poems in Kao's collection mentioning Chang by name, and more than forty poems and prose pieces mentioning Hsü Pen, often calling them his "friends of *pei-kuo*," the quarter of the city close to the northern city wall. Hsü and Chang were both pressed to join Chang Shih-ch'eng's regime soon after the rebel leader arrived in Soochow. Both may have accepted appointments briefly, but they quickly made their escape by becoming recluses. They were attracted to the mountains of Hu-chou (modern Wu-hsing) on the southern shore of Lake T'ai, and they went there together and built rustic cottages on adjoining mountains, so that they could devote themselves entirely to study and self-improvement. Chang specialized in the study of the *I-ching*, the *Book of Changes*. Hsü had broad interests in study, but seems to have been drawn particularly to the texts of Taoism. Both were suitable fields of study for men fleeing a troublesome world, and seeking better understanding of it. But both Chang and Hsü returned eventually to Soochow, and to the world, and both had official careers in the early Ming.

Indeed, as recluses Hsü Pen and Chang Yü had no more real desire to cut themselves off permanently from the world than we would expect of the youthful Kao Ch'i; the hermit's role was a temporarily useful one. The following extracts from a commemorative essay which Kao Ch'i wrote, at the request of Hsü, on Hsü's "Study on Mount Shu," referring to the place in Hu-chou, show clearly that Kao and his friends had their attention on practical and worldly matters even when living the life of the recluse:

"My friend Mr. Hsü is the man of the study on Mount Shu; that is the place in which Yu-wen [Hsü Pen's courtesy name] pursues his studies. Yu-wen has written me a letter from Wu-hsing saying: 'Mount Shu is east of the city a few miles. My house on the mountain consists of a few rooms. The books in my room consist of a few volumes. The mountain, although small, is exceedingly beautiful. The house, although rustic, is roughly adequate. The books, although not numerous, are enough to provide me with reading. I shall complete my studies here. Would you do me the favor of writing a commemorative piece about this for me? . . .'

[Kao explains that he is unqualified to offer advice such as a commemorative essay might be expected to give, but he comments:] . . . Yu-wen is now just at the age of early manhood. He possesses talents that could be employed. Yet he is not hasty in his pursuit of advancement and reward; rather, he devotes himself to study in order to seek knowledge beyond that which he has as yet encountered. Is this not a scholar of great purpose? And myself,—beyond the northern wall I have some land. In the home at my eastern village I have books. Both were left to me by my forebears. Encountering times of many troubles, I have left the lands to fall to weeds and thorns, have left the books to deteriorate through dust and insects. Blindly I rush about doing unimportant things, not knowing to return to reason. Such frantic, unworthy conduct shames me before Yu-wen. Who am I to write this commemorative essay for him? Nonetheless I have written this, not refusing him, because I did not want to deny his request, and also in order to spur myself on thereby."[5]

Note that Hsü is praised for his purpose, or ambition (*chih*), a worldly term. This purpose is described as something ultimately of practical value. He has been offered positions employing his talents, but he is not anxious to achieve fame and rank too early; he would rather prepare himself more fully, the implication being that he will then be able to employ his talents in the world even more effectively. The mood of all the writings of Kao Ch'i and his circle from these years is one of eager and expectant preparation for great deeds in the world of human affairs. At first they shied away from the opportunity to accomplish this in the Chang Shih-

---

[5] FTC 1/5a-b; note similarity of "Sung Hsü I-wen hsü" i.e., "Preface on Sending off Hsü I-wen," where Hsü's courtesy name is given as "I-wen" instead of "Yu-wen," FTC 3/6b-7a. A poem written to send Hsü Pen off to this place of retreat is far more "heroic" in the martial sense; it is perhaps the most extreme expression of the romanticized heroism of these young men, but it defies translation. See CCSC 4/10b.

ch'eng rebellion, not yet ready to believe that it could prove
to be the proper vehicle for their ambitions. Later, when
Chang himself was pardoned and granted legitimate status,
and when other alternatives became even less appealing, some
of them were for a time attracted, without, however, giving up
all of their skepticism. Most of them seemed hopeful that
something good could come of the rebellion, and several of
them entered into some kind of relationship with it. In the
case of Kao Ch'i himself, it seems clear that he also shared
some of this hopeful feeling, at least for a time in the early
1360's.

When we look at Kao Ch'i's other friends and associates,
this character becomes all the more evident.

Even during their lifetimes Kao Ch'i, Chang Yü, Hsü Pen,
and a fourth poet of their age named Yang Chi were classed
together as the *ssu-chieh*, the "four outstanding figures," in
poetry of the early Ming period, in analogy to four young
poet-friends who appeared early in the T'ang dynasty in the
seventh century and who ushered in the greatest age of Chinese poetry. It may be difficult to say which one of the four
T'ang poets was the greatest, but all critics have agreed that
Kao Ch'i was the best of the Ming group. And if any contemporary rivalry existed among them, it was of the friendli-
est kind.

Yang Chi, the fourth poet, like Hsü Pen, was of a displaced Szechwanese family, and was born in Soochow. But
he did not live in that section of the city inside the north
city wall, and therefore is not listed among the Ten Friends
of the north city wall. But Yang and Kao Ch'i became very
good friends, and exchanged much poetry. Yang, too, was a
youthful prodigy who gained early fame. When he found
that the disorders of the time blocked his ambitions, he retired to the family home in the western suburbs of Soochow
and devoted himself to study. But soon he came forth again,

enticed out of his premature retirement by Jao Chieh, chief official for literary affairs in Chang Shih-ch'eng's government. He did not actually hold an official position, but he became one of Jao's unofficial staff, a "guest" of Jao's household. His duties were to accompany the older man at parties for literary figures, to discuss and compose poems, and to make brilliant conversation with a literary flavor. One should not assume that Yang Chi debased himself in this association with Jao Chieh. He did not do it for material gain, nor, in the strict sense, for personal advantage. He was a brilliant young poet, receiving the reward which his society granted such brilliance —the favor and attention of the great, applause and fame, and the stimulus that the company of fellow spirits could bring. Such men looked upon their literary revelries as "heroic gatherings," and felt they were emulating the great men of the past in their most noble and valuable experiences. More-over, there was another significant aspect to the matter: an auspicious association of values, the power and rank repre-sented by Jao Chieh as a leading official of Chang Shih-ch'eng's regime with Jao's cultivation of literary and intel-lectual talent. An ideal government should cultivate these values, should honor brilliance, should encourage talent. In the eyes of everyone, the government gained dignity from its patronage of men like Jao Chieh, and through him of men like Yang Chi. Kao Ch'i, Yang Chi, and all such men could hope that this augured well for the future, and they may not be considered too foolish for believing, for a few brief years, that indeed it did.[6]

The character of certain others of the Ten Friends is also

[6] Hsü Pen's collection of poetry is called *Pei Kuo Chi*, Chang Yü's is called *Ching Chü Chi*, and Yang Chi's is called *Mei An Chi*; all three are to be found in SPTK, Series Three. Although not cited here, all three have been extensively relied upon in building up the information about Kao Ch'i's circle. Yang Chi's collection in particular is of interest and value, both as literature and for the information it contains.

very revealing. One, called Yü Yao-ch'en, before coming to Soochow to make his home near Kao, had already seen service on the staffs of high officials in northern Chekiang, and was credited with important contributions, as a civilian advisor and literary assistant, to the defense of the region. But he too had become discouraged with the late Yuan situation, and had withdrawn from active service to lead a life of literary leisure and hopeful watching in Soochow. Many of Kao Ch'i's poems attest that Yü's home was the frequent scene of feasts and drinking gatherings of the whole circle of friends; they also reflect the respect in which Yü was held for his knowledge of government and military affairs.

Another of the Ten Friends was Sung K'e, a native of Soochow. He was tall and broad of frame, and, although given a thorough classical education, was attracted by temperament to swordsmanship, horsemanship, military history, and battlefield tactics and strategy. Sung wanted to offer his services to the government, but found that the rebellions of the times made travel to the north impossible. On entering Soochow, Chang Shih-ch'eng made an effort to recruit Sung K'e's services, but without success, for he "barred his gate and practiced calligraphy." Kao Ch'i had the greatest respect for Sung and wrote a biographical sketch of him,[7] telling how he had dissipated his fortune in riotous living as a very young man, but then had reformed, acquiring a sense of serious purpose; he had taken up his study of military affairs and finally turned to the study of calligraphy and literature. Clearly here was a man of action and of thought, of practical abilities and great ambition, yet of a high moral sense of purpose, who demanded a great and worthy cause before he would serve it, and who grieved that none could be found in the degenerate age in which he lived. That Kao Ch'i should admire him and cultivate his company is not surprising.

[7] FTC 4/1a

Another of the ten was Lü Min. He became a Taoist adept, it is said, because the Yuan government forbade the wearing of the traditional Chinese garments of the literati class except to Taoist adepts, and Lü Min preferred becoming a Taoist to wearing the regulation "barbarian dress." Earlier he had been a student of the classical Confucian education in preparation for the official career, and after the establishment of the Ming dynasty he served in office. While dressing as a Taoist in the troubled years of the 1360's, he also lived for periods of time in Buddhist temples. Kao Ch'i's poems to him make it clear that Lü Min's unusual mode of life was primarily for the sake of evading the chaotic conditions of the age; he was a student of Taoism, to be sure, but not to the extent of really wishing to forego the world for the sake of the Taoist kind of spiritual enlightenment. Rather, his turn to Taoism expressed his resentment of Mongol rule. His rebellious spirit, coupled with his cultivation and his literary interests, made certain his inclusion in the group of Ten Friends.

The two friends of the group of ten who remain to be mentioned are Ch'en Tse and T'ang Su. Both were well known for their learning and literary ability, and both earned their living in these years by teaching the classical learning to young men preparing for the official life. Both subsequently served as local directors of Confucian studies in the early Ming period. In a preface written at a farewell party for T'ang Su, when he was leaving to take an education post in a nearby city in the mid-1360's, Kao Ch'i speaks of the activities of these friends, and how he regrets seeing the group scatter—Hsü Pen and Chang Yü going off to the mountains near Hu-chou to study in seclusion, Kao Hsün-chih having gone elsewhere, and now T'ang Su who must also leave. When at the farewell party at his house Kao Ch'i raises this complaint, "another guest" reminds the friends that they will always be one in their *chih*, their purpose, their will, and that they will always be united in their *tao*, their fundamental philosophical orientation. Kao Ch'i accepts this, and says that even if, on their distant travels, they should fall into the hands of savages (literally the *hu* and the *yueh*, an historical allusion from Han times, which in the Yuan period might well be taken to refer to the Mongols as well as to the Red Turbans or other rebels), this unity of spirit would keep them together as if they were still in the north wall quarter of Soochow.[8] Throughout Kao Ch'i's poems and other writings for these friends, the feeling of unity of spirit is strong. This spirit is not merely the product of their common interest in literature and learning, and their enthusiasm for composing poetry. Beyond that there existed among this group of brilliant young men the spirit of participation in the affairs of their world, of readiness to examine the events of their age, to analyze the right and the wrong of military and political developments, to give expert judgment about what should be done. Their learning and their intelligence made them confident in their own judgments, and confident that they possessed the qualifications to serve heroically and ably to set the world aright, should the opportunity arise. Even though some of them were forced temporarily to evade some difficulties of their surroundings by fleeing or withdrawing, in these confident youthful years they did not value withdrawal for its own sake. Rather, theirs was eagerness and optimism, and the desire to prove themselves.

Beyond this group of Ten Friends of the north city wall, there were other friends who also fit this pattern. The most remarkable of them is a young man known in Kao Ch'i's poetry as the monk Tao-yen. The son of a doctor of medicine in Soochow, he showed unusual proclivity for study, but after

[8] This preface is in part translated above, Chapter 4, page 95; it is to be found in FTC 2/3a.

receiving a sound classical education, turned to Buddhism. He was one year older than Kao Ch'i, and about the time that the poet was setting off on his travels to the south, this youth was taking the vows to become a monk, shaving his head and donning the patched tunic. He was a very unusual Buddhist monk. Instead of devoting his energy to sutras and Indian metaphysics, he became the apprentice of a Taoist adept in a Taoist temple near his Buddhist monastery, and acquired from this man his profound knowledge of the writers on military subjects, political forces, and worldly affairs. It is said that he concealed himself, however, and did not seek to make his special talents known. A learned man, meeting him and visiting with him, remarked: "You are no ordinary monk. You are the equal of Liu Ping-chung!" Liu Ping-chung was a monk who gave up his religious life, to serve Kubilai Khan for thirty years as advisor and confidant, virtually as prime minister throughout the period when Kubilai was creating the Yuan dynasty and establishing Mongol rule over China. The comparison was an apt one.[9]

The monk Tao-yen later encountered the Prince of Yen, fourth son of the Ming founder, who admired his vast ability. This prince forced the monk to give up his monastic profession and resume his worldly surname. As Yao Kuang-hsiao he served the prince, later the emperor, throughout the usurpation and through most of the Yung-lo reign, until his death in 1419, virtually as prime minister and chief advisor. That this young man's talents should have been recognized by Kao Ch'i and that they should have become very intimate friends is not, then, surprising. There are a dozen poems which Kao Ch'i wrote to him, as well as a preface for a volume of the monk's poetry dated 1370. These display the high respect in which Kao Ch'i held him, for his broad

[9] This may be an apocryphal story, told with the benefit of hindsight, which would make its aptness less startling.

learning, profound judgment of affairs, and literary talents. There is a short poem whose title is an explanation of the circumstances under which it was written: "Going to Visit Yen Shang-jen at the Western Stream." "Shang-jen" is a polite form of address to the monk.

> The evening sun colors the remaining patches of snow;
> Through the haze the Western Stream appears dark.
> If it were not that the Master lives so far away
> What reason would I have to come so deep into these
>   mountains?[10]

The other poems written to and about Tao-yen also in most cases say little, but similarly give evidence of the intimate understanding and close friendship that existed between them. That the monk was a "heroic figure," a poet, a man of thought but a man capable of action as well, is the key to their relationship.

These friends were all men devoted to a particular ideal of heroism. In their civilization, this meant displaying a combination of moral courage and intelligence. It further meant displaying the cultivation that their education had given them. It also meant maintaining a romantic attachment to the ideal of the hero, the man who used that cultivation to accomplish great things that would gain a man the eternal gratitude of his descendants and earn him a place in history. It meant to be the noble and wise official in a time of trouble, to supply the holder of power with profound advice. It meant possessing the ability to make a realistic appraisal of the world's needs, and formulate plans that would set the world aright again. This was the real ambition of this group of young poets. Poetry was their language. It gave the clearest evidence of their worth, and it had an undying value, in that it could bring permanent fame to the poet. Beyond the ad-

[10] CCSC 16/16b

miration which their civilization bestowed upon poetry and poets for technical and artistic perfection, poetry was regarded as the sign of a man's moral worth. The poet would be judged as an artist, but even more, he might in his poetry display the heroic qualities that could be communicated in no other way, unless perchance the opportunity came to him to perform in deed as well as in word. It was this opportunity which they all hoped for, and their confidence in each other's heroic abilities was confirmed by the poetry in which they exposed their otherwise inexpressible inner selves to each other. Normally they had no need to proclaim themselves more prosaically on these matters; the spirit of their poetry, the loftiness of its mood, the vastness of its poetic conception accomplished this. The poem itself becomes a heroic act, in addition to displaying the poet's capacity for other heroic acts.

There are poems in which Kao Ch'i speaks more directly of these things. For example, there is a long poem written for his friend Sung K'e, who had had a successful career as a military advisor and administrator before moving to the north wall quarter of Soochow. He speaks of Sung's wild youth, in gambling on fighting cocks, racing horses, engaging in fights and feuds, and caring only for swordsmanship and athletic skill. Sung K'e gradually learned to discipline this wild spirit, and apply it to learning and worthwhile pursuits. In this poem Kao Ch'i tells Sung K'e that they are kindred spirits: "Although you may see me as but a useless scholar, there was a time when I too stood out above all the rest."[11] In historical allusions, he describes his youthful ambition to be like the heroes of history who commanded troops, led campaigns, arranged alliances, earned the ruler's confidence, and helped bring peace to the world. In another poem, when he meets a man from K'ai-feng named Kao who turns out

[11] CCSC 4/1a-2a

to be a distant kinsman, from the same clan descended from the founder of the Ch'i dynasty, he is anxious that this martial northerner not despise him as a mere bookish southerner. (The first quatrain is translated on pages 39-40.) Heroic blood flows in both our veins, he tells the kinsman. He describes the other's martial appearance, his great strength and courage, and the glory that will come to him as his heroic qualities and utilized. Then he speaks of himself: "Do not think of me as any soft white-faced courtier; my youth too was one of hardship and struggle." They sing a hero's song together, a song of noble sentiment, and down heroic quantities of wine. "Together with you, cannot misfortune be turned into rejoicing? In the west there appears the evil red glow. Do not say it is too late to apply the whip; the difficulties are far from having ended."[12] These lines also contain allusions to heroes of history. Of greatest interest, however, is the allusion to the evil red glow in the west. While superficially it might be taken as a reference to the evil of war, it also might be seen more literally as a reference to the Red Turban menace, based up the river to the west of Soochow.[13] In any event, Kao Ch'i wants this newly met distant cousin, a man of heroic temper, to look upon him as a fellow spirit.

Nor did all of these aspirations exist only in the poet's empty imagination. Kao Ch'i and his friends really strove to acquire the heroic abilities they admired. Kao Ch'i practiced swordsmanship and other forms of military exercise, and tried to become an expert on military strategy, studying the military writers of the past. This goal emerges only indirectly, from inadvertent admissions, it would seem, as if later he chose to suppress this aspect of his early career. In

[12] CCSC 4/16a-b

[13] After the establishment of the Ming dynasty, references to the Red Turban origins of the dynasty were taboo; only infrequently does one run across oblique references that could be explained in another way and hence were not expurgated, or for some other reason escaped the notice of the expurgator.

one of the prefaces written on the occasion of one of Hsü Pen's departures from Soochow to go to his mountain study near Hu-chou, Kao speaks of the company they kept: "Valiant and strong, tall and robust, with far-ranging command of debate and invincible in argument, how they drank wine and laughed and joked; how many friendships were gained thus, through this spirit of mutual accord."[14] In another place he writes of his friendship with a young man named Ni Ya. Ni was proud to the point of arrogance, and normally would not condescend to make friends with people. Kao writes:

"When I was young and before I had experienced the setbacks and difficulties of the world I was proud and fond of argument. I always wanted to overcome everyone in any argument before I would give up. One day I met Mr. Ni in an inn. He was my junior in years yet possessed a spirit that surpassed mine. I engaged him in a discussion of the writings of the militarists. We talked through the whole day, but I could not overcome him. Hence I looked upon him as an unusual person, and he at the same time did not despise me. In consequence we formed a fast friendship. After that every time we met we would take along books of history to criticize the personages in order to determine the reasons for their successes and failures, and use the maps to study the geography and topography with reference to strategic features. Or we would call for wine and drink together, singing songs overflowing with the spirit of valor and gallantry. We urged ourselves that merit and fame would readily be achieved by us. . . ."[15]

And he writes on of the ideals they held, and their heroic projects. That they were drawn together by their mutual respect for the other's mastery of military affairs is revealing.

But there is still more explicit evidence that Kao Ch'i

[14] FTC 3/6b-7a   [15] FTC 2/3b-4a

was the leading spirit among a group of men to whom political and military strategy was a chief interest. Two brief biographies of him were written, one by a close friend and neighbor within a year of his death, and the other by a student of his within a decade or two after his death. Both, because of the conditions in the early Ming period, and the circumstances leading to Kao Ch'i's death, would have wished to conceal any possible connection between Kao and the Chang Shih-ch'eng regime, and thus emphasize that Kao was not among those flatterers who ingratiated themselves with Chang for the sake of immediate advantage. In this they undoubtedly are correct. But even so they reveal other very significant facts, indirectly and perhaps without realizing how important they are. The friend's biography tells that leading officials of the Chang regime, like Jao Chieh, who considered themselves patrons of literature admired Kao very greatly, and that in addition to his skill as a poet, Kao Ch'i "was particularly fond of strategy and policy. When he discussed affairs, he startled his hearers, and thus his interests perfectly matched those of Jao Chieh. His friends such as . . . [some of the Ten Friends and some others are listed] and the like were men of boundless literary talent, outstanding ability and cultivation. In discourse and debate they were brilliant and facile. Confidently they felt that the world depended upon no one but themselves, and at the time all the martial and courageous followed their leadership."[16] The biography written by his student says much the same thing. We see him as a young man whose understanding of affairs was looked upon as startlingly profound, and whose judgments were so apt that people sought his opinions and accorded him great respect for the wisdom they displayed. The young poet was a man of the world, and the world honored him for it.

[16] Biography prefaced to FTC, in SPPY ed., vol. I, prefatory materials, "Pen chuan," p. 11a

All of this heroic sentiment which can be revealed by reconstructing the activities of Kao Ch'i and his circle seems to be of the kind that lends itself readily to caricature as mock-heroics. To so caricature it would be an error. The Chinese have been as sensitive to the distinction as have we in our Western traditions. The cultural symbols vary, and the "translation" from that environment to our own should not be done in terms of superficial equivalences. Poets with exaggerated notions of their own value and importance, downing heroic quantities of wine while bewailing their times and their personal fates, may appear slightly ridiculous and as such quite familiar to us, at first glance. Kao Ch'i and his circle should be neither. This group did not greatly exaggerate their own value. They did in fact represent the most significant concentration of the literary talent of their age. Their numbers included several who still rank as important painters. They represented a braintrust of great competence in political and military knowledge. One of their number eventually became the leading official of the empire, and several others had abilities that this official felt to be fully the match of his own, even though they were not granted the opportunities for equally spectacular careers. In short, it would be impossible to isolate a more remarkable group of men in the mid-fourteenth century in China.

Nor should they seem familiar figures, by analogy to Western history, for the cultural symbols had different significance. The poet in China was not an eccentric figure, a minority phenomenon on the periphery of the arena of important events; he was more nearly the typical figure, at the epicenter of the world of important affairs. He was by no means self-conscious about his poetry and his achievement as a poet, for to think as a poet was natural, even though greatness in poetry was a rare and difficult achievement, as greatness must always be. Mock-heroics in the

Chinese scene might much more readily turn on the man who should have had the poet's sensibilities but who made himself ridiculous by displaying his lack of them. The mock-heroic figure in Kao Ch'i's world was the unsuccessful rebel Chang Shih-ch'eng himself, who, to be sure, had displayed himself as an upstart youth of great daring at the beginning of his career, but who thereafter was quickly transformed into a demoralized prince, a sadly ridiculous figure whose vision was not large enough to match his opportunities. Kao Ch'i and his friends, in contrast, truly possessed the hero's vision and the heroic abilities, as their age and their civilization defined them.

That Kao Ch'i became deeply involved with Chang Shih-ch'eng's government seems indisputable. There is ample evidence that in the years immediately following his return to Soochow in 1360 he spent much time in the company of certain important members of Chang's regime. There are four extant poems and four prose writings mentioning Jao Chieh specifically, and often giving information about the circumstances under which they were written. Several commemorate excursions to neighboring scenic places, when Jao was host to groups of literary figures, and when the recreation included composing poems on the scenery or discussing historical parallels to current events, as well as feasting and drinking. One written in 1362 relates how Chang Shih-ch'eng won Jao Chieh over to his service, and how he entrusted great responsibilities for the planning of his government to Jao. Kao comments: "Ah, how auspicious this is, nor is it mere chance. For when Heaven is about to cause a man's state to flourish, then it is sure to supply him with scholars of brilliance and of extraordinary abilities, to assist him on the right and on the left, by proposing and advising, so that he can undertake great deeds. . . ."[17] Thus Kao describes a kind of role

[17] FTC 3/7b

which he, no less than Jao Chieh, must have wanted to fill. In another of these essays, he mentions the time when he had been a "guest" in Jao's home; the term is somewhat ambiguous, but it can mean a person accepting the patronage of another.[18] In a poem written in lamentation for Jao Chieh after Chang's regime had fallen and Jao was a prisoner of the new Ming dynasty, facing execution as an enemy of the state, Kao speaks of the debt of ten years' friendship which he owes Jao.[19] From all of this it is evident that Kao Ch'i was an intimate associate of Jao Chieh, and thus his relationship with Chang's regime was not as insignificant as his early Ming biographers would have us believe.

But the most important of Kao's connections with Chang's regime was not that with old Jao Chieh; rather, it was probably his friendship with Ts'ai Yen-wen. Ts'ai was a man in his fifties who had had a long career in government at the provincial level in the Southeast triangle area prior to the Chang Shih-ch'eng era. He was a learned and vigorous administrator, a man of deep thought and a man of action. Moreover, he was a poet, and was fond of cultivating the company of the leading poets of his time. It is then not surprising that Kao Ch'i found him congenial. He came into Chang's government about 1360, nominally as a Yuan government official, since Chang was at that time in the service of the Yuan government, but actually an appointee of Chang's. Although he never held one of the highest ranking positions in Chang's organization, he was one of the two or three most influential of Chang's officials. If Kao Ch'i intended to bring his ideas to bear on Chang's policies, he might well have felt that through Ts'ai he had surer and more direct access to Chang's councils of state than even Jao Chieh could have provided. Thus his friendship with Ts'ai assumes great sig-

[18] FTC 5/4b   [19] CCSC 12/5b

nificance. The poems he wrote for Ts'ai, mentioning him by name and telling why they were written, show that Kao Ch'i came to know Ts'ai Yen-wen through mutual friends, and that he came to develop a very great respect for his character and ability, and an appreciation of his importance in the Chang government.[20] Kao Ch'i had several other friends serving in the Chang government, and all of them must have served as important points of contact, but none more so than Ts'ai Yen-wen.

Thus we know that Kao Ch'i the poet was more than just a youthful genius developing his sure powers as an artist; he was a man whose ambitions went far beyond the realm of literature and were inspired by a romantically conceived heroic ideal of the man of action in the world of human affairs. This double career might seem almost incongruous in Western civilization, but it embodied the highest values of Kao Ch'i's civilization, and was not without many glorious precedents for him to emulate. Beyond that, he lived at a moment and in a setting in history where the strong possibility of realizing these ideals seemed to present itself. The hope of finding so immensely satisfying an opportunity for action, in times that had become frustrating to most men, was a great spur to the young poet's imagination. Undoubtedly his youthful ardor magnified the possibilities that the situation seemed to hold. There is evidence that he repeatedly became discouraged, and yet did not wholly give up his faith that "The standstill comes to an end. First standstill, then good fortune." He tried desperately to bring about the transition from evil fortune to good. But eventually he came to realize that the situation did not really hold the promise which he had foreseen.

[20] Kao's extant works mentioning Ts'ai Yen-wen by name are the three poems in ccsc: "Yen K'e . . . ," 4/18a-b; "T'uei ssu chai . . . ," 4/18b; "Kan huai . . . ," 14/19b; and the essay "Sung Ts'ai Ts'an-chün hsü," FTC 3/9a-10a.

CHAPTER FIVE

THE HERO DISILLUSIONED

KAO CH'I was intermittently discouraged with the situation that faced him in Soochow after his return there in 1360 from his travels through nearby regions to the south. As early as 1361, at the age of only twenty-five, he wrote a poem speaking of himself as disillusioned and enlightened, prematurely aged, and ready to put the folly of his youth aside and settle on less ambitious goals. The youthful folly apparently was the travel to the south and the hope of finding a position that would utilize his talents, but the poem is also very critical of those who have found high position in the government of the time. Such disapproval can only refer to the *nouveaux riches* of Chang Shih-ch'eng's regime. The poem evidently was written in a moment of discouragement, when both the folly of the dashing bravo's career and the hopelessness of the civil servant's career in the Chang regime made him feel that the recluse-scholar's life, here described in conventional terms that exaggerate its rusticity and simplicity, was the best.

The poem was written for an acquaintance by the name of Hsüeh Chien, someone who himself held high office and who urged Kao to do the same, and for whom Kao must not have had very warm feelings. Some extracts from this long poem follow:

As a youth I delighted in name and fame,
Scornful of everything, I was brave and reckless.
I regarded myself as a most unusual man,—

Of imposing dignity, tall and impressive.
I expected that two or three stratagems of mine
Could enable the ruler to restore peace to our time.
Highest rank would be mine for the taking;
I would not have to wait until I was an aged servitor.
Now looking back, how many years has it been?
Suddenly I am grown old and worn.
Of my original intentions, none has been brought to pass.
Difficulties and danger, alas, have always been my fare.
Returning, I now see that yesterday as false.
Now I plow, while my wife gathers mulberry.
Cutting trees, I roam the wilds
Singing odes in praise of the Sage emperors Yao and
    Shun.

.   .   .   .

[Mr. Hsüeh objects to this idealized path of with-
drawal, and urges him to take the proffered office.
Kao is scornful:]
Just look how people in these times
Ride their prancing horses through the courts of riches
    and rank.
They possess no talent; they only know how to curry the
    favor of the powerful.
Before long such persons will all have fallen into dis-
    grace.

.   .   .   .

To live in peace, and accept one's destined lot—
Is that not in the best of all courses?
Oh, speak to me no more
About those foolish thoughts that I have long since
    sought to forget.[1]

[1] ccsc 6/20a. Hsüeh's name is given as Yüeh-chien in some editions.

The tone of disillusionment is strong in this poem. It reflects the passive wisdom of the *Book of Changes*: "The superior man falls back on his inner worth in order to escape the difficulties. He does not permit himself to be honored with revenue." But this tendency to blame fate and accept discouragement, while always present as an alternative, did not easily satisfy a man like Kao Ch'i. We know that in these years of the early 1360's he was more often in the heroic mood, eagerly looking to the Chang Shih-ch'eng regime for hopeful signs. For example, there is an essay written to commemorate an excursion to the T'ien-p'ing Mountain, some fifteen miles west of Soochow, on the ninth day of the ninth month in 1362. Custom demands that one "ascend a height" (*teng kao*) on this day, and it always is an excuse for a lighthearted outing. Kao Ch'i in this essay records a very buoyant mood, as he goes to keep the engagement which had been long set with a group of friends, whom he calls his *t'ung-chih*, men of "similar purpose." He describes the natural beauties in forceful descriptive prose, tells how the group paused to rest and drink wine into which they have put chrysanthemum blossoms, for this flower is associated with the fall festivals. He concludes the essay:

"Happily we drank until about half of the wine was gone, when I stood up and addressed the group, saying: 'Today the world has been convulsed in disorders for a decade. The princes are unable to protect their fiefs, and the great lords and ministers are unable to protect their homes. How many people have been forced to flee and scatter to the four directions! And yet I, and you gentlemen, thanks to the power of our overlord can remain at peace in our fields and villages, and when a festival occurs we can ascend famous mountains and gaze into the distances, raise our wine cups and get ourselves drunk. How rare a privilege is this! But I fear that there is no constancy in the alternations of prosperity and adversity; whether there shall be unity or discord is difficult to guarantee. Let us inscribe this on a stone here so that we can come again next year, and have some record of it to refer to.' All agreed, and I have written this to record it."[2]

Here is gratitude to Chang "our overlord." References to "princes" and "fiefs" adopt the conventional terms appropriate to antiquity, but obviously refer to the great and powerful of Kao Ch'i's own time. The companions with whom he made this excursion are not identified, but it was in this same year that he wrote the essay praising Jao Chieh and Chang Shih-ch'eng's government, and, from the tone of this essay, some men of the Chang regime may well have accompanied the group.

The next year, on the ninth day of the ninth month, however, he did not return to T'ien-p'ing Mountain; a dated poem written that day is one of the most discouraged poems in his entire collection. It is entitled simply "Kuei-mao, chiu-jih" or 1363, the Ninth Day (of the Ninth Month):

> The wine has mellowed, but why have the chrysanthe-
>   mums not yet bloomed?
> On the weed-grown paths of my little garden I pace to
>   and fro.
> I do not go with all that company to ascend a height
>   today;
> I fear it would bring me only sadness to look into the
>   distances.[3]

The wine is ready for drinking, but something is lacking— represented by the chrysanthemums which have not bloomed. It may be some personal sadness that spoils this day for him this year, but it also may be his discouragement with the recent turn of events. In the same month of this year Chang Shih-ch'eng had again proclaimed himself a rebel, had re-

2 FTC 1/3b-4b   3 CCSC 18/19a-b

* 118 *

nounced the titles and honors bestowed upon him by the
Mongol government, and had refused to send the grain shipments to Peking. Men like Kao Ch'i who had hoped for the
best in Chang's regime while, to be sure, fearing its instability, as his essay written on the previous Nine-Nine Festival
shows, must have found this turn of events more than enough
to make them thoughtful and apprehensive. Chang Shih-
ch'eng, the defender of the region on whom they had relied,
whose chief officials had been the patrons and friends of Kao
Ch'i and his circle, once again was a rebel. Jao Chieh and
Ts'ai Yen-wen, and even his friend Yang Chi who served on
Jao's staff, were now bandits, in the eyes of the imperial
government and in the eyes of history. Kao Ch'i himself may
have wondered if his connections with the regime were of a
kind that could be broken off, or if he was now committed to
stay with it, rebel or legitimate, and hope that it might be
able to protect them all.

The sobering reflection into which this must have plunged
Kao Ch'i probably caused him to re-evaluate the Chang Shih-
ch'eng movement. He had been conscious of its weaknesses
prior to this, and his hope that it might prove to be a worthwhile venture probably was aroused by the fact that Jao and
Ts'ai and other worthwhile men had been willing to tie their
fate to it. But the hope was that men of ability and integrity
could bring strength to an otherwise weak movement. It was
probably for Ts'ai or for Jao that Kao Ch'i had written another essay, his "Discourse on Love and Fear," which very
clearly was an attempt to reform the Chang regime, particularly its military organization. It is probable that the essay
was an outgrowth of discussions among Kao's friends and
these officials of the regime, and that Kao hoped that his
essay, through them, would reach Chang himself and would
in that way bring about the corrections that were so clearly
needed.

The "Discourse on Love and Fear"[4] is a short and tightly organized essay of about eight hundred words,[5] aimed at the problem of how to discipline and effectively use military forces. Kao notes that the troops of the period are either vagrant, dispossessed peasants from the countryside, or are drawn from the irresponsible and criminally inclined men of the towns and the city streets, people without proper homes or regular work, untaught and undisciplined, lacking moral self-restraint and subject to no externally applied prohibitions. Military service is to them an opportunity to pillage and plunder; they have no will to fight, no awareness of any larger purpose. With such material, Kao argues, one must not rely on benevolence, and he quotes the writings of the late sixth century B.C. militarist Sun-tzu, who noted that soldiers who fear the enemy do not fear their own leaders, while those who fear their own leaders will not fear the enemy. The only way to make them fear their own leaders, thereby to submit to discipline and become reliable and effective soldiers, is to punish their grave infractions of discipline by death. This, Kao argues, in the long run is benevolence, for the fighting effectiveness it brings about will protect them from the enemy, enable them to protect the state from the enemy, and furthermore protect the civilian population from their undisciplined depredations. Kao believes that such fear must be balanced by love, but he apparently feels that in the present situation there is a deficiency of fear, not of love, for he does not emphasize the need for it. This, he concludes, is not merely a problem for generals to concern themselves with. For if the emperor practices it, the empire can be well governed, and if the governor of a region observes it, the region can be well ordered and strong. It is not merely a technical military problem, but a problem of government.

[4] FTC 1/1a-2a
[5] An English translation would run to several thousand words.

The reference to the emperor means the Mongol emperors of the Yuan dynasty, and the regional governor of course means Chang Shih-ch'eng and his government at Soochow. Thus this essay must have been written before the fall of 1363, when Chang still was, in name at least, an official of the Yuan state. It shows that even in that time the breakdown of morale and discipline in Chang's armies had reached serious proportions, and the historical accounts confirm this. Before crossing the Yangtze in 1356 to invade the rich Southeast, Chang apparently was a vigorous and effective leader. After becoming the master of Soochow and the surrounding area, he became ever more lax and concerned himself ever less directly with the problems of rulership.

At first Chang delegated chief authority to his younger brother Chang Shih-te, who was an able field commander and a far-sighted strategist. But Chang Shih-te was captured in a siege of Ch'ang-chou in 1358, and died while a captive of Chu Yuan-chang and the Red Turban rebels of Nanking. After that Chang delegated chief authority to another younger brother, Chang Shih-hsin, who was a man of little ability and who had an insatiable rapaciousness for material wealth and sensual pleasure. Under his influence, Chang Shih-ch'eng's military arm became an agency for one vast looting operation. His chief generals emulated Chang Shih-hsin in devoting themselves to the acquisition of wealth and the enjoyment of pleasure. They became arrogant and insolent, insubordinate and ineffective. Bastions at the front became scenes of music and feasting, as the officers revelled with dancing girls and entertainers, and the soldiers pillaged the local population. Generals ordered to undertake field campaigns were known to ignore the commands, making vague excuses. Chang Shih-ch'eng became a soft and indulgent leader, unwilling to apply punishment, confident that with the great wealth now at his disposal he could purchase reliable service from his subordinates. His nearest rival, Chu Yuan-chang, based up-river at Nanking, had neither the population nor the surplus wealth to draw on, but he had a rigorously disciplined movement and generals who were eager for combat. One can well imagine that to Kao Ch'i and his friends, concerned with military strategy as with principles of government, the contrast between the two movements was a cause for grave concern. The earnestness of Kao Ch'i's "Discourse" reflects accurately the apprehension with which a thoughtful man viewed the situation. We can believe that Kao Ch'i alternated between hope that wise men could bring constructive influences to bear, and despair that their influence was not great enough to accomplish what was so urgently needed.

The only other formal discourse to come down to us from Kao Ch'i's pen also reflects this same background. It is a definition of the four kinds of minister who are indispensable to the state.[6] These are: (1) the loyal official who will serve the dynastic interest in a fashion that will deter enemy states from daring to attack; (2) the discriminating, perceptive official who understands the secret springs of the cosmic balance, and who is never at a loss to know the appropriate policies to adopt; (3) the remonstrating official who dares to inform the ruler of his errors and who fears neither the anger of sycophants nor the reprisals of a tyrannical ruler; (4) the official who maintains the law, upholding proper administrative procedures, serving no special interests and bowing to no pressures, before whom the wolves and the foxes slink away. Only when the ruler encourages the services of all four kinds of minister can the state be strong. This somewhat longer discourse analyzes vividly the causes of disintegration and dissolution of the power of the state, and must have been intended as warning and advice to Chang Shih-ch'eng.

[6] "Ssu ch'en lun," FTC 1/2a-3b

"Even an ordinary man selecting his friends, hopes to find in them such qualities," Kao admonishes, "how much more the emperor of the nation! How much more the governor of a region!"

Kao Ch'i's concern was that of an intelligent man who felt that he knew what was wrong and that he possessed the ability to correct it. His was not the cynical criticism of a neutral bystander; it was the analysis of a participant. It displays clear identification of interest with the regime he was criticizing. His hope, in the earlier years when he was more optimistic, was that of a man who believed in his own powers and in the effectiveness of the ideas he was advancing, which were the traditional ideas of Chinese statecraft. He would have thought of these as originating ultimately in the Confucian classics, but we might better see them as an amalgam of Confucian idealism and administrative realism, stemming in large part from a background of the actual experience of more than a thousand years of the Chinese empire. His views were an intelligent analysis of the needs of his time, presented by a man who believed in man's ability to perfect the human world in which he lived. As Kao's optimism was slowly eroded away, he did not lose that belief, nor his faith in the traditional political wisdom on which it was based. But he came to see that human shortcomings in the Chang regime were greater than he and his friends could overcome. His pessimism was no less thoughtful than his former optimism. He came to accept more of the passive wisdom of the *Book of Changes*, to withdraw and turn his attention to other things. He did not cut off all connection with the Chang regime overnight, but as he grew more critical of its failures, he associated less with his acquaintances in it, and more with his own circle of friends, especially the Ten Friends of the north city wall, most of whom like him-

self also gave up their connections with government. He retired to inaction.

Late in 1362 Kao moved away from the city to a rural
residence on the Lou River, the name for a section of the
Wu-sung River east of the city, close both to his father-in-
law's home at the Green Hill and to his own family property
at the Village of Tall Trees. For more than three years, until
the year 1365, his Lou River retreat served as his home. It
was a withdrawal from the city, and symbolically an estrange-
ment from the political activity centered there. It is the disillusioned hero, frustrated by fate, who turns thoughtfully back
to the country, and to the values he can find there. These lay
chiefly in his poetry, and it is Kao's poetry which records
both his sad feelings on having to make this move and his
gradually achieved contentment with the life he found there.
A poem called "On Moving to the River's Edge, and Taking
Leave of My Old Home on the East Side of the City" must
have been written just at the time of moving. The old home
on the east side of the city probably refers to the north city
wall home, the old family home which was in the northeast
corner of the city.

> It is only human to feel fond attachment to one's old
>   home;
> Who would happily be a far-roaming[7] wanderer?
> That I go surely is not that I would choose so.
> In truth, it is these chaotic times which force me to go.
> Desolately I look on the little hills;
> Grieving, I bid farewell to loved ones and family.
> I fear troublesome worries if I do not go,
> But even wanting thus to go, I am overcome with the
>   sadness of parting.

[7] "Far-roaming" is a poetic license, describing a move to a country
residence only a few miles away.

Though my wife and children are to go with me
My resentment lingers on undiminishing.
I step through the gate, but cannot bear to set off
And linger sadly through the whole day.[8]

A second daughter had been born to Kao this year, and his immediate family were going with him. But the comfort to be derived from his family's presence could not offset the sadness of having to leave.

Another poem written the same year is somewhat more philosophical about the move; it is called "Moving to Temporary Lodgings on the Lou River." A home away from one's ancestral home might be called "temporary lodgings" even though one lived there for decades.

A man is lodged in this corporeal frame less than a
    hundred years
During which time it now moves, now rests, without
    certainty.
I have lived just three times nine years[9]
And my shuttlings back and forth no doubt will not
    end with this.
Last year I lived at the foot of the hills;
This year I move to the edge of the river.
My rude nature delights in rustic simplicity;
My aim is no more than merely getting by.
Idly, from my window I look over an expanse of fields.
My secluded gate is close by this remote stream bank.
Have I forgotten what it might be to live in a palatial
    dwelling?
Yet neither should it be said that I am not content with
    this.
I have cleared away the weeds on coming to this place;

[8] ccsc 6/16a
[9] Twenty-seven *sui*, or twenty-six years of age by Western reckoning.

I have exposed myself to the chilling frost and dew.
But who says I've left loved ones all far behind?
I find delight here in company with my students.
In the house I have noble wines—
The year is at its end; I pace about aimlessly.[10]

Many of the lines of this poem have figurative as well as literal meaning. Some of these are not entirely clear, but the reference to palatial dwellings in which Kao Ch'i might have lived concerns the rewards which high office could have brought him, and which he has, not without some pain, foregone in order to take up this simple life of a country teacher. He insists that he is content, yet he ends pacing aimlessly about at the New Year's time, the time when one reflects on the year just past and on those things which the new year may bring.

Immediately on moving, in 1362, Kao Ch'i devoted his energy largely to poetry. Perhaps the line in the poem above about "clearing away the weeds" refers to the task that he set himself of going through his accumulated poems and deciding which ones to save by including them in a collection called the "Draft of Poems from the Lou River" ("Lou chiang yin kao"). This collection was never published, but it probably circulated in manuscript form at the time, for the preface that Kao wrote for it is a kind of explanation to the world of his present course of leaving the world of affairs to do nothing more important than write poetry. It is a revealing statement:

"In an age when the world is not troubled, scholars possessing vast and outstanding abilities and who find no place to utilize them often go off to mountains or forests or wastelands of grass and marsh, to keep the company of farmers and old rustics; they drink until deep in their wine, and sing

[10] CCSC 6/1a-b

aloud, and in these things find pleasures that satisfy them. But, because of this they never become known abroad in the world. However when the world is troubled, such persons can join together in the common cause, the brave ones utilizing to the full their strength, the learned ones applying all their stratagems, and those skilled in speech winning others to their views. Such activities all display the ways by which men can utilize whatever abilities they possess to advance their careers and gain for themselves merit and fame. Nor, in such times, could they restrict themselves to the company of farmers and old rustics and be content with idle pleasures. But in either case [whether in troubled or untroubled times], they would be acting in accord with the times.

"Today the world is in a state of disintegration and collapse. Campaigns and military expeditions are underway on all sides. This can indeed be called an age of troubles. Persons who are capable of presenting invincible stratagems in the council tents, or of performing warlike deeds within the military forces, or of carrying out important missions beyond the borders, all are needed by the rulers. All of these await the appearance of scholars who are wise and brave and skilled in speech. If such were to exist in the mountains or forests or wastelands of grass and marsh in a time like this, who among them would *not* be willing to come forth, in response to the needs of the ruler, to utilize his special talents? Who would willingly remain to shrivel up and die of old age, wearing only rough homespun and eating only coarse foods?

"I live in such an age, but I am truly lacking in those abilities. Even though I might want to rouse myself into action, it would be like a man who lacked a strong carriage and good horses yet wanted to set out on a journey of a thousand miles;—would that not be too difficult? Therefore it is that I have ensconced myself on the banks of the Lou River, and content myself with mean status.

"Sometimes I climb a hill and gaze out where the Yangtze's waters race past for a hundred miles, to pour into the sea. The tumbling and tossing of its waves, the dark mysteries of its mists and haze, the flowering and dying of plants and trees, the soaring and drifting of birds and fishes, in fact all sorts of things that can move the mind and entice the eye have been here set forth in poetry. For it is in this way that I have been able to dispel disquieting sadness by forgetting both myself and the world, granting to matters of gain and loss no more than a laugh.

"From the first I paid no attention to the matter of these poems' poetic workmanship; they have just accumulated until they fill a volume. I have named this a 'Draft of Poems from the Lou River.' If one finds himself in a rustic cottage or under a thatched roof, when there is mellowed wine and a fattened pig, and he drinks with farmers and old rustics until all are drunk together, and should he then strum on an old pot and sing these verses, that will be enough to bring out all that they have to say. Thus my preface, by way of introduction, in which to make known that I have turned myself out to dwell among the rivers and lakes because I am a man of no ability; it is not as if I had ability but would not utilize it."[11]

This preface is apology and self-defense. It is also a retreat from the earlier attitude of eager confidence, and it has the pathos of defeat and retreat. But it also gives false though conventional explanations for the new attitude. In these years Kao Ch'i certainly did not lose confidence in his own powers, nor in the correctness of his political philosophy, but he is willing to describe himself as an incompetent in order to escape responsibility for failing to exert himself positively

[11] ccsc, prefatory section of vol. 1, p. 1a-b

for the local political powers. At twenty-two, before experiencing active involvement, he had proclaimed himself the Man of the Green Hill, the poet banished to this lower world, intent only on poetizing, and contemptuous of this world's affairs. Now, a mere four years later, he has traveled and has returned, he has known close association with the men of power and has decided to forego the great worldly rewards that they could give him. But he does not say that he scorns the world. He is no longer a banished immortal, intoxicated only with poetry. Nor is he the hopeful and self-confident hero, seeking tasks to try his powers. He is the hero disillusioned, the would-be statesman who sadly and with difficulty comes to the conclusion that he cannot give this cause his talents. He withdraws to the Lou River, not drunk on poetry, but to find thoughtful solace in it. Poetry is the most enduring value of this world of non-involvement to which he now confines himself. There are poet-friends, and there is wine, and there are still occasions which bring pleasure and satisfaction. But they do not wholly cover the pain of frustration which the self-denial of this passive world has brought him.

This was a period of intense poetic activity for Kao Ch'i. His nephew, writing a preface to a collection of his poems some twenty years after his death, tells that he "lived as a recluse by the Wu-sung River, barred his gates, and studied. He concealed his traces among peasants and fishermen." However, the preface continues, he spent his time in the company of friends and of his father-in-law and his wife's five brothers; they "whiled away their days in cordial company, giving themselves up to wine and to chanting poetry, giving vent to the feelings that moved them."[12] Many poems have dates or titles indicating that they come from these years,

[12] Chou Li, Preface to CCSC

and many from their content seem to have been produced out of this experience, Kao Ch'i strove to content himself with this way of life, but he clearly had not forgotten other things, as this poem indicates:

> I have borrowed a place to live beside the eastern fields.
> Idle, I seek out my old fishing rock.
> In the morning rain the willow trees look dark.
> Midday brings wind that rustles the sparse rice flowers.
> I have stepped aside but temporarily; I'm ashamed to be
>   called a recluse.
> Yet I've only just come away, so do not ask me about
>   returning.
> I fear my scholar's cap would startle the simple people
>   here,
> So, like them, I too wear the clothing of a rustic.[13]

This ambivalent attitude about what he was doing shows in other poems as well. One that from internal evidence also seems to date from this time is called "On Watching the Farmers":

> This morning, in a rush of good spirits,
> Taking stick in hand, I walked far through the empty
>   fields.
> The spring plowing is just commencing;
> Ridges of earth turn upward to receive the warm sun.
> There's a twitter of birds warbling off in the valley,
> And splashing of springs flowing in their courses.
> The year's labors now must begin;
> How busily the farmers must toil!
> Yet my limbs recline in indolence.
> I hide away uselessly in my shabby hut.
> Thus I must bear hunger and need.
> Inactive, I sigh, irresolute.[14]

[13] ccys 3a, *Chiao-shu tsa-fu*, No. 2   [14] ccsc 6/14b

The "hunger and need" of this rustic way of life can be dismissed as only relatively real, relative that is to the life of a high official. Kao Ch'i's simple country life of these years was one of other strains than those of economic hardship, and even these strains were often forgotten in the pleasures of friends and wine-drinking, conversation and poetry.

Thus passed three years, until in 1365 Kao returned to the city, to his home inside the north city wall. In 1364 Chu Yuan-chang, the future Ming founder, had disposed of his enemy to the west in the central Yangtze, and now in 1365 turned his armies against Chang Shih-ch'eng to his east. In the summer of 1365 these Nanking armies succeeded in wresting away large portions of Chang Shih-ch'eng's territories north of the river, and concern became urgent in Soochow. It undoubtedly was for reasons of safety that Kao Ch'i moved back within the protecting walls of the city. In the early part of 1366 Chu Yuan-chang ordered his chief commander, the awesome General Hsü Ta, to undertake direct attack on Chang Shih-ch'eng's main strongholds. Hu-chou and Hangchow to the south quickly fell to the Ming armies.

From June onward Soochow itself was threatened, enclosed in an ever-tightening siege under Hsü Ta's command. Chang's defending forces were drawn into the environs of the city itself, and finally within the city walls. These forces had been vastly reduced by the series of defeats north of the river, and by the surrender to Hsü Ta of sixty thousand troops and three leading commanders at Hu-chou in November of 1366. Chang's generals continued to surrender to Hsü, who advanced on the city from the south. Soochow was isolated and completely surrounded in December. Yet Chang and his remaining forces held out desperately, foraging out from the walls to raid the besieging army, fighting fiercely for an opportunity to break through the siege. Hsü Ta was unable to devise a means to break into the city, and the siege lingered on. Within the city, conditions became unbearable. "The price of rats soared to a hundred cash, and when the rats were all gone, people boiled the leather straps of their sandals and ate them." Finally, in August of 1367, Chang decided that the situation was hopeless, and surrendered. The people of Soochow who had survived could eat again, but they faced the fearsome prospect of being ruled by a Red Turban bandit lately turned self-proclaimed "Prince of Wu," soon to call himself founder of a new Great Ming dynasty. This Chu Yuan-chang, the victor, hated Chang Shih-ch'eng as the last of his rivals, the man who had held out longest against his rule. He resented the people of the Wu region who had helped Chang to resist him so long. The people of Soochow with good reason were apprehensive about what might lie ahead.

From 1365 when he moved back into the city until the collapse of Chang's regime in August of 1367, Kao Ch'i was within the city walls. The return to the city brought increased contacts with friends. The Ten Friends were mostly again in the city, like Kao Ch'i forced to seek the safety of the city's walls, but not at first feeling directly threatened by the advancing warfare. By this time, Chang's government had degenerated, the character of his personal leadership had changed. He and his brother and his leading lieutenants were subverted by the luxuries of high life, and they turned increasingly to pleasure-seeking. Whatever identification of interest with the regime Kao Ch'i and his friends had felt several years earlier, they now were alienated from it and watched its decline and fall as spectators, as unwilling sufferers, not as active participants. Thus they engaged in what pleasures were still possible, chiefly the pleasures of keeping each other's company, drinking and talking and writing poetry. In 1365 and 1366 they still could go out of the city on pleasure excursions to the nearby scenic regions, pay calls on learned monks in their monasteries on T'ien-p'ing Mountain and on the shores of Lake T'ai, and make brief visits to their country places. Many poems speak of these activities. One, which may have been written in the spring of 1366, is called "Inviting a Friend To Go Out for an Excursion":

> Irrepressible melancholy of spring—and dragging idleness.
> I want so much to go out beyond the West Gate and see the lovely hills.
> I address myself to my drinking friends, seeking a companion in wine.
> One tankard and we'll be drunk, 'midst the blossoming apricot trees.[15]

Another is "Addressed to My Friends of the North City Wall":

> As youths we rushed off to famous cities;
> How earnestly we desired to be noble men.
> These foolish sentiments were at odds with the times;
> The more actively pursued, the more regret there followed.
> Rest your travels, return to your humble homes!
> Don't set yourselves again upon the highways.
> Though living in poverty will you be without companions?
> You will find three or four whose spirits match your own.
> We have gathered often under the tall pines,
> Sitting and drinking in total informality.
> After passing the goblets back and forth
> The talking and joking sometimes have been a bit too free.

[15] CCYS 12a-b

Although that could be called excessively open and
    direct,
Still, it has never involved matters of great importance.
We let ourselves go in the woods and the wilds;
Why not, for the time, free our spirits in this way?[16]

Here Kao Ch'i urges his friends to let themselves enjoy
their fun, even though it might in ordinary times be considered too frivolous. These times permit no activities more
meaningful. But sometimes this frustration brought inescapable sadness, which the wine and the company could not
disperse. We see this in a song called "About Myself":

Boundless ambition for fame! Scorn for bookish men
    [such as I am]!
What physiognomer ever approved of my counte-
    nance?[17]
But all my life my fierce will has driven me on; I blush
    to be compared with those ordinary persons.
The wine takes hold; heroic the talk,
My sword bolsters my proud spirit;
I compose a poem, in lines that startle the hearer.
But the winds are adverse; they still do not permit the
    great bird to soar aloft.

For what have I wandered alone through this dusty
    sphere?
North, South, East, West—ten years I've been a trav-
    eller.
I've feared only that the likes of Ch'en Teng would
    scorn me; therefore have I ignored my own chickens
    and millet patch.
The flute recalls distant mountains and passes; the wine
    brings back those days and months.

[16] CCYS 1a   [17] "Ever predicted success for me."

I turn aside, transfixed by thought.
I'm not yet old; why should my gleaming tears fall like
    rain?[18]

This intensely personal poem is full of allusions, some of
which defy translation. Ch'en Teng was a martial figure of
the period of the Three Kingdoms, the symbol of the heroic
figure who ignored self-interest (his chickens and his millet
patch) in order to devote himself to larger ideals. The first
stanza refers to the heroic ideals of Kao Ch'i's earlier years,
his years of wandering and his earlier ambitions with regard
to service under Chang Shih-ch'eng. The second stanza
speaks of his disillusionment, and the discontented resigna-
tion of the present.

    The theme of sadness brought on by the sound of the flute,
suggestive of the loneliness of the unhappy wanderer, is a
common one. Kao Ch'i has written of it in another poem,
"On Hearing a Flute":

    The flute has only commenced, and my tears already
      flow.
    The cold lamplight reflects the rain without my river's
      edge lodging.
    I trust you not to play the songs about farewells;
    In this chaotic age everyone is easily moved to grief.[19]

    The tone of sadness is intensified in the poems dating
from the year 1366-1367. As the warfare drew closer after
the middle of 1366, the people were confined to the city.
They watched from the city walls when the fighting was not
in progress, and gathered soberly in each other's homes to
seek what diversion was still possible. It is not surprising
that the poems from these days are deeply reflective and

[18] KHC 1a   [19] CCSC 17/3b

somewhat sad. One, "Spring Prospect in the Rain," bears
the poet's notation that it was written during the siege:

> From high atop the city's gate towers I spy the river's
> bank.
> Spring excursions in gaily colored carts are not to be
> this year.
> Crab apple and pear blossoms have all fallen in the
> rain of the day of cold food;
> Only the chirping birds do not know sadness.[20]

The "day of cold food" (*han shih*) is a day in spring, just
before the Spring Festival of Visiting Graves. It is a time
when people want to be able to travel out to visit the graves,
and when the joys of spring are tempered by thoughtfulness.
Poets have traditionally mourned rain at this time, but this
year for Kao Ch'i the season is one of unusual melancholy.

None of Kao Ch'i's extant poems describe the distress of
the months of siege in detail; a few make mere passing reference to it, such as one which speaks of a neighbor's children crying in hunger, or another which speaks of the sounds
of warfare that echo into the city. If he wrote other poems during those harshest months, he did not keep them. The sad-
dest recollection of those difficult months was that of the
death of his second daughter, a little girl of five (six *sui*),
who died of some illness in the spring or early summer of
1367, during the siege. The following spring, seeing the
flowers bloom again reminded him of an incident that recalled her to mind, and he wrote the following poem,
"Written on Seeing the Flowers, and Remembering My
Daughter":

> I grieve for my second daughter,
> Six years I carried her about,

[20] CCSC 17/6a

Held her against my breast and helped her eat,
Taught her rhymes as she sat on my knee.
She would arise early and copy her elder sister's dress,
Struggling to see herself in the dressing table mirror.
She had begun to delight in pretty silks and lace
But in a poor family she could have none of these.
I would sigh over my own recurring frustrations,
Treading the byways through the rain and snow.
But evenings when I returned to receive her greeting
My sad cares would be transformed into contentment.
What were we to do, that day when illness struck?
The worse because it was during the crisis;
Frightened by the alarming sounds, she sank quickly
    into death.
There was no time even to fix medicines for her.
Distraught, I prepared her poor little coffin;
Weeping, accompanied it to that distant hillside.[21]
It is already lost in the vast void.
Inconsolate, I still grieve deeply for her.
I think how last year, in the spring,
When the flowers bloomed by the pond in our old
    garden
She led me by the hand along under the trees
And asked me to break off a pretty branch for her.
This year again the flowers bloom.
Now I live far from home, here by this river's edge.
All the household are here, only she is gone.
I look at the flowers, and my tears fall in vain.
A cup of wine brings me no comfort.
The wind makes desolate sounds in the night curtains.[22]

[21] This probably some months after her death, and after the end of the siege.
[22] ccsc 6/16a-b

There is little else in Kao Ch'i's poetry that speaks directly of the military conquest of Chang Shih-ch'eng by Chu Yuan-chang's armies, and of the perilous circumstances under which the poet and his family and friends existed through those fateful months. But there are a few poems which record the mixed feelings with which they went out from the city the first times to look about and survey the changes that the fighting had brought, and the welcome evidence of the return to normal conditions: "Distant sails once again moving on the river, fortifications empty, the happiness on finding that friends are still alive, or the sadness on hearing from them that others have not survived."

The new Ming government that proclaimed a new dynasty commencing with the first day of the New Year in 1368 was not long in making itself felt, and in realizing some of the apprehensions of the citizens of Soochow. True, the armies of Hsü Ta were well-disciplined, and Chang Shih-ch'eng's surrender was accompanied by no looting or pillaging. But Chu Yuan-chang immediately ordered his civil and military officials to replace those of Chang Shih-ch'eng. Lung-p'ing again became Soochow, now a mere prefecture under direct rule from the central government at Nanking. Thousands of the rich of the Wu districts, and men who had held office under Chang, were banished to the Huai region, the arid and desolate area from which the new Ming founder himself had come, to suffer hardship and learn about the stern way of life there on the edge of the North China Plain. At the same time, new taxes, punitive by intent, were imposed on the Wu region. The new government was efficient, well-organized, and thorough—all of the things that the Chang Shih-ch'eng rebel regime had failed to be.

Kao Ch'i, objectively considering these contrasts, must have approved of many of the changes. In many ways they echoed the advice he had tried to give Chang five or six years earlier, when hope of reform still seemed to exist. But it is doubtful that he could be wholly pleased. The banished thousands included most of his friends. The harsh taxes affected him, his wife's family, and all his friends and neighbors. True, there were many auspicious signs to be observed at Nanking. The new emperor appeared anxious to divorce himself from his Red Turban rabble background. He had surrounded himself with famous men of learning, had called for a return to the noble institutes of T'ang and Han government, and had issued proclamations resounding with the tenets of traditional Confucian government. He had called for all men of learning and ability to come forth and serve a vigorous new dynasty, and his armies in the field were quickly and smoothly bringing the people again under the control of one Chinese government. There was no doubt that the Mandate of Heaven had shifted, and that Chu Yuan-chang, the Hung-wu Emperor of Ming, was its bearer. But there were signs that his crude background made him violently suspicious of men of learning, and that his rigorous government was to be little tempered by gentler humanistic concerns. Most clearly of all, the resentment that he bore the Wu region deterred men of Soochow from flocking immediately to his standard.

Chang Shih-ch'eng's regime had ended in a way that kept its memory alive in the minds of the people of Soochow. His wife and concubines had nobly immolated themselves in a burning tower, rather than suffer disgrace at the hands of the Ming conquerors. Many of his commanders had wanted to fight to the end, but had been dissuaded from the hopeless cause by Chang's command to spare the citizens further suffering. Chang himself was captured, trussed up, and taken off to Nanking in a cage; there he resolutely starved himself and refused to speak to his captors. His defiance only further angered the Ming founder, who had hoped to force Chang to submit and acknowledge his new dynasty. Many of the people of Wu were said to remain loyal to Chang; they concealed his two little sons to prevent their capture by Ming agents, and secretly sacrificed to Chang's memory. The Hung-wu Emperor could impose a government on the Wu region, but he could not destroy the feelings that lingered on, loyal to his old rival there.

He tried intimidation. The people of Soochow received a constant stream of reports from Nanking, telling of the punishments meted out to captive officials. Kao Ch'i had close friends among the victims. Ts'ai Yen-wen, Kao Ch'i's literary friend in Chang's government, and two other literary men, had been chief advisors to Chang's younger brother and chief minister, the dissolute Chang Shih-hsin. These three were held responsible for the laxness and corruption of the rebel regime in decline. The Ming founder had heard the popular jingle blaming them for incompetence, and predicting their downfall; he had made a point of contrasting their foolish, bookish ways with his own diligence in governing. He ordered the three brought to Nanking. One was strangled, Ts'ai and the third man were beheaded, and their corpses were displayed for a month as a warning to the public. Even old Jao Chieh, the chief literary ornament of Chang's regime, was carted off to Nanking and executed as a war criminal. Kao Ch'i wrote a moving poem, lamenting his death,[23] as did many other poets of the time. Jao was genuinely respected as a man of great talent, talent which fate had not permitted him to use. That the Ming founder should have felt it necessary to eradicate men like Jao Chieh must have given Kao Ch'i pause. What of his own connections with Ts'ai and Jao? What about the members of the literary circle who had been actual officials of Chang Shih-ch'eng's ill-fated rebel

[23] CCSC 12/5b. "K'u Lin-ch'uan kung"

dynasty? A few had escaped the net by fleeing, abandoning family and property, disguising themselves and changing their names. Many others of Kao Ch'i's friends and men of his class were included in the general lists of the exiled, and were no doubt fearfully expecting to be singled out for further punishment. Kao Ch'i had escaped, but his elder brother, who had been a minor official stationed north of the Yangtze, seemed to have disappeared. Kao Ch'i made no attempt to escape; he remained in Soochow, living quietly, if apprehensively.

It was at this time that he received a long-delayed letter from his brother, and learned that he had been banished to Shou-chou in the Huai region. Kao Ch'i replied with a poem, commiserating: "As you crossed the waves of the Yangtze and the Huai, it must have been in sadness; now you can wander 'midst the rivers and hills of home only in your dreams."[24] Yang Chi and other friends in exile also wrote to him, sending sad poems. In response to one of theirs recalling more joyous occasions in the years before, when they had listened to singing together in Jao Chieh's pleasure garden in Soochow, Kao reminded them:

Flowers are falling in famed gardens, but drunken revels
　　have ceased;
My friends too no longer know their elegant pleasures
　　of old.
In that strange place where you are, mourn not that
　　you hear no songs
For if you heard music now, your grief would only
　　increase.[25]

Soochow's famed gardens saw no music and revelry in those first months and years after the Ming victory. Kao Ch'i, left

[24] ccsc 14/18b　　　　[25] ccsc 17/15a

alone in Soochow, could be as apprehensive about the future as were his brother and friends in exile.

Soon after the end of the siege, he moved out of the city, back to his old dwelling on the Lou River, and again devoted himself to his poetry. Once again he went through his accumulated poems, culling out the best, no doubt changing many references to political events that might now be better forgotten, preparing a new collection. He called it "Fou-ming Chi," "The Earthen-Pot Resounds," and in his preface he stated that it contained 732 poems dating from the ten-year period 1358 to 1367. The title is odd. Superficially it appears to be a reference to the rustic custom of strumming on an earthen pot to mark the cadence for chanting songs. His poems, Kao tells us in the same preface, are the ingenuous works of a common poet who merely wants to express his naïve thoughts and has no skill at learned polishing of elegant phrases. Perhaps this is all Kao Ch'i intended. But his own friends and later writers have felt that the name required explanation. The earliest usage of the phrase about strumming the earthen pot, the *fou*, is in the *Book of Changes*, under the thirtieth hexagram, and Kao's title for his new collection of poetry undoubtedly called that passage to the minds of his learned friends. Is it significant that there it is a reference to uncertainty? The passage in which it occurs reads:

> In the light of the setting sun,
> Men either beat the pot and sing
> Or loudly bewail the approach of old age.
> Misfortune.[26]

[26] The quotation from the *Book of Changes* follows the Wilhelm-Baynes translation, Vol. I, p. 128; for further discussion of this hexagram and the meaning traditionally associated with it, see Vol. I, pp. 126-29, and Vol. II, pp. 178-82.

Perhaps the "light of the setting sun" suggests the "red glow in the west," the Red Turban rebellion from which has evolved the new government at Nanking, to the west of Soochow. Or perhaps, taking the hexagram more literally, it merely means that as time passes and the transitoriness of this life comes home to one, one can either enjoy simple pleasures or fruitlessly bewail his fate. The traditions attached to this passage offer many possible allusions which Kao Ch'i may have found relevant to his own situation, but he leaves the point unclear.

This preface, curiously in the view of subsequent happenings, also stresses the point that some poets, Kao included, are so addicted to expressing themselves in poetry that "even should they because of it bring disaster to themselves, suffer imprisonment or banishment, yet they would be unable to desist." To many this has seemed a presentiment of Kao Ch'i's own tragic fate.

He completed his self-imposed task of editing before the end of 1367. After that, he continued to live in the country, by the river bank, on into 1368, the first year of the new reign-period *hung-wu*, observing the transformation of his nation under the vigorous actions of the new dynasty. His own poetry reflects the melancholy brooding of one who is not sure what these times mean. Seven poems written in the late autumn of 1367, "Setting Forth My Innermost Thoughts on an Autumn Day, While Living by the River," convey the mood most clearly.[27] Each of the seven poems turns on the word *ch'ou* ("sadness") or *yu* ("grief") or *hen* ("vexation") or the like. The last line of the first poem seems to echo the thirtieth hexagram, lamenting the premature approach of old age—although the poet was only thirty-two. The fifth poem contains the lines: "At one time I too harbored the desire to seek fame; I congratulate myself that in recent years I've

[27] CCSC 15/15a-16a

gradually put that aside." Perhaps the fourth of these seven poems most clearly sums up his feelings in the late autumn of 1367:

> Battered and decimated are the ranks of the old scholar-clans;
> Alone I lodge now by the river's edge, and few the pleasures here.
> In the lane before my gate the insistent tax collectors are making their rounds.
> Among my neighbors here there's no place to borrow books to read.
> An insistent hum of insects in the fields betokens dusk's advance;
> Blossoms drip down from the peas on the fence, and the rain brings a feeling of chill.
> If I do no more than stay on in this village, I should have no cause for regret;
> It is only that I fear in these tossing waves there is still no certain safety.[28]

The insistent tax collectors, like the insistent hum of evening insects on all sides—repetition of the word in the original makes the analogy inescapable—the waves still tossing, the decimated ranks of his natural associates, all symbolize the threatening power of the new dynasty, and the uncertainty of the poet in the face of it. But at least there was solace in poetry.

[28] CCSC 15/15b

CHAPTER SIX

NANKING, 1369-1370

IF WE ARE ACCUSTOMED to thinking of pre-modern times as possessing a comforting stability, a languid pace as compared to the history of our own hectic century, Kao Ch'i's life should be instructive. He was nineteen when the legitimate imperial government, already cascading dramatically into decline, lost control of the Wu region, to be replaced there by contending rebellions. During the next twelve years the political fortunes of the rulers of Central China were unpredictable from one year to the next, and the citizens of a great city like Soochow could never be sure what manner of life might be visited upon them. In a man like Kao Ch'i there is manifested a bewildering alternation of attitudes, shifts from involvement to detachment, which give the history of the time as seen through his eyes a fluid character comparable to that of any transitional period of our own times.

It is not surprising that Kao Ch'i did not immediately recognize in the fall of Chang Shih-ch'eng to the enemy from the west in the late summer of 1367 the beginning of one of the long periods of stability in Chinese history. The hindsight of history enables us to see the Ming founding as an inevitable recovery of unification and strong centralization; of reassertion of dominant forces and trends; of the beginnings, even, of the crystallization of Chinese society which ultimately gave it the seemingly "unchanging" quality so misunderstood by nineteenth-century Europeans. Kao Ch'i at the age of thirty-one, in the autumn of 1367, was dazed by the year-to-year uncertainty of life, and quite prepared for more of the same. He received a poem that autumn from his wife's brother in exile who wrote complaining that the Mid-Autumn Festival (coming only a month or more after the fall of Soochow) has been passed in desolate loneliness, despite the beauty of the full moon. From his riverside retreat, Kao Ch'i wrote a long poem in return, telling that his own cares and troubles were at least as great as those of his brother-in-law in exile. He remarks on the rapid pace of unpredictable events. Two years ago they had all feasted and drunk, watching the full moon at a family gathering in his father-in-law's garden. Then, one year ago, they were all within the besieged city, "No different from a lost pig, fallen into a deep trap," awaiting the captor's violence. They have escaped the trap, but this year things seem very little better. "This year I've moved to lodgings by the river's edge, briefly encouraged at least that the disorders of the Southeast have just been settled." But he feels isolated and lonely, and he feels pressed by the insecurity of poverty. Moreover, he associates only with shepherds and old farmers who have little appreciation of his values, and the vanished refinements of his ideal way of life. "After living long in this countryside village I begin to scorn myself. Dissipated completely are my heroic thoughts and my irrepressible enthusiasms. Battered by the world's storms, I'll never again know the flush of youth. I'm ashamed to meet people who may ask my name. My friends have all been dispersed; my world emptied. My older brother and myself are separated by vast distances...."[1] And he goes on to catalog the sorrows of this fleeting existence.

But one year later, a new chapter in Kao Ch'i's life had begun. In that year, his world must have changed greatly, taking on features of certainty and stability. The first year

[1] CCSC 8/22a-b

of the calendar of the new dynasty had seen an unbelievably rapid extension of Ming military might in all directions. The Mongols had been driven from their capital at Tai-tu, modern Peking. Simultaneously, Canton and the south had been conquered. The upper Yangtze and the northwest were under attack, and presented no formidable opposition. Nanking clearly had become a great new imperial capital, its greatness evident in the vastness of the imperial design and the thoroughness of its realization. All of this obviously was not to be compared with Chang Shih-ch'eng's pretensions to imperial dignity. The new dynasty was an awe-inspiring development. Kao Ch'i could feel no familiarity with it, or with any of the men in it, and the fear of reprisal which hung threateningly over his head must have worked to increase the awe with which he viewed this new dynastic enterprise. But his fluid world, for better or for worse, had congealed and stabilized; the outlines of the future were becoming quite discernible—if not yet his own personal future, at least the future of the world in which he would have to work out his own destiny.

By the winter of 1368 that destiny seemed to hold the promise of greatness. How unexpected it must have been! The vengeful hand of Nanking had not fallen upon Kao Ch'i; in its place there came a summons to honor, recognition of his literary genius, and the promise of that high and noble career in public life that his civilization valued above all other careers. There must have come to him some probings and inquiries through intermediaries in the summer or fall of 1368. All we can know from the official accounts is that with the fall of the Mongol capital in the late summer of that year, the Yuan dynasty records and archives were captured. The Ming founder ordered them sealed and transported to Nanking, there to be opened and examined by officials of his government, who would perform one of the

important tasks incumbent on a new dynasty—the preparation of the history of its predecessor. The Ming founder
acted in unusual haste to do this. In the twelfth moon of
the first year he ordered that a historical bureau be established, and by the second moon of the following year (March
1369) the historian-officials of the bureau had been recruited
and brought to the capital to commence their work. Kao Ch'i
was one of sixteen historian-officials appointed for this task.
He must have indicated his acceptance of the position during
the twelfth moon, for in the first days of the New Year he
set off for the Ming capital, a high official-appointee of the
glorious new regime which a mere two or three years ago had
seemed a rabble movement threateningly poised to the west.

The head of the historical commission for the compilation
of the *Yuan History* was Li Shan-ch'ang, one of the Ming
founder's oldest adherents and one of the highest civil officials of the new dynasty. But his position was nominal. The
work would actually be under the direct supervision of two
literary figures who had served the Mongol government and
who had more recently come into the service of the Ming.
These were Sung Lien (1310-1381) and Wang Wei (1321-
1372), famed litterateurs, poets, men of the Southeast, of the
generation older than Kao Ch'i's, but in every sense men of
his kind. Other members of the commission were mostly
scholars who had not previously served the Ming, men of
ability and accomplishment, whom Kao Ch'i undoubtedly
was prepared to look upon as congenial fellow spirits. Moreover, it was obvious in the nature of the situation that the
Yuan History commission was to be, to this specially selected
group of men, a short cut to high administrative office. The
Ming founder faced a great shortage of qualified and trust-
worthy bureaucrats to staff his rapidly expanding government.
Commissions concerned with primarily literary and scholarly
responsibilities gave the government a chance to administer,

as it were, a dignified and honorable test to men who in the normal course of events would have passed their civil service examinations earlier; the candidates belatedly gained an opportunity to prove themselves in tasks to which great prestige attached. An ambitious man could make up for years wasted in the frustrating conditions of the late Yuan, when normal avenues of advancement were not open. He could serve at court, be passed upon by the emperor himself, make acquaintances and form associations in the higher officialdom, and securely place his feet on a rung midway up the ladder of officialdom, instead of starting at the bottom in competition with mere beginners who were his inferiors in years and accomplishment.

The opportunity could only have been immensely attractive to Kao Ch'i. He would secure at once the respect of his community, honor, freedom from pressing economic worries, an opportunity to help his family and friends, an outlet for his suppressed ambitions. We can well imagine that the pessimism expressed in the poem addressed to his brother-in-law in the autumn of 1367 now gave way to cautious hope, that he ceased to scorn himself, and that the flush of youth returned to his cheeks. He could abandon his obscure life among shepherds and farmers, put on his scholar's cap and gown, and know again the exhilarating association with his intellectual peers. His wife's family would be proud of him; his friends would envy him. His name might even be preserved as one of the meritorious officials of a glorious new era in history. The opportunity suddenly to reverse the evil trend that had until this moment beset him must have left him dizzy. Could it be possible that there was no flaw in this? Was it simply that the Time of Standstill, the Image of Decay, had passed; that, in the words of the *Book of Changes*, "First standstill, then good fortune"? Great new events clearly were bringing unexpected opportunities to men, and auspicious changes of fortune were in order. Was his fate to be linked to the new, detaching itself from the frightening undercurrent that the men of Wu felt with the Ming take-over? Kao Ch'i must have permitted himself at least cautious optimism at this moment, as he prepared to hasten to Nanking immediately after the New Year's celebrations in 1369.

The haste is evident from the fact that he left home on the tenth of the first month, before the full holiday season had ended; a poem written that day concludes with the lines: "The only cause for sadness is that the messenger so urgently presses us to depart; unfinished still are all the expressions of feeling of those who have come to the river's edge to see me off."[2] The messenger from the court delivering the imperial commission is under instructions to return with all haste, but Kao Ch'i does not sound sad or reluctant as he leaves his native city this time. A poem written taking farewell of his wife suddenly takes on a curious formality, like the public utterance of a man in official life. It contains standard literary allusions metaphorically but not literally appropriate to his own situation, such as that in the first line about preparing his carriage for a journey that we know was to commence by boat. Kao Ch'i is now playing a role. He is acting a part which he has long idealized and for which his cultural tradition supplies him with all the precedents; he is now doing and saying the things which a great official does and says. But he has not ceased to be Kao Ch'i the poet, and his poem of farewell to his wife also contains some intimate and tender lines:

> Called for the Compilation of the Yuan History and About to Leave for the Capital, I Take Leave Of My Wife

[2] CCSC 15/18a

In receipt of the imperial command, I hasten to prepare
    my carriage;
Comes the dawn, I must depart for the Capital.
Is not this fine commission a thing imparting honor?
I hesitate only because I must bid you farewell.

Ever since you came into my household
You have long shared my humble poverty.
Yet within your rooms joy and happiness have prevailed;
I honor all your goodness; I do not judge only by a stand-
    ard of beauty.

The season is cold and the house empty of provisions.
How can I bear to go off so far like this?
But the ruler awaits me to work on the archival records,—
I have no time to be concerned about my own affairs.

As I rush about, I'm touched by your devoted aid,
And that you've cooked the setting-hen for me.
Leading our children by the hand, you see me off in
    tears
And ask when the homeward journey will be.

The journey is to be a distant one.
Moving clouds gather low on the river's edge.
The Sages forbade pleasant idleness;
Would I dare linger on at ease in my thatched hut?
It has been my firm purpose gladly to serve my country;
That it has come about in this way is my good fortune.

Eat well and take care until we meet again—
Don't give way to loneliness and sad thoughts.[3]

The allusions, most of which do not emerge in the translation, become almost pedantic, but despite them there is a
genuine feeling of warmth and of concern for his wife, and

[3] ccsc 7/2b

there is simultaneously a feeling of anticipation about the journey and what lies at its end. These same mixed feelings are apparent in all the poems Kao Ch'i wrote on the five- or six-day journey to Nanking.

He left by the Ch'ang-men, the west gate of the city, which led down to the docks on the Grand Canal. On the first day his canal boat seems to have gone no farther than the Maple Bridge, about ten *li* from the city, and there stopped for the night. Spending a chill night as a traveler on a boat tied up at Maple Bridge outside the city of Soochow, hearing the sound of a distant bell from the temple on Han-shan, the Cold Hill, is precisely the situation described in a famous T'ang poem by Chang Chi.[4] Kao Ch'i could not resist writing a pair of quatrains, borrowing half the phrases in Chang Chi's poem, and turning them to his own uses:

I.

The ravens call through the frosty moonlight; the night
    is silent and lonely.
I turn and look back at the city, left not yet far behind.
This then is the night when homesick thoughts begin—
The distant bell, the solitary boat, passing the night near
    the Maple Bridge.

II.

A moonlit haze drifts o'er the sandy shore; the traveller
    still has not slept.
Sounds of singing, lamps and lanterns, there in front
    of the inn.
How is it that just out of the Ch'ang-men we should
    stop for the night?
It's as if we were already spending a night on the boats
    of the Ch'in-huai River.[5]

[4] M. Davidson, *A List of Published Translations from Chinese*, Part II, "Poetry," tentative edition, New Haven, 1957, p. 269, lists a dozen translations of this famous poem.
[5] CCSC 17/11a-b

Here are perfectly mirrored two aspects of Kao Ch'i's thoughts as he set forth for Nanking in February of 1369, still in the lunar New Year season. The first poem has the melancholy air of a lonely traveller thinking about the separation from home, while the second responds to music and gaiety ashore, anticipating the famous pleasure-boats of the Ch'in-huai quarter of Nanking, also made famous in T'ang poetry. Both sets of allusions were virtually inescapable; Kao Ch'i succeeds in using them meaningfully and intimately.

En route, perhaps the next day, he meets a friend from Soochow who is traveling the other direction, home from the capital. He records the encounter in a brief poem:

> I am on my way, and you, instead, returning.
> We meet, and stand long at this stopping place en route.
> I want to send word back home by you
> But first must ask all about affairs in the capital.[6]

Is it eager anticipation about what lies ahead, or is it still a feeling of uncertainty, that makes inquiries about the capital and the new government there drive thoughts of home into secondary position? It may well have been a fair mixture of both.

The *Soochow Prefectural Gazetteer*[7] of 1379 describes the journey from Soochow to Nanking as one of seven stages by water, a total of five hundred and eighty-eight *li*, or almost two hundred miles. Kao Ch'i's poems written en route are not dated precisely or numbered in sequence, nor do they make clear the passage of time, but we know that he said farewell to friends seeing him off on the tenth of the first lunar month, and that he arrived at Nanking on the six-

[6] ccsc 16/14a
[7] Lu Hsiung, compiler, *Hung-wu Su-chou-fu chih*, Peking National Library rare books microfilms (Library of Congress) ch. 1, p. 11a. This work is an invaluable source for all aspects of life in the lower Yangtze region in the first years of the Ming dynasty.

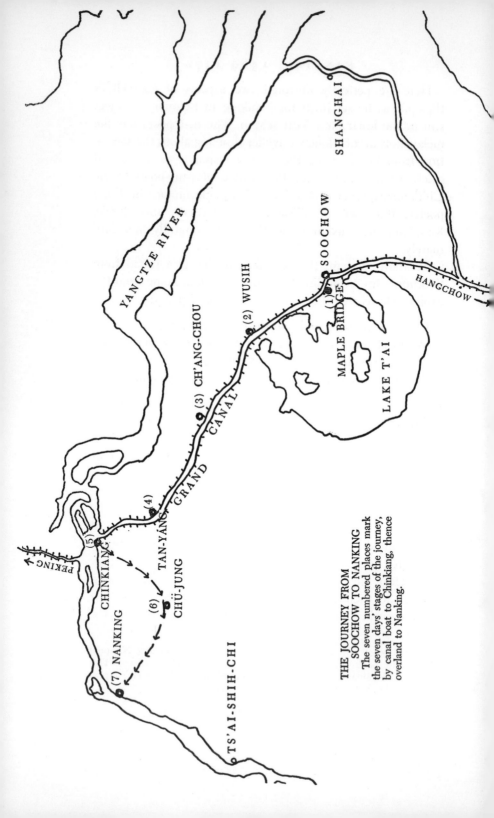

SHANGHAI

SOOCHOW

HANGCHOW

MAPLE BRIDGE (1)

WUSIH (2)

LAKE T'AI

CH'ANG-CHOU (3)

YANGTZE RIVER

GRAND CANAL

TAN-YANG (4)

CHINKIANG (5)

PEKING

NANKING

CHÜ-JUNG (6)

(7)

TS'AI-SHIH-CHI

THE JOURNEY FROM
SOOCHOW TO NANKING
The seven numbered places mark
the seven days' stages of the journey,
by canal boat to Chinkiang, thence
overland to Nanking.

teenth, and we can locate some of the points at which he stopped along the way. Wusih, a hundred *li* from Soochow, probably was the second night's stopping place. Another poem is called "Spending the Night under the Walls of Wusih":

The boat rests temporarily in the long channel, 'midst
    ancient willow trees;
The cock is unwilling to announce the morn so that the
    gates can be opened.
In the high gate tower, near at hand, is heard the chill
    sound of the water clock;
Far off, when the guard-fires flare, mountains are visible
    through the night.
The walls and battlements still bear the traces of warfare
But these routes will not again witness difficulty in trav-
    elling to and fro.
In my lonely boat I sit staring at the lamp, thinking my-
    self less fortunate
Than all those residents here, lost in their peaceful
    dreams.[8]

Ch'ang-chou was another ninety *li* away, and Kao Ch'i probably reached it the next night, his third on the way. He referred to it by its ancient name, P'i-ling, in two poems written there, again on his canal boat at night, thinking of the warm wine and lanterns and laughter of the farewell party for him, as "I clutch the quilts tightly about me, listening to the wind and the rain."[9] This must have been a lonely and rather desolate night. The next night, at Tan-yang, he makes preparation for a more cheerful evening.

Buying wine, I come inquiring at the gate of this water-
    way station.

[8] ccys 5a   [9] ccsc 18/25b

In the boat next to mine lanterns are lighted, and there's
    the sound of voices through the dusk.
This morning I for the first time really felt far from
    home;
Here I am in a little village, outside the walls of Tan-
    yang.[10]

The next night Kao Ch'i was in Chinkiang, staying in the
famous and ancient Kan-lu Ssu, the Temple of Sweet Dew.
His journey had brought him to the place where the Grand
Canal crosses the Yangtze, and he seems to have left his boat
to travel overland on to Nanking, rather than continuing upstream on the Yangtze. This night he finds more comfortable
lodgings in the historic old temple, and his poem is full of
allusions to its past. It is a clear and starlit night, as he
lingers in the temple courtyard ". . . sitting idly talking about
former dynasties."[11]

The fifth night Kao was apparently forced to stay in some
small village without proper lodgings, halfway between Chinkiang and Nanking. In two poems written on the two days of
overland travel, he speaks sympathetically of the great difficulties experienced by the cart-drivers in getting the vehicles
up the hills over bad roads, and safely down again. Sharply
feeling the difficulty of travel, he writes: "I think how it was
at home, each day so pleasant, knowing only comfort. Why
is it that I undertake this travel, so far, through the frost and
cold, laboring in such urgent haste? The ruler's work I did
not dare decline,—nor was it that I sought the trifling emolument."[12] He passed the next day through Chü-jung,[13] and on
the afternoon of the sixteenth at last entered the capital.
He immediately went out to observe the display of lanterns,
although it was a day late: the fifteenth day of the New Year

[10] ccsc 17/11b   [11] ccsc 12/12b-13a
[12] ccsc 7/2b-3a   [13] ccsc 7/6b-7a

is the festival of lanterns, when the people of the great cities in the south parade at night holding aloft specially designed lanterns of curious form and many colors. On the sixteenth day and for several nights thereafter the lanterns are still to be seen, and he wrote "Don't laugh at the traveller for arriving a bit late; there are still as many spring breezes as there were last night."[14] The traveller moved into the T'ien-chieh Temple, the largest and most magnificent Buddhist temple compound within the capital city. Part of it was temporarily being used to house the *Yuan History* Bureau and its historian-officials who did not have homes in the city. It was to be Kao Ch'i's home for a year.

The T'ien-chieh Temple had been built in the 1320's as the palace of the Mongol imperial prince who in 1330 ascended the throne as the Emperor Wen-tsung. After coming to the throne, the new emperor ordered that the name Nanking (then Chien-k'ang or Chin-ling) be changed to Chi-ch'ing. The palace in which he had lived through a very uncertain decade, in which his life and fortune were constantly in doubt, was to be named Lung-hsiang Ssu, or "The Temple of the Soaring Dragon," in recollection of the fact that the dragon had soared—that is, the emperor had ascended the throne—from this place. The president of the Board of Works was sent to enlarge the already splendid compound, and construct additional buildings, "all needed materials to come from the imperial treasury, and no expense or effort to be spared."[15] The temple was located in the middle of the city, a comparatively quiet island in the midst of the bustling traffic and crowded movement of the capital. When the Ming founder's armies took Nanking (Chi-ch'ing) in 1356,

[14] CCSC 17/11b
[15] Yü Chi, "Lung-hsiang Chi-ch'ing Ssu Pei," in *Chin-ling Fan-ch'a Chih*, ch. 16/3a-6b. The justly famous Lung-hsiang Ssu pictured in this valuable history of the temples of Nanking, however, is the one rebuilt outside the city walls near the end of the fourteenth century.

it was the most splendid set of buildings in the city, but he did not confiscate them for his own use. The place had become a leading center of Buddhist learning, housing some very famous monks, and the Ming founder, who had himself spent several years as a novice in a Buddhist monastery, respected it. To be sure, he ordered the name changed, perhaps to avoid the auspicious association with Yuan dynasty fortunes, to T'ien-chieh Temple, the "Temple of the Boundaries of Heaven." He came there occasionally to talk with some of the monks, famous for their learning and their spiritual powers, and he patronized the temple, giving it hundreds of acres of "incense lands," tax exemption, and other privileges.

Kao Ch'i has left very little record of his life at T'ien-chieh Temple, or of his work on the compilation of the *Yuan History*. There are references to long conversations with Sung Lien and Wang Wei and others of the history bureau, and there is evidence in Kao Ch'i's poetry and in the poetry collections of these literary associates at Nanking during those two years that the friendships formed there were of enduring significance. Kao Ch'i must have been deepened and broadened and greatly stimulated to new realms of thought by the contact with these men, and they, though often his seniors, respected and admired him. The number of occasional poems, written in response to the dictates of etiquette on certain types of social occasions—to mark a gathering of friends, a celebration of one kind or another, or most commonly of all, to send off a friend leaving on a journey or to take up a post in local government somewhere—is very great. From these we can see something of Kao Ch'i's associations and the activities of his daily life. But of life at T'ien-chieh Temple he tells very little. There are poems about climbing the bell tower and gazing out over the roofs of the palaces and houses of the capital[16] and describing the atmosphere and activity of the temple compound, where "Incense lingers in this secluded realm of the Buddha," and "Ten thousand shoes gather to its bell, and a thousand lamps flicker in its mirror-reflectors; this place of meditation also has room for the traveller, who does not feel that he has tarried here too long."[17]

But if Kao Ch'i could occasionally escape the feeling that he had stayed too long in the capital by drawing on the aura of peace of the temple environment, such occasions must have become increasingly infrequent. For the largest number of poems from Nanking, commencing with those written only shortly after his arrival there, compare life in Nanking unfavorably with life in Soochow. Irritation and discontent begin to seek expression in his more intimate and reflective poems. As early as March of 1369, the Spring Festival of Visiting Graves, a time when everyone longed to be at his own home in order to tend the family graves, he wrote a poem addressed to his colleagues of the history bureau, including the lines, ". . . At the time for visiting graves (*ch'ing-ming*) there is no traveller who does not have thoughts of home. . . . I'm glad to have the company of friends here among my colleagues in the emperor's service; I shall buy some of the spring wine, and we'll be drunk midst the capital's splendors."[18] Here the thoughts of home do not seem to be overpowering in their sadness. But that same spring he wrote "Hearing Rain in the Night, and Thinking of the Flowers in My Garden at Home":

> The imperial city, and spring rains seeing out the last
> of the spring;
> A night of rain. I hear it sadly; the traveller's pillow is
> cold.

[16] ccsc 15/11b, and 17/12a   [17] ccsc 12/7a-b
[18] ccsc 14/9a-b

Don't go as far as my garden at home, and make all
those flowers fall—
Leave one branch of blooms 'til I can return and see it.[19]

In this poem the traveller is sad, and soon he is writing still
more pointed comparisons of Nanking and home. There is a
poem called "Sitting at Night in the Western Porch of T'ien-
chieh Temple":

The moon rises over the Eastern Hall
And shines on me as I sit at the forecourt porch.
All the monks have long since settled for the night;
I feel deserted, with no one to talk to.
Through curtains of haze fireflies pass softly by;
In breeze-stirred branches the cicadas have ceased their
clamor.
Although this pure scene brings pleasure to the be-
holder,
It is not, alas, my own garden at home.[20]

When he eats "New rice, white as shining jade, transported
far, all the way from Soochow,"[21] he thinks of his own bit of
rural property, and idealizes the simple life he had once
known there. And when friends and relatives send the new
wine of Soochow to him in Nanking, he finds it makes him
drunk in a special way, for this wine conveys feelings that
stir the traveller's deepest thoughts.[22] When his wife writes
a poem to send to him, he replies in kind in a very homesick
mood: "The breeze comes in from my old home, bringing
your poem all the way to the capital; reading it I see your
heart therein. I would prefer only to be able to see your face."
And he goes on to assure her that the glittering splendor of
the capital does not divert his thoughts from her, that

[19] CCSC 17/11b
[21] CCSC 7/4b-5a
[20] CCSC 7/4b
[22] CCSC 17/12a-b

". . . there comes a time when even drifting clouds must meet again," and that the sadness of separation is aging him.[23] As the year wears on, his poems become sadder and sadder.

There is little reason to doubt that homesickness played a large part in Kao Ch'i's feelings of dissatisfaction. But it is also quite probable that the work in the history bureau was less than exciting, and that the rigorous pattern of official life was unexpectedly distasteful to him. Even these facts might have mattered less, had he been able to feel confident in his new status and optimistic about his future as an official in the Ming founder's government. However, his brother and his old friends were still in exile, and harsh measures against his Wu region were just then being carried out. Moreover, the emperor was already displaying signs of the unpredictable wrath and the cruel fury that transformed him eventually into the most violent tyrant in all of Chinese history. This wrath and cruelty seemed to fall most frequently on the innocent heads of literary courtiers like himself, especially men who had suspicious backgrounds or past associations with the emperor's former rivals. This was not necessarily so, for even Liu Chi, the most illustrious of the emperor's advisors, and the man who had made the greatest civil contribution to the founding of the dynasty, had aroused the emperor's suspicions, and had been sent home to Chekiang the year before. He was seemingly permitted to go home because of his wife's death, but everyone at court knew that he had angered the emperor.[24] In a few months Liu was recalled, but his honest and conscientious expression of opinion had created a gulf between him and the emperor, who was both indebted to him and dependent on him.

Other officials were demoted and punished with great frequency, and some had been put to death for what seemed

[23] CCSC 7/5a-b
[24] Hsia Hsieh, *Ming T'ung Chien*, ch. 1, p. 30a

slight breaches of conduct. By 1370 Soochow had already
had its first four Ming-appointed prefectural magistrates,
each of whom had served very short terms, only to be demoted or banished. Despite the great shortage of personnel,
and repeated efforts of the government to recruit educated
men into government service, an air of suspicion and intimidation was beginning to be felt. The spectacular outbursts
of imperial wrath, which often condemned hundreds and
thousands to death, had not yet begun to occur, but some
foretaste of the emperor's unfathomable character undoubtedly already caused men to discuss in private the uncertain-
ties of public life. Kao Ch'i must have begun to feel discouraged about government service, and to wonder if it was indeed the career he had sought so eagerly a decade earlier.[25]

Moreover, the *Yuan History* itself must have seemed a less
than satisfactory task. It was being rushed to completion,
carelessly thrown together without adequate expenditure of
time and thought. The Mongol court archives included *Veritable Records* for thirteen of the reigns of the dynasty, but
stopped short of the last reign, which had lasted almost thirty
years. These records were incomplete and poorly prepared,
and beyond them there was little else. In the space of seven
months, the historian-officials somehow made a dynastic history from inadequate materials, but it is notorious as the
poorest of dynastic histories, incomplete, inaccurate, poorly
edited. The emperor's instruction to the historian-officials
was to make clear the reasons for the Yuan dynasty's rise and
fall, for "A dynasty can be destroyed but its history should

25 The *Veritable Record* (*Ming t'ai-tsu shih-lu*) of the *hung-wu* reign
shows in these first two or three years the extreme instability of public
office. While reasons are not given and punishments are often not mentioned, the turnover of personnel in cabinet level posts is remarkably
rapid, it being quite common for a major post to have five or six in-
cumbents in the space of a year.

not be destroyed."[26] The members of the history commission, writing at a time when the emperor under whom they had lived for more than twenty-five years was still alive and claiming to be the legitimate ruler of China,[27] and writing for a new dynasty whose emperor was to most of them still mysterious, must have found it difficult to know how to judge the history of the dynasty about which they were writing. Not surprisingly, they adopted the rule of omitting the customary sections of discussion and judgment from the beginning and ending of each chapter of biographies,[28] for it is in these sections especially that the historians must express a coherent view of their subject and display their evaluations of it. The *Yuan History* contains no coherent view of the period, and was too close to its subject and too uncertain of its own orientation to be capable of evaluations. Why the Ming court insisted on rushing the task in such unseemly fashion is not quite clear; it is probably to be explained by the great pressure of governmental business that year, the year in which the conquest of the Chinese world was being completed, and government was being extended to all of the new tasks entailed therein. The historians themselves were needed for those other tasks. And the low regard which the new government and the literate public at large felt for the old dynasty made the writing of its history perhaps a merely perfunctory duty at best.

[26] *Yuan History*, Po-na ed., pref. "Chin *Yuan Shih* piao," p. 2a, line 4; see also *op.cit.*, "*Fan-li*" and *Veritable Record*, ch. 37, p. 1a-b, where the emperor's instructions to the history commission are recorded in other words. After this book went to press there appeared an excellent discussion of the compilation of official histories, with specific reference to the Yuan History; see Lien-sheng Yang, "The Organization of Chinese Official Historiography" in W. G. Beasley and E. G. Pulleyblank, eds., *Historians of China and Japan*, London, 1961, esp. pp. 46-47.

[27] Although already driven out into the Mongolian steppe, Shun-ti did not die until the 4th moon of 1370.

[28] *Yuan Shih*, "*Fan-li*," No. 5.

In the eighth lunar month of 1369, on the thirteenth day, Li Shan-ch'ang, Sung Lien, and the whole staff appeared at court and presented their history. It was in manuscript, bound in 120 large volumes, containing 161 chapters and a total of more than 1,360,000 words. Rather than deal with the last long reign, the staff had been ordered simply to omit it for the time being. Knowing that the history would be considered incomplete, and that some further work would be necessary, they had the excuse of insufficient materials for the last decades of the dynasty. The following year the emperor ordered the history bureau reopened, and new materials sought, so that it could be continued to include the last reign, thereby making the work we know today as the *Yuan History*.[29] But except for Sung Lien and Wang Wei and one other member of the commission, that further work was to be done by a different group of scholars;[30] Kao Ch'i and his colleagues could emit sighs of relief that their task was accomplished. Kao Ch'i recorded the ceremony of formal presentation in a poem, in which he quotes some of the words of the emperor's instructions to the history bureau, and notes that he, a mere commoner, is privileged to take part in the imposing audience ritual, based on Han dynasty models.[31] Two days later, the fifteenth of the eighth month, the officials of the just disbanded bureau held a celebration at T'ienchieh Temple, to mark both the Mid-Autumn Festival and

[29] See *Veritable Record*, ch. 42, p. 4b, day *yi wei*, where it notes that the emperor dispatched Ou-yang Yu and eleven others to Peking and the north to gather materials relevant to the last reign ". . . for the further compilation of the *Yuan History*. At this time the group of scholars compiling the *Yuan History* have about completed their work, and they are hereby commanded to submit that part which can be finished first, the deficient sections to wait until later to be filled out." This was in the 7th moon, prior to the completion of the task on which Kao Ch'i was working; that was finished and submitted in the following month.

[30] See *Veritable Record*, ch. 49, p. 3a, day *yi-ch'ou*

[31] CCSC 14/8a

the completion of their common task. Kao Ch'i wrote a poem commemorating this event, and introduced it with a preface explaining the occasion:

"On the thirteenth day of the eighth month of the second year of the reign *hung-wu*, the *Yuan History* was completed and submitted to the throne by the chief minister [Li Shan-ch'ang]. The sixteen scholars who had compiled it were rewarded by gifts of silver and cash,[32] moreover they were presented in audience and commended, and were appointed to various official posts; the old and sick among them however were granted permission to return to their homes. Two days later, on the Mid-Autumn Festival, in view of the completion of their historiographical work and the arrival of the festival, further overjoyed by the generosity of the imperial favor to them and regretting that their days as colleagues in the same bureau were about to end, these gentlemen borrowed the central hall of the T'ien-chieh Buddhist Temple in which they were lodged and had spread there a feast, so that they could find pleasure in the appreciation of the moon, and distribute rhymes on which each could make a poem to commemorate the event. I, Kao Ch'i, got the rhyme 'ch'ü.' "

The poem itself tells little more, except that some of the monks of the temple joined with them in the feasting and that the wine soon overcame formality. It was truly a memorable occasion; the poem ends "Next year when we again see this moon, we shall all think back to this and heave long sighs."[33]

"The old and sick among them however were granted per-

[32] *Veritable Record*, ch. 43, p. 4b-6a, day *kuei-yu*. After quoting the text of the memorial of submission of the *Yuan History*, it is noted that the emperor "ordered the work copied and published. He rewarded Wang K'e-k'uan and the others of the sixteen men [including Kao Ch'i] with 32 ounces of silver and 4 bolts of patterned silk each, with double this amount for the Editor-Officials Sung-Lien and the others." This was a handsome reward, by the standards of the Ming court at this time.

[33] ccsc 7/9a-b

mission to return to their homes." Kao Ch'i could not claim
to be either old or sick. His appointment to the history bureau automatically carried with it title and rank in the Han-lin
Yuan, under which the history bureau was organized.[34] Kao
Ch'i apparently retained that rank and title, and was assigned to other Han-lin duties. This now meant attending
court regularly, serving as instructor in the school for imperial princes and sons of high officials, being "on duty"
through the night at some of the offices that required twenty-
four-hour duty, drafting documents, attending embassies, accompanying the emperor and court on outings in the palace
gardens and at sacrifices in the temples to Heaven and earth
in the suburbs, and many other kinds of more or less day-to-
day assignments. The Han-lin Yuan served as a pool of talent
that could be employed in these miscellaneous tasks to service the varied activities of the court. Junior men in it like
Kao Ch'i could expect to be called forth shortly from this
personnel pool to appointment in one of the administrative
organs or to a magistracy in local government. Meantime, he
had the opportunity to learn more about the court and the
government, and the leading personalities in it, above all the
awesome emperor himself.

Kao Ch'i had certainly seen the emperor already, presum-
ably on the occasion of receiving instructions to compile the
Yuan History, and again on its completion. We can imagine
the curiosity that possessed him to gain a look at this Son of
Heaven, this peasant's son who had been monk and bandit
and Red Turban rebel-chief. Rumor had it that he was tall
and gaunt, with a jutting lower jaw, a snout like a swine, and
a high-domed skull with a pronounced ridge from front to
back across the top of it. He was a man of great energy, of

[34] His essay *Chih Meng* ("Recording Dreams") FTC 5/6b-8a states
that he was formally appointed Han-lin Compiler only in the second
month of 1370, but he must have had some kind of provisional Han-lin
rank before that.

penetrating shrewdness and decisive judgment, one who could readily be accepted as the man destined to rule the world and to found an enduring dynasty. His court was arranged so that he presided over it from a high dais, far removed from his courtiers, who strained from a distance to see his face and guess his mood. In these years he was usually in a good mood, for reports of victory came to him every day from his armies in the field. From dawn until well into midday he met his court, and conscientiously studied all the memorials and routine administrative reports, asking for opinions and precedents from history, and pronouncing judgments. But his wrath had been known to flare, and his decisions in the most routine matters frequently took his court by surprise. His court undoubtedly had confidence in him, and high officials of wisdom and of vision could feel that this new government merited their respect. But the emperor wanted no affection from his courtiers. There was no spirit of camaraderie among this group of men who together were rebuilding the world. He remained aloof, and seemed consciously to cultivate a reputation for unpredictability. If Kao Ch'i still retained the romantically conceived ideal of sharing in heroic action, this emperor's unfathomable character must have extinguished it. Romantic ideals were out of place at the business-like court of the Ming founder.

Kao Ch'i's romantic ideals had already suffered repeated rebuff, and he himself had put them aside as a delusion of youth. He had already known repeated disillusionment, and as he took up the duties of a busy courtier in the late autumn of 1369, he probably told himself that he would try to seek a solid and respectable career. Whatever the task demanded, he would give it full measure of his energy, and soon it would lead him into a satisfying series of official appointments. So we find him staying on in Nanking, continuing for the time being to live at T'ien-chieh Temple, and deeply involved in the varied and often colorful life of the court.

Embassies came, offering tribute to the new Son of Heaven and seeking legitimation from the new dynasty through enfeoffment of their kings. In this year they came from Korea, Annam, and Cambodia. Kao Ch'i was present at their audiences, and at the feasts with which the emperor entertained them. He wrote poems for these occasions of such formal and learned tone that they obviously are public pieces, not his own personal records of the events. In the ninth month of 1369, on the day before the emperor's birthday, the prime minister led all the officials of the court in ceremonies petitioning for permission to congratulate the emperor and celebrate the august occasion. Kao Ch'i was present, and again contributed a formal commemorative poem.[35] A month later a heavy "sweet dew" fell on the cedar trees of the inner palace grounds. The emperor called the court to see it, hanging in pearl-like beads from the ancient trees, and they pronounced it an auspicious omen, of a kind for which glorious precedents existed. Again Kao Ch'i contributed a poem laden with historical allusions.[36] At the winter solstice he accompanied the emperor and court at sacrifices at the newly constructed Temple of the Earth outside the south gate of the city. The emperor's father, posthumously enfeoffed the "Benevolent Ancestor," also was sacrificed to on this occasion, and Kao Ch'i's poem again displays his vast learning and his skill in combining a great number of literary euphemisms into an appropriately formal poem.[37] This skill undoubtedly was applauded by all, and no courtier used it more successfully than Kao Ch'i, but it is to be doubted that when his friends read his poetry for pleasure, or when he himself sent

[35] ccsc 13/14b   [36] ccsc 13/15a
[37] ccsc 14/7a-b. Note a number of very formal poems in the following pages, all referring to official duties in the court.

copies of his poems to his intimate friends, these command-performance pieces were included.

Less formal occasions permitted less formal poems, like those written about the elephant and the deer in the imperial palace park, which he saw when commanded to attend a pleasure outing there with the court.[38] The poem written on viewing a captive tiger in a cage at the Hsüan-wu Gate is a very effective evocation of the fearsome beast, but here as in many of his Nanking poems, Kao Ch'i draws heavily on Han dynasty allusions.[39] One wonders if he finds it necessary to join in the suggestive flattery which virtually became the official line, since the emperor had taken to seeing himself as a second Han Kao-tsu, the only other founder of a great imperial dynasty who had come from very humble background.[40]

Composing poems as an adjunct to his official duties was not all that Kao Ch'i did. Life in Nanking offered possibilities for private activities, and some of his now very limited leisure was spent in pleasant excursions and drinking parties of the kind he had known before. The poems written on these occasions breathe a freer air. The magnificent setting of Nanking, with its vast curving walls set in hills and lakes, and the mighty Yangtze just beyond, stirred his sensitive appreciation. The "royal air" which hung over the city, signifying that it was meant to be the seat of imperial power, was apparent to him. Even when highly allusive, his poetic descriptions of the great city show the richness of his creative imagination and the ever-increasing depth of his poetic powers.[41] Once with a group of friends he visited Ts'ai-shih, the

[38] ccsc 9/18b-19a [39] ccsc 9/10a
[40] Chao Yi, Nien-syh shih Cha-chi, ch. 32, item No. 1.
[41] Note especially ccsc 14/7b-8a, "On Climbing the Southern Ridge of an Evening, and Gazing over the Palace Roofs of the Capital City," and another poem probably written on the same occasion, "On Climbing Nanking's Rain Flowers Terrace and Gazing at the Great River," ccsc 11/10b.

village nearby where the Ming forces had made their crossing of the Yangtze in 1355 before taking Nanking. The place is famous for its associations with the T'ang poet Li Po as well, and in the spirit of these associations Kao Ch'i and his friends drank wine and listened to the songs of girl entertainers, and rented a boat so that they could view the moon from the middle of the river.[42] There are many poems indicating that the poet was not left to fret away his hours in lonely isolation, that he saw the sights and attended parties, and that he had many friends with whom he could share interesting conversation. Yet from the poems of these busy months in Nanking, written at a time when he was an admired member of the intellectual-literary circle of the court, and also a successful courtier with a promising career ahead, there emerges no air of elation, no sense of satisfaction or achievement. Kao Ch'i from the beginning was not happy as a courtier-official of the Ming dynasty.

Moreover he began to find the details of an official's life and the rigorous regimen of court service irritating and unpleasant. He writes of the bitter cold of the capital in the winter of 1369:

The north wind rages, the scudding clouds are dark;
Deep winter's cruelty saddens both Heaven and earth.
Dragons and serpents burrow deep in the mud, and wild
    animals hide in their caves.
Misshapen stones freeze and crack, and are marked by
    broken lines.

Below Lin-ts'ang Temple the air is filled with swirling
    snow;
At the Yangtze ferry-crossing frightened waves race by.
In the deserted mountains the trees stand all stark and
    dead

[42] CCSC 12/10b

Awaiting the sun's warmth to penetrate deep to their
   roots again.

By his thatched hut there sits an old man without even
   a rough coat,—
He raises his head and looks hopefully where the dawn
   is about to break.
Bitter cold like this is least of all good for the traveller;
I sigh that at the year's end I'm still a wandering soul.

Usually, at home, we could find pleasures indeed.
By the bedstead there would be a pot of well-aged wine,
In our mountains the charcoal is cheap, and the floor
   stove always warm,
With the children we'd sit encircling it, forgetting for-
   malities of rank.
The flight of birds even stopped, let alone the visits of
   friends—
For ten days at a time we might not dare even open our
   gate.

But now, having come to the capital, I get up and go
   out at dawn
Forcing my way, by cart and horse, to get to the palace
   gates.
By the time I return my face is the color of earth.
In my shabby room in the evening I perch like a hungry
   falcon.
At the corner wine-shop the wine is mercilessly dear
Yet who could argue about the price, even if it cost three
   hundred cash the pint.
I can't wait to get drunk, then fling myself down to
   rest,
But the padding is thin in my cotton blankets, and
   warmth never comes.

Then I think about those husky fellows, now campaigning off in the Northwest,—
There for a thousand miles the snow stretches, all the
way to the K'un-lun Mountains.
The ice of frozen rivers is splintered by the hooves
of their horses.
By night they storm firm fortresses, capturing armies
of *ch'iang* and *hun*.[43]

But scholars like me only know how to use their jaws;
I lack the strength to repay the court's gracious favor.
Would it not be better to submit tomorrow a petition
to resign?
Then as an old commoner I could go home and fish in
my southland village.[44]

Winter intensified the discomfort of arising at dawn to attend the court; this practice has often seemed the hardest
part of the life of a court official. No one has ever expressed
it with as much feeling as Kao Ch'i in this poem, and he
also has other poems on the same subject.[45] Even when it is
not bitterly cold, he resents the early morning duties, and
thinks about the pleasant sound of the rain heard while lying
under the matting cover of a little fishing boat, idling away
his time in the middle of some stream near Soochow.[46]

Early in 1370 Kao Ch'i evidently decided that his dissatis-
factions would vanish if he had his wife and family with him,
and could live a less lonely and more normal kind of life
at the capital. The year before, soon after his arrival, he had
visited Chung-shan, the magnificent mountain overlooking

[43] Tribal people of the Northwest border region—an allusion to Han
historical parallels.
[44] CCSC 10/10b-11a
[45] e.g. "Ching-shih tsao ch'i" to the tune of *Pu-suan-tzu*, KHC/5a,
and "Hsiao ch'u ch'ü ch'ao," CCSC 7/9b
[46] CCSC 17/23a, "Feng yü tsao ch'ao"

Nanking just outside the walls of the city to the east.[47] Now he found a house there to which he could move from T'ien-chieh Temple, and make a home for his family. It was government housing for officials, not his own property, but it pleased him. There he had a beautiful view, he wrote in a poem about his change of residence, but he concluded with the lines: "Who says that this new house is good? It is not, after all, as good as returning home."[48] Nonetheless, when his family at last arrived, worn and dirty from their trip, too full of emotion to speak, he writes that he is overjoyed. And in this happy moment, although he fondly reviews the pleasures of his simple life back home, he concludes that he will gladly forego those pleasures in order to repay his ruler's beneficence to him.[49] If more than a polite reference to the throne, this represented a fleeting mood.

There was an interlude in the late winter and early spring of 1370 when Kao Ch'i's duties did not require attendance at court, and when, perhaps, he had no regular duties at all. Why this occurred, or how long it lasted, cannot be determined. The only evidence for it is indirect, derived from three or four of his poems. He was at this time living at Chung-shan, outside the city, and the quiet ease of this mountainside suburb brought him as close to acceptance of his life away from Soochow as he ever came.

One poem tells about leaving Chung-shan early to enter the city, and finding the city gates still closed for the night. A crowd of impatient people gathers in the frosty morning, their horses neighing and stamping, as they wait for the dawn to come up so that the guards can open the gate. Some are officials who must soon be at court. Kao Ch'i observes: "I pity those waiting there with me; many of them are not people at leisure."[50] Kao Ch'i in this interlude of leisure sees

[47] CCSC 9/22a-b
[49] CCSC 9/22b-23a
[48] CCSC 12/8a
[50] CCSC 12/7b

little that is enviable in the busy life of a courtier; his pity for them is new, something that would have been inconceivable to him before his coming to Nanking.

Also dating from this brief respite from official duties is a set of three poems written at Chung-shan. The first follows:

> Who says my former recluse life was wrong?
> This quiet village and I suit each other very well.
> Green trees covering all outside the city wall—
> Blue mountain and temple just opposite my gate.
> Official duties now leave me free; I do not have to attend
>   early court.
> I've been a traveller so long now that I seldom even
>   dream of going home.
> I'm busy only pawning my court robes, now that spring
>   has come,
> Saving out merely those which I once received as gift
>   from the emperor.[51]

Pawning one's court robes after leaving court is an allusion to a poem of the T'ang poet Tu Fu; its significance is to emphasize with wry humor the simple ease, verging on poverty, that he now enjoys. Is Kao Ch'i hinting that he needs a regular appointment with a better salary (emphasizing his loyalty by his reverence for the imperial gift), or are these polite conventions covering his delight in the freedom from official duties? The rather ambiguous allusions of the other two poems in this set of three do not really clarify his feelings. In any event, this leisure did not last long. Soon he was again busy at court, and again dissatisfied with court life.

As his second spring in officialdom passed, he was again in an unhappy state of mind. A poem written at his Chung-shan home that spring begins: "I had always thought that with the coming of spring, the traveller's sorrows would

[51] CCSC 12/11a

lessen, but now spring has come and my sorrows are twice those before."[52] What are his sorrows now, when he no longer is separated from his wife and children? He is preoccupied with thoughts of his former friends, and his brother and sister, and other former associates. He wrote many poems at the capital expressing his concern for Hsü Pen, Yang Chi, Wang Hsing, and others of the Ten Friends. He worries that his older brother is still away in exile, and he dreams about his older sister (or is it his brother's wife?), concerned that she is alone back at Soochow, at their old family home on the Lou River, neglected and perhaps in need of his care. "If I were not bound up in the ruler's tasks, how could I bear to be separated from my flesh and blood? East of the city there is the home of my fathers, and in it there are books to read. Should I not perhaps resign and return there? I could then cook a porridge for my older sister."[53] The last line in an illusion to a man of T'ang times who cooked a porridge for his sick elder sister, of whom he was very fond. It is easy for Kao Ch'i to imagine that duties to family and friends reinforced his own desires to leave officialdom and return to Soochow.

Are these reasons, of sentiment and of taste, adequate to explain Kao Ch'i's final decision? Although the historical records say nothing more specific about him, and although he alludes to nothing else in his poetry, it is possible to see still further and far more pressing reasons for his decision to resign from office. One is that the official life held for him the real prospect of humiliation and danger. And to a man of Kao Ch'i's temperament, it is also quite possible that office-holding came to be seen as something unworthy. In large part the unpleasant character of official life was natural

[52] ccsc 14/12b, "Ch'un lai"
[53] ccsc 7/10a-b. There is no other evidence that he had a blood sister; the term "sister" is often loosely used.

to it. The Ming court in these first years was fraught with tensions caused by ambitious men playing a ruthless game of politics. The leading civil minister, Li Shan-ch'ang, held his high place chiefly because of seniority and not by reason of ability. The emperor was increasingly impatient with him, and he was clearly marked for downfall. Several ambitious men struggled to advance at his expense, and factions contested underhandedly, sometimes resorting to rumor and slander.[54] This, it might be said, is natural to politics, and Kao Ch'i should have learned to live in that kind of environment. Perhaps he could have in another age, under another emperor. However, add to the unpleasantness of this political jockeying the awesome character of the Ming founder, and the situation was one that gave brave men pause. The leader of one of the shadow factions at court at last overstepped, and in the seventh month of 1370 the emperor's wrath descended on him. He and his chief cohort were seized at court, denounced, and immediately sentenced to be executed.[55] The whole court, men who had seen the issue developing and who had talked about it in private and perhaps even expressed personal sympathies in the affair, must have felt threatened and intimidated by the fierce ending of this political struggle.

Kao Ch'i might not have felt immediately endangered by

[54] See Hsia Hsieh, *Ming T'ung Chien*, ch. 5, p. 23b. In discussing the downfall of Yang Hsien, Hsia Hsieh tells of the increasing irritation of the emperor with Li Shan-ch'ang, and of the other tensions in the court.

[55] Yang Hsien, Minister of the Right of the Secretariat, and some of his cohorts were the victims; see *Veritable Record*, ch. 54, p. 7a ff. Wang Kuang-yang, another leading official, had been suddenly cashiered the previous month. The *Veritable Record* contains a number of references in these months to the emperor's unpredictable temper, but on the whole leaves most of the story untold. Some of the feelings of officials in the court must be read between the lines; for example, in ch. 59, p. 11a-b, there is a discussion of why black spots have been observed on the sun. An earnest official turns his answer into a plea for less violent punishment of scholar-officials, and less hasty execution of punishment. The rising fears of the new Ming scholar-officials can be guessed at.

such political factionalism. The possibility of his becoming involved in it was perhaps not very great. But the violent resolution of the struggle must have removed much of the luster of official life for an idealistic man. Another event of that same year may have damaged court life in his eyes even more. One of his associates in the Han-lin was the venerable old scholar Wei Su. Wei had served on the historical commission in the Yuan dynasty that had written the histories of the Sung, Liao, and Chin dynasties, and had been in the Yuan dynasty Han-lin and in other prominent posts as well. His whole life was one of vigorous defense of traditional morality in government, as well as of scholarship. Kao Ch'i had come to know him, and wrote a poem expressing his respect.[56] Wei's service to the new Ming dynasty was not casually undertaken; on the fall of Peking to the Ming conquerors, he had tried to commit suicide by attempting to jump into the well of the temple courtyard, where he lived at the time. The monks held him back, and persuaded him that he had an important last service to perform in loyalty to the Yuan dynasty. "Except for you, no one knows the history of our dynasty; if you die, the history dies with you," they urged him. Wei agreed to live, and was instrumental in saving the manuscript copies of the *Veritable Records* of the first thirteen reigns of the dynasty and other archival materials at the time of the entry of the Ming forces. He accepted service at the Ming court with honorable intentions, but the Ming founder did not permit him to serve on the historical commission. Nonetheless, the emperor seemed to show Wei signal honors, permitting him in view of his advanced age, to ride in a little cart at court, to be absent from the early convening of the court, and the like.[57] But one day

[56] CCSC 12/7b-8a
[57] Such courtesies were also accorded other very old and much respected officials; note the case of Lo Fu-jen, whose biography appears in the *Veritable Record* in ch. 64, p. 4b-5b.

the unpredictable emperor heard Wei's old shuffling footsteps down a corridor, asked who it was, and proceeded to
humiliate him, deriding him for his failure to show the ulti-
mate loyalty, as had the famous hero Wen T'ien-hsiang at
the end of the Sung dynasty, by dying rather than accepting
office from the successor dynasty. A sycophant censor submitted a memorial immediately thereafter, saying that Wei
was unfit to be ranked with the great ministers of court, and
the emperor suggested that perhaps all he was good for was
to tend the shrine of Yü Ch'üeh, a loyal late Yuan official
who had so died. With this Wei Su was dismissed from
court; he died the following winter, so it was said, of humiliation.

Wei's humiliation took place in the fourth month of
1370,[58] and the sudden punishment of Yang Hsien, the factional leader at court, took place in the seventh month. By
that time Kao apparently had made up his mind to extricate
himself, and seems to have sent his family home to Soochow.
But how would he extricate himself? It could prove very
dangerous, for it might indicate to the suspicious emperor

[58] The *Veritable Record* gives very little of this story, and none of the
facts of Wei's humiliating treatment. It mentions only that he "was
again appointed" to his position in the Han-lin Academy (ch. 51, p.
11a) without having mentioned that he had been removed from office.
But Hsia Hsieh (*op.cit.*, ch. 3) states that the emperor humiliated Wei
in this month. The last mention of him is in the 6th month (ch. 53,
p. 11b-12a), where he is reported discussing Sung and Yuan history
with the emperor. The *Veritable Record* does not mention his dismissal
or his death later that year. Ming informal writings contain many
stories of Wei's cruel treatment. Yeh Tzu-ch'i, *Ts'ao-mu-tzu* (orig. pref.
dated 1378, edition cited is that of 1878), ch. 4, p. 17b, states: "Because of his moral failure [i.e., failure to remain loyal to the Yuan], the
emperor repeatedly humiliated him." Huang P'u, *Hsien-chung chin-ku
lu* (in *Chi Lu Hui Pien*, ch. 129, ts'e 41, p. 2b), describes an elaborate
insult to Wei Su which the emperor contrived, forcing him to appear at
a court banquet wearing placards bearing insulting jests. Ho Meng-ch'un,
another later Ming writer, in his *Yü Tung Hsü Lu* (in *Chi Lu Hui Pien*,
ch. 148, ts'e 51, p. 17b-19b), gives a long discussion of the pros and cons
of Wei's case, which was a celebrated and much discussed one in later
ages.

that Kao despised him (which may well have been true) or
that he did not value above everything else the honor and
the reward which official service could bestow on a man
(which certainly was true). We cannot know how he prepared his way safely out of office, but it must have involved
consultations with his superiors like Wang Wei and Sung
Lien, highly placed men who could understand his feelings,
and who could speak potently on his behalf. We know only
that on the twenty-eighth of the seventh month,[59] Kao Ch'i
and his friend Hsieh Hui, a fellow native of Soochow and
colleague in the Han-lin as well as in the history bureau,
were handed an imperial summons to attend the emperor at
an audience, where they were commended for their work, rewarded, and appointed to high office. Kao Ch'i was appointed to a vice-ministership, i.e. Vice-President of the
Right of the Board of Revenue, a promotion from seventh
rank as a Han-lin compiler to the third rank.[60] This was a
great step upward into the higher officialdom. But his plea
must have been well-prepared. He thanked the emperor for
this undeserved honor, and stated that the overwhelming responsibilities were beyond his limited abilities. He wrote in
an essay describing dream-premonitions of the event: "I
begged permission to resign with the reasons that I was too
young, and had had as yet no experience in the management
of fiscal matters, and that moreover I did not dare to ascend
so suddenly to such weighty responsibilities."[61] Hsieh made

[59] Hsia Hsieh, *Ming T'ung Chien*, ch. 3, p. 18a, and some other
sources, say ninth month; Kao Ch'i himself dates this in the seventh
month in his essay "*Chih Meng.*" (ftc 5/6b-8a), and in the preface to
a poem written for Hsieh Hui on this occasion (ccsc 7/10b "*Ch'ou
Hsieh Han-lin liu-pieh*").

[60] His salary rank would have been raised to 400 piculs of rice from
80 piculs—assuming that salaries in 1370 were roughly those stabilized
by an order of the first month of 1371 (see *Veritable Record,* ch. 60,
p. 10a).

[61] See essay "*Chih Meng,*" cited in note 59 above.

similar excuses, and the two were both granted gifts of silver and permitted to return to their homes. Kao Ch'i claims that both Hsieh and he foresaw these events in dreams. The dreams in which Kao Ch'i and Hsieh Hui so curiously foresaw these events must have been nightmares, following sleepless nights of planning their withdrawal maneuvers. But Kao wrote a very polite poem describing the great honor, and his unfortunate necessity of refusing it[62] and left immediately by boat with Hsieh and Hsieh's family for Soochow.

A curious chapter in Kao Ch'i's life, apprehensive but hopeful in the beginning, still apprehensive but now quite disillusioned, had concluded. There are preserved only two or three short poems written on that homeward journey; perhaps he did not dare put his true thoughts on paper. One of these two poems is about visiting again Kan-lu Ssu, the Temple of Sweet Dew at Chinkiang, where he had stayed overnight on the journey to Nanking almost two years earlier. It contains the word "happiness"—happiness on again visiting this famous old temple—and it contains no word "sorrow," which has been the recurring theme of his Nanking poetry. Beyond this hint of the elation that he felt, the poem is preoccupied with a thoughtful but not grieved recognition of the transitoriness of his life; it turns on the lines: "Clouds come and clouds go, but the mountains remain the same; the tide falls and the tide rises, but the river flows on unheeding; . . . The immemorial nature of river and mountains will never be exhausted, while men come and men return, their heads inevitably growing white."[63]

[62] CCSC 14/18a-b   [63] CCSC 15/32b

CHAPTER SEVEN

THE POET LIBERATED

IN THE EIGHTH MONTH, early autumn, of 1370, as he approached Soochow after almost two years at court, Kao Ch'i's reserve about recording his feelings on the return journey vanished. At the sight once again of the familar scenery between Lake T'ai and his home city, and on hearing again the dialect of Wu, which was his own, he was overcome with the ecstatic realization that he had gained his freedom. Perhaps until this moment the tense mood of escape had been strongest in his mind, but now the fact of success superseded, and he was like a prisoner liberated, numbed senses restored, savoring the delightful feeling of being home and free again. When he reached the Maple Bridge, only ten *li* west of the Soochow city walls, where he had spent the first night aboard his canal boat on the journey to Nanking and the point to which friends seeing him off had accompanied him that cold February day, he recalled the earlier parting in a brief poem:

"Reaching Maple Bridge on the Return East"

Old friends saw me off that day, as I left to go up to the capital,

And here the boat stopped; we were drunk as the sun went down.

I feel shame before that willow there by the water's edge; its branch was broken long ago,

Yet it still has smiling eyes to greet the traveller returning.[1]

---

[1] ccsc 17/14b

The branch of a willow is broken and planted at the water's edge when bidding farewell to the departing one, to hasten his return; it is supposed to bring him back by the time that it again puts out its green buds. Kao Ch'i is almost a year late, but the same willow tree nonetheless has green buds waiting for him—"green buds" being a cleverly employed double meaning, signifying also a friendly expression of the eyes. Thus he recalled briefly the moment of parting.

A longer poem written at the same point in his return looked forward to what lay ahead:

"Reaching Maple Bridge on the Return to Wu"

(Original note: There once was a Pagoda here, which has now fallen to ruins)

From far off I see the city's walls, and still doubt that it's really so.
I can't make out the green hills; only faintly glimpse the old pagoda.
Office and rank bestowed on me must have been falsely gained;
But my native dialect reaching my ears again is proof that I've truly returned.
The temple is hidden in the sunset haze, but the raven's call is here;
With the autumn stream and the empty bridge, and the fledgling ducks flying.
I have written home longingly to my village, but now the longing can cease;
My brocaded robes now have already been exchanged for a rustic's costume.[2]

Here again the levels of meaning are too complex for translation. Kao Ch'i employs again the words of the famous

2 ccsc 15/26b

青邱先生像

Kao Ch'i in Court Attire

This woodblock copy of the original drawing was first published in Chin T'an's annotated edition of Kao Ch'i's poetry, preface dated 1728. Chin T'an added the comment that he obtained the original, from which he had this woodblock made, in a collection of portraits of early Ming worthies of the Wu region which he chanced to come across in a bookstall at Tiger Hill (Hu-ch'iu), near Soochow, in 1727. Unsigned and undated, its historical authenticity is difficult to evaluate.

T'ang poem written at this spot, as he had in his two poems written here on the journey to Nanking,[3] but he has turned the mournful associations into expectant ones. In the last line he alludes to an old saying about the traveller who returns to his native village, decked out in brocaded court robes and in glory, signifying success achieved in his journeyings. Kao Ch'i anticipates that his village and his family will see him as a returning hero, for he had served gloriously and had declined high office to return, but he is not making a triumphant return, parading his success. Putting aside his brocaded robes is more than a gesture to him; his triumph must be a secret one, disguised in attitudes of respect and humility.

Perhaps he felt he could better affect this disguise by living in the country, at the Green Hill again, instead of living at his home inside the city. Or perhaps the longing for the simple life of the country, for the quiet fields and streams and his old fishing rock, was too powerfully appealing to be denied after the life in the capital. Once again, he turned his energies in withdrawal to poetry. For a year at Green Hill, seeing few friends and doing little else, he devoted himself to reading and writing poetry. At the end of the following year (actually January of 1372 by the Western calendar) he had finished a collection of 123 poems, which he called *Ku-su Tsa Yung*, or "Various Poems About Soochow." *Ku-su* is an old literary name for Soochow; *yung* means a special kind of poetry embodying most often one's response to persons and places and events in history. What better mask than that of the antiquarian?

His own preface to this collection describes very well the life and the mood of that first year after Nanking:

"Soochow is one of the famous cities of antiquity. The most imposing of its mountains and streams and of its per-

[3] See page 152.

sonages are to be encountered with great frequency in the poetry of such noble men as Liu and Po and P'i and Lu.[4] On days of leisure I have sought out the curious and visited the unusual in deserted fields and deep valleys, so that my footsteps have taken me almost everywhere hereabout. But my poems commemorating these places are in many cases lacking.

"Since returning from the capital I have lived in seclusion at the edge of the Wu-sung River. My books are scattered and lost. Friends and guests never come. Inside my ever-closed gate, sitting too long in silent thought, lacking any diversion, I accidentally came across the gazetteer of the prefecture and have been reading it. Reading there its accounts of the mountains and streams, terraces and pavilions, gardens and ponds, shrines and graves, there come clearly before my eyes again all of those places that I have sought out, through mists and clouds and in the midst of wilds and woods, places where I have lingered long and gazed thoughtfully afar. In response to the place one thinks of the person, and seeks an explanation of his successes and failures, his rise and fall. One cannot but be moved by it.

"Therefore I have selected the most prominent of these, and for each I have written a poem to enshrine it. The phrasings and language of these is crude and inelegant, and they are unworthy of being preserved in this region.[5] And yet, one's feelings on ascending a height or gazing into a great distance, one's intent in cherishing the virtuous and eulogizing the past, one's expressions of joy and admiration or of sadness and mourning on encountering events and observing objects, as one looks up and down through the span of thousands of years, are perhaps sometimes capable of pre-

---

[4] In Soochow it was customary to refer to the T'ang poets Liu Yü-hsi, Po Chü-i, P'i Jih-hsiu, and Lu Kuei-meng as the most eminent of the earlier literary residents who had written poetry about local scenes.

[5] i.e., *pang*, "country," Soochow with its rich literary tradition.

serving a cautionary warning or of demonstrating the causes of success and failure. At the very least, it may be better than merely filling one's stomach all day long every day and never concerning one's mind about anything at all. All the more so in my case, for I have the good fortune to be a retired servant of this enlightened dynasty. Living on the edge of the river and the lakes, I sometimes take out one of these pieces and while the fishermen beat cadence, sing long and loud my song of joy at the profound grace which our sovereign has bestowed upon me. Is this not reason for happiness?

"Thus I could not bear to discard all of these poems, and I have collected and arranged them into a volume, which I call *Ku-su Tsa Yung*, containing in all 123 pieces in all *genres*, both ancient and modern."[6]

Here we have Kao Ch'i depicting a year of cautious withdrawal, living a bucolic if somewhat isolated existence, deeply immersed in a thoughtful and loving re-evaluation of the historical associations of his native Soochow. It may well be that he turned to this merely to escape boredom, as he says, fortuitously inspired by the reading of the local gazetteer. But it must have suited his mood completely. Here was the opportunity to ponder again the motives of the great men of the past, their springs of action and the ideals that inspired them. His own ideals must have demanded thoughtful reappraisal, as he sat by this same river bank to which he had withdrawn twice previously, to re-examine the frustration he had felt on those occasions, and to reconcile it with the contentment that possessed him now. He was certain that his course was right this time. It involved no sense of frustration, of missed opportunity, of being the possessor of abilities that were unrecognized and talents that were unemployed. If it involved a feeling of resentment against the new govern-

---

[6] Quoted from the prefatory section (*yüan hsü*) to ccscc, p. 2a-b

ment, against the emperor whom Kao Ch'i in all probability
feared and despised at the same time that he acknowledged
his legitimacy and the achievements of his reign, it does not
show. The polite references to the throne are conventional,
indicative of nothing.

This is a different Kao Ch'i from the young poet who twice
fled involvement in Chang Shih-ch'eng's regime. It was probably this same year, 1370-1371, that he wrote the best poetic
expression of his newly gained self-knowledge, a poem called
"In Imitation of Lo-t'ien." Lo-t'ien is the T'ang poet Po
Chü-i, whose simple and direct style he here imitates:

Who says I've been too long of humble status?
In a glorious age I've known official emolument.
Who says I'm suffering in lowly poverty?
My empty bins still hold a bit of grain.
I took leave of the court in order to go into this retire-
    ment.
Returning to one's home certainly is not banishment!
The old house has my shelf of books,
The unkempt garden still a few clumps of chrysanthe-
    mums.
My worldly affairs are the concern of my wife,
My household tasks are borne by a servant or two.
By nature indolent, it is natural that I early seek leisure,—
What need is there to rush about on into one's later
    years?
I still wear my court-scholar's hat
But I've newly had made for myself this rustic's robe.
Deep my cup, and deep am I in wine by afternoon;
Warm my blankets, and sound is my morning sleep.
Others laugh at my lonely uneventful existence,
But a lonely uneventfulness is precisely my desire.
To the end of my days, what further might I seek?

I fear only to lose this present good fortune.
Fame and glory are like a delicious flavor
In which to dip your finger once and taste is forever
    enough.
Why seek a surfeit of it
When it can only cause a poison in one's bowels?
Remember if you will that Marquis Liu retired from
    court
And was far better off than the whole clan of Chu-fu.
I therefore follow Lao-tzu's dictum;
"Know satisfaction with what you have, and feel no
    shame in humble status."[7]

Here Kao Ch'i expresses his keen satisfaction with his
chosen course, and introduces an ominous comparison with
events of the founding of the Han dynasty, a historical paral-
lelism that the Ming founder himself delighted in. Marquis
Liu, better known as Chang Liang, and Chu-fu Yen were
both men of great ability who aided the Han founder in his
rise to power and in the early governing of the empire. Chang
Liang retired from court, returned home to study Taoist philosophy, and lived out his life in peace. Chu-fu Yen was so
able a talker that everyone feared him; his abilities led to
ever higher office, but also to implication in plots that caused
the suspicious emperor to have him and his whole clan ex-
terminated. This was a daring comparison for Kao Ch'i to
indulge in, but it is not the only poem in which he employs
the comparison. Chu-fu Yen became at this time the symbol
of the disaster that Kao Ch'i himself sought to avoid. He
used it again in another poem written at this time, called
"Planting Vegetables in My Eastern Garden":

I am not of the right stuff for the world of affairs;
It's more appropriate for me to learn gardening.

[7] ccsc 7/12b-13a

Planting vegetables, living here at my eastern garden,
I hoe and irrigate, and dare to quit when I'm tired.
Since the coming of summer the winds and dews have
    been heavy,
The growing greens have become a tangled mass.
For my morning meal I gather my own cress;
For my supper I pick my own mallows.
These are delights that the humble know how to savor;
Wildly spreading weeds cannot destroy this.
How true the words spoken by Chu-fu,
How real the dangers of eating in lordly style![8]

That Kao Ch'i would express himself so clearly and unequivocally about the fears that led him to resign from office
is truly striking! He must have counted on the humility of
the sentiments, the lack of personal ambition which he
claims for himself, as well as the conventionality of the meta-
phors, to keep the poems from attracting undue attention.
Clothed in such metaphor, his attitudes probably would not
be marked, but if noticed and reported to the court, at least
he would appear a harmless and simple-minded man, not a
man capable of action and of vast vision, or a man driven by
ambitions to embark on a course of adventure. Or would the
incongruity of his past and these new attitudes in itself stir
suspicions? Despite the all too apparent incongruity, it is not
really to be doubted that Kao Ch'i was sincere in the new
goals that he set for himself, and sincere in relinquishing his
earlier ambitions. Kao Ch'i had now acquired a measure
of self-knowledge that he earlier lacked. Now he can say
with complete sincerity that he does not want a life of
power and of responsibility in the world of affairs. Has he relinquished his ideal of heroism, or has he merely redefined it
again? At first, for a year or two, he probably would have said

---

[8] ccsc 4/20b

that he had abandoned it. Eventually he was to discover that it had in fact persisted, but was to emerge in a new conceptualization of the hero's true role; ultimately this pursuit of the heroic life was yet to bring about his tragic end.

Late in 1372, a little more than a year after returning from Nanking, Kao Ch'i for some unexplained reason gave up his "eastern garden," as he called the old family property at the Village of Tall Trees, and moved back closer to the city. His movements at this time are unclear; there is a suggestion that he lived briefly at some place just west of the city, but it could not have been for more than a few months, and perhaps it was merely a borrowed house used while making ready a new home outside the south gate of Soochow. From early 1372 at least, and perhaps from the end of 1371, he was living in the house south of the city. This home, whether rented, borrowed, or purchased, is not clear. Why he made this move also can only be speculated upon, but the fact that neither he nor anyone else bothered to explain it seems to indicate that there was no momentous reason for it. Perhaps he merely wanted to be again closer to the city, for the convenience of social contacts or for his teaching activities, and yet could not forego the pleasures of living in the suburbs.

Kao Ch'i wrote several poems to mark this change of residence, and all of them display a measure of sadness. His constant moving about, never living for more than two or three years in one place, reminds him of the uncertainty of life. The separation from friends and neighbors on each moving is an additional cause for at least temporary sadness. But there is also a note of contentment with his humble lot in most of these poems, as in the closing lines of this one, called simply "Moving to the New Residence South of the City":

Poor and struggling in middle life, still with no house to live in;

Long I've had to seek lodgings first here, then there,
carrying with me only a bag of books.
Always unable to evade the world, forced instead to
lean on the world—
Is it possible that I'll move again; still have to seek
another place to live?
My neighbor's garden is full of leaves; haze hangs heavy
over all;
Bamboo stretches to the monastery nearby; rain falls
now heavier.
What need have I of Hsü Po's princely dwelling at
Ch'ang-an?
This house, rustic and crude, is already more than I
need.[9]

The allusions again are to the Han dynasty. Hsü Po was a
relative of the Han emperors who lived in lordly style at
Ch'ang-an, the capital. In another poem written on this same
occasion, Kao Ch'i again marks the helplessness of the individual before the cosmic forces that buffet him now this way,
now that; the poem closes with the lines: "How sad the feelings as the village elders come, reluctant to bid us farewell;
back and forth we are moved aimlessly, drifting in the wake
of the cosmic changes."[10] Human feelings avail not at all
before the forces that move our lives, the poet sadly concludes at a moment like this. And throughout these last years
of his life, Kao Ch'i's mood is often one of displeased recognition of many of the conditions of human life, but at the
same time of satisfaction with his own course of adjustment
to those conditions. The way he has found is not doubted.

The move to the new house south of the city wall ended
a year of self-imposed isolation, and brought him into increased contacts with the reviving intellectual-literary life of

[9] CCSC 15/2a   [10] CCSC 14/21b

Soochow. The last desperate years of Chang Shih-ch'eng's regime had scattered many of the leading literary figures of the region, and the wholesale banishment of the wealthy and officially connected families by the Ming conqueror immediately thereafter had done even more to drain the city of its great and famous men. After these numbing blows, it was several years before the banished returned, often surreptitiously, and before a new gathering of cultivated men made possible the reconstitution of the city's traditional literary life. Kao Ch'i has left the remark in several places that after his return from Nanking there were at first none of his old friends there except for Wang Hsing. In an essay dated the second month of 1371 Kao wrote: "Last autumn I left office to return to the river's edge. My old comrades were mostly scattered, the ranks of my friends virtually emptied. . . ."[11] And in another place, writing about visits to friends among the monks in a temple near his north city wall home, he tells that for some years he had not been able to visit the place, because: "Later on I moved to the suburbs, and thereafter was on official service in Nanking, so it had been some years since I had been there. Since that return, the first time that I have passed by the place again was in the spring of this year. The monks Wu-yen and Pai-yün have both passed away, and many others of the monks who used to be there also have gone away or have died. The bamboo groves and the trees, the monks' quarters and temple buildings are largely in a state of decay and disorder. Count shows that of all those of us who formerly visited this place so often together, only Wang Hsing is still in this city; all the rest have gone out into public service or have withdrawn into seclusion, each to some far quarter of the world. I look about and pause to ponder, saddened and grieved by this thought. . . . "[12] From this one

[11] FTC 2/12b, "Sung Ting Chih-kung . . . hsü"
[12] FTC 3/2b-3a, "Sung Shih Shang-jen hsü"

can gather something of the calamity that had befallen Soo-chow in these years of transition, and of the depths of stagnation from which it had to recover its old vitality.

Recover it did, and quickly. But Kao Ch'i's old circle of friends was never reconstituted. Their concentration in the city in the late 1350's and 1360's was in large part the result of abnormal circumstances, as was the existence of the spirit that dominated their feelings at that time. Kao Ch'i became part of a new circle of fellow spirits; the spirit that they shared in common was different from the bond that had existed among his old friends. Yet he continued to cherish those old friendships, and to write fond poems about the old times and the friends who had shared them. Although Wang Hsing alone of the group was still in Soochow, Kao Ch'i must have seen little of him. There are no poems mentioning him that clearly date from this period, and we know that Wang in these years stubbornly refused insistent calls to office and lived in rigorous seclusion at a place in the suburbs called Stone Lake. Of the other Ten Friends of the north city wall, and the other important friends of the pre-Nanking years, the three outstanding poets were also the three most important as friends. Of the three, Yang Chi and Hsü Pen had been exiled in 1368 to the Huai region, and Chang Yü had moved away, to a place of retreat and seclusion near Hangchow. During his first year in Nanking, Kao Ch'i had dreamed that he received the news of Yang Chi's death, and wrote a poem in his memory. Then Yang showed up in the capital and visited Kao, who showed him the poem. They both wrote poems to commemorate the happy outcome, saying that each had been deeply concerned about the fate of the other in those troubled times.[13] But Yang Chi, who probably was the one among his friends whom Kao Ch'i held in greatest respect as poet, then went his own way, a troubled

[13] See ccsc 13/17b and Yang's *Mei An Chi*, sptk ed., ch. 1/17a

way of alternate banishment and office-holding, and the two never again lived near each other. They could at best send letters and copies of their recent poetry back and forth from time to time.

If Yang Chi was the recipient of the greatest respect, Hsü Pen probably was the one of whom Kao was fondest as a friend and fellow spirit. He wrote far more poems and essays to Hsü or for him or mentioning him than the others, and many poems were written "thinking fondly of Hsü Pen." Hsü too was in exile in the Huai region, and he too was able to get released from exile and visited Kao in Nanking. Then the next year he visited him again in Soochow, and they saw each other briefly on several occasions. On one such occasion, Hsü Pen was on his way back to the mountainous region near Hu-chou, where he had gone into seclusion a decade earlier.[14] Kao sent a poem-message by him to Chang Yü. Eventually Hsü and Chang both saw official service under the Ming, but Hsü never again lived near Soochow and Chang returned there only briefly.[15] Kao's great friend, the monk Tao-yen, who shortly after this began a spectacular rise to prominence in his forced return to secular life as Yao Kuang-hsiao, was called to the capital from Hangchow in 1370 and visited Kao Ch'i there at his Chung-shan home. Kao wrote a preface that year for his collection of poems, called *Tu An Chi*.[16] The two poet-friends continued to correspond, and may have occasionally seen each other again, but, like the others, Tao-yen never returned to live in Soochow. Those who were still alive among the other friends were scattered even farther.

[14] See especially ccsc 15/27a, "Sung Hsü Shan-jen . . ."
[15] Chang's first attempt to enter the government of the new Ming occurred shortly after Kao Ch'i resigned his office, but it was unsuccessful. See *Veritable Record*, ch. 64, 4th month of 1371, pp. 5b-6a, under day *keng-tzu*.
[16] See FTC 2/12a-b, and ccsc 14/10b-11a, "Yen-shih chien fang . . ."

If the old circle of friends was irrevocably broken up, the normal life of Kao Ch'i's native city was slowly recovering in the 1370's, and a revived intellectual literary activity began to develop there again. Kao Ch'i inevitably was part of this life, and his move to the south of the city signalled an increased measure of his participation in it. He now was held in great respect, and was widely known, because of the recognition he had been granted at the capital. All of Soochow looked up to him, and he in turn could not easily have evaded a central role in the cultural life of the place. The character of the new circle of which he was part is best exemplified by Wang Yi, an old acquaintance who became a new close friend.

Wang Yi and Kao Ch'i had surely known each other for years, but had not been intimate friends earlier. About Kao Ch'i's own age, Wang had achieved a kind of fame as a very young man for attacking Yang Wei-chen (1296-1370), the grand old man of late Yuan poetry. Yang's influence on poetry was dominant in the 1350's and 1360's, and had led to the development of a somewhat freer song-form in imitation of the ancient songs of the Wu region. His poetry was very romantic in conception, and bold in technique; unfortunately, especially among its many imitators, it tended toward frivolity and decadence. Wang Yi wrote a youthful essay denouncing Yang as the "devil of literature," blaming him for an evil influence contributing to degeneracy in an age of moral decline. At that time, Kao Ch'i probably had held Yang Wei-chen in far too great respect to want to associate himself with so extreme a view; his good friend Yang Chi was something of a protégé of Yang Wei-chen's, and Kao himself had participated in poetry contests at which Yang had been the judge. If Wang Yi's rather puritan views had ill matched Kao's own strong tendency toward romanticism in those years, now changed circumstances made close friends of them. Wang's literary gifts were by no means insignificant, and the outraged morality evidenced in his youthful attack on old Yang Wei-chen sprang in fact from an upright character coupled with sound scholarship in the institutions of antiquity. As Wang grew older and wiser, he displayed many qualities that Kao Ch'i could respect. Moreover, Wang Yi had been summoned to Nanking a year after Kao Ch'i, in 1370, to work on the continuation of the *Yuan History*. This was completed a month or two following Kao's return to Soochow. Like Kao, Wang too had been summoned into audience with the emperor, commended and rewarded, and appointed to high office. Like Kao, he had declined. His excuse for doing so displays well the subtleties of Neo-Confucian morality. He had an old widowed mother at home, he said, who was distressed at the thought of adjusting to a new environment, and it was his filial duty to return and care for her there, since he could not (under the principle of avoidance of one's native place) serve in office in Soochow, and she would not accompany him elsewhere. He stated this so piously (and no doubt with some sincerity) that the emperor could only praise him and send him home to Soochow. Filial piety, in the last analysis, was paramount in the hierarchy of virtues; it took clear precedence over second-ranking loyalty to the emperor.

Although Wang and Kao had not worked on the *Yuan History* at the same time, they shared in common an experience, and perhaps their reactions to it. They became fast friends now. Kao wrote a commemorative essay explaining to the world Wang's motives in declining office,[17] and they must have discussed with deep mutual understanding their private motives for the same. A number of poems testify to the frequency of their visits to each other. A simple but deeply expressive poem written at this time, when they happened to run into each other unexpectedly on a short journey away

[17] FTC 1/12a-b

from Soochow, shows the depth of the friendship that had
come to exist between them:

> My old friends are all scattered and gone; you alone
>   remain,
> In wind and rain we meet here at this seaside village.
> Our tankards of wine are almost finished, but our talk
>   is never-ending,
> And we linger on before the low candle that gleams now
>   through the dusk.[18]

Their fates were to become inextricably intertwined in the
two or three years of life that remained to them.

No other single friendship of these later years was to be so
important to Kao Ch'i as that of Wang Yi. But a group of
friends among the Buddhist monks were of importance, and
the fact that philosophical discussions with monks came to
replace the high-spirited gatherings of heroic-minded youths
is indicative both of Kao Ch'i's increasing age and maturity
and of an accompanying shift in his own thinking. The question of whether or not Kao Ch'i became a Buddhist is of
course misleading. A Chinese of his time and his background
seldom became a Buddhist in a formal sense; even to define
the formalities that would have been involved is a difficult
and perhaps meaningless task. For, short of shaving the head
and becoming a monk or nun, there are no clear-cut steps to
formal Buddhist affiliation; even the secondary vows of lay
Buddhists to forego meat and engage in regular devotions
and to patronize the *sangha* were often made by persons who
retained attachment to non-Buddhist practices and to concepts of a kind that we might consider to be in conflict with
Buddhism. Merely to warn, however, that China's religions
were non-exclusive, and that the average layman simultaneously participated in all of them, does little to describe the

[18] ccsc 17/24a-b

actual relationships that functioned among Buddhism and Taoism and Confucianism and the popular religious practices and the religious-philosophic systems worked out in the syncretizing spirit of the centuries of Neo-Confucian dominance. A man of Kao Ch'i's temperament was interested in the philosophic content of his Confucian tradition. When his interests were extroverted, as in his youthful years when he sought excitement and action, the ethical and practical sides of that tradition concerned him the most, but as he came to renounce the world of action, he saw his life moulded by cosmic forces and dominated by fate. The metaphysical realm of Neo-Confucian thought absorbed him increasingly, not to the exclusion of the ethical and practical, but supplementing it and providing him personally with more meaningful problems to speculate upon. The affinities of this aspect of Neo-Confucian thought for Buddhist and Taoist thought were not always obvious to an educated man of Kao Ch'i's time; the spirit of Neo-Confucianism had been to proclaim itself opposed to and superior to Buddhism and Taoism. Like many men Kao Ch'i was reared in prejudices contemptuous of Buddhism as a perverter of traditional morality and as a superstitious religion suitable only for women. Like many men of his time, he had to make his own discovery of Buddhism. He alluded to that discovery in an essay written for a monk friend named Hsü-pai. His essay begins:

"Originally I had no desire to form friendships with Buddhist monks. Then I read Su Tung-po's 'Preface to the Poetry of the Monk Ch'in,'[19] and noted there how he praised the Monk Ch'in as a worthy man, saying: 'Were he to be ranked among the scholar-officials, he would not fail to live up to the expectations of [his sponsor and friend] Ou-yang Hsiu.'

"Subsequently I have been grieved about the long-continu-

[19] In Su Shih's literary collection, SPTK ed., Series 1, ch. 56, pp. 7b-8b, the title is given "Ch'ien-t'ang Ch'in Shang-jen shih-chi hsü."

ing decline in the standards of scholar-officials, and have
found pleasure in the discovery that there are Buddhist
monks with whom one can associate in friendship, among
whom I count Monk Hsü-pai. . . ."[20]

The remainder of this essay, in its condemnation of the
degenerate ways of Confucian scholar-officials, appears to be a
denunciation of the grasping, self-seeking crowd that came to
dominate Chang Shih-ch'eng's regime in its last years. The
essay bears no date, but from this internal evidence it seems
to belong to about 1365 or 1366. The reference to Ou-yang
Hsiu, the eminent Confucian scholar-official and patron of
literary and political talent of the Northern Sung period, is
very meaningful. Ou-yang had done more than any single
man to establish the ideals of the Neo-Confucian revival, and
in this essay Su Shih (Su Tung-po) clearly states that Ou-
yang did not like Buddhism and Taoism, but that he would
not fail to say a good word about their followers who had accomplishments in classical learning and in literary pursuits—
evidence to Ou-yang (as to Su and to Kao Ch'i) of their
moral worth. The fact of Ou-yang's respect for Monk Ch'in,
and of Su Shih's approval of him as man and as poet, are
adequate precedent for Kao Ch'i in his own beginning recognition of the worth of some Buddhist monks. Noting that
Buddhism also has its unworthy followers, Kao Ch'i nonetheless commends the Monk Hsü-pai above most men. "In
his worthy qualities," Kao wrote, "the Monk Hsü-pai not only
surpasses my kind, but also surpasses his own kind. And thus
I delight in his friendship, and never tire of his company."

The integrity of some learned monks, noteworthy in the
degenerate conditions that developed in Soochow in the mid-
1360's, had begun to prepare Kao Ch'i to accept monks as
friends. His friendship with Yao Kuang-hsiao, the Monk Tao-
yen, developed in those same years. That Tao-yen had de-

[20] FTC 3/4b-5a

* 199 *

cided to shave his head and take up the patched robe and
begging bowl of a monk, Kao Ch'i did not find incompre-
hensible. In a poem to Tao-yen, he wrote: "Master Yen originally was a student of Confucian learning; broad and clear
of brow and face, he stands out far above the crowd of ordinary men. . . ."[21] In the remainder of this long and allusive
poem Kao writes with highest praise. He tells how the monk
had once worn the garb of a Confucian scholar, and had
studied the writings of the Neo-Confucian philosophers
Chou Tun-yi and Shao Yung, but subsequently, encountering
evil and disorderly times, had sought Buddhist wisdom. Kao
praises his courage, his character, his learning, and the excel-
lence of his poetry. In Tao-yen, Kao Ch'i found a man who,
although a monk, not only merited his admiration but was a
person with whom he could become the most intimate of
friends. In his preface to Tao-yen's collection of poetry,[22]
written about 1370, Kao Ch'i makes no patronizing conces-
sions to the monk as a man who surprisingly also possesses
learning and talent, as had Su Shih in his preface to the
poetry collection of the Monk Ch'in; Kao writes in this preface only of his theory of poetry and of his friend's wonderful
achievement as a poet. He even wrote a poem to him, twit-
ting him about the inconsistency of his growing fame as a
poet and his monkish disregard for worldly fame; the second
quatrain follows:

> Recently you have been visiting famous temples, there
> to discourse on the Dharma,
> Now you are returning to your former cloister, to settle
> into deep meditation.
> Your Buddha-mind is profoundly aware that all is empty
> illusion,

[21] ccsc 5/18a-19b
[22] "Tu An Chi Hsü" FTC 2/12a-b

But is helpless to prevent your fame as a poet from
spreading throughout the world.[23]

In all likelihood this intimate friendship had succeeded in
removing from Kao Ch'i's mind all sense of strangeness to
the Buddhist mind. In Nanking, living for a year in the great
T'ien-chieh Temple, he had further opportunity to observe
appreciatively and sympathetically the life of the monastery,
and to become acquainted with some of the leading monks
of his age. His much respected superior in the *Yuan History*
Commission, the eminent essayist and scholar Sung Lien,
was particularly intimate with Buddhism, and able to con-
verse about Buddhist philosophy as a sympathetic Confucian
scholar. In a poem written to Sung Lien on an occasion when
he served with him on night-duty in the Han-lin Academy,
it is significant that Kao compares him to Wang Wei, equally famous in the T'ang period as Buddhist believer and as
poet-scholar.[24] Kao's appreciation for Buddhist thought increased in the thought-provoking years in Nanking, perhaps
as a result both of his association with Sung Lien, and from
his direct contacts with monks there. A poem written at
T'ien-chieh Temple in 1369 describes "An Evening Sitting in
the Cell of the Ch'an Master Lo." The monk Tsung-lo referred to in the title was the most famous of the T'ien-chieh
monks, a man whom the emperor himself honored with occasional visits.[25] Kao describes a scene of oncoming evening:

> Green shadows about to overflow the Temple,
> Birds singing, following a spring rain.
> With nothing to do, in a moment of leisure to read,
> I sit by the window, scanning his monkish books.[26]

[23] ccsc 15/13a   [24] ccsc 12/7b
[25] See *Chin-ling fan-ch'a chih*, ch. 16, p. 22b, for a biographical sketch
of the monk Tsung-lo; and pp. 5b ff. for Yao Kuang-hsiao's account of
his part in the history of the temple.
[26] ccsc 16/14a; see also 15/2b

So we know that Kao Ch'i was on intimate enough terms with one of the most powerful Buddhist personalities of his time to go to his cell and read his Buddhist books.[27] Thus on his return to Soochow after Nanking, in the mood in which he found himself then, it is not surprising that increasingly Kao Ch'i's friends included learned monks. He wrote of visits to them: "Sitting close by the incense burners, in the morning, listening to explanations of the Dharma; to the sound of clanging begging bowls from the window, discussing poetry through the night."[28] And they often visited him. "When was it we parted last at your western stream; so soon again I am pleased by your visit to my garden,"[29] he wrote to a monk friend. The last quatrain of a poem he wrote to another monk friend who was going off to the famous Ling-yin Temple at Hangchow shows the depth of understanding that Kao gained of Buddhist ways:

> The bell hastens you to rest your walking staff at the temple;
> Lamps already shine from the river boats tied up for the night.
> As for the meaning of the Dharma, ask no farther—
> To be wordless,—that is *ch'an*.[30]

Ch'an, or Zen, is well within the scope of his sympathetic appreciation. Perhaps this ability to commune with his learned monk friends is best conveyed by his simple poem, "On Going to Visit Master Yin, at the Same Time He Was Visiting Me, So That We Missed Meeting":

> I went to seek out your secluded cloister
> While you, reverend master, were calling at my small garden.

[27] In the poem "Sung Lien Shu-chi tung kuei," ccsc 7/3b, he uses very similar phrases in talking about reading Buddhist sutras with the monks of T'ien-chieh Temple.

[28] ccsc 14/20b "Sung Chi Shang-jen. . . ." [29] ccsc 12/16b
[30] ccsc 12/20b

No need to say we did not meet,
And had we met, there would have been no need to
    speak.[31]

Kao Ch'i's circle of friends in these post-Nanking years
provided an atmosphere quite different from that of the high-
spirited group with whom he had so expectantly discussed
fame and glory, politics and war, a decade earlier. Kao Ch'i's
liberation was complete, and many-faceted. He was free from
the vicious trap of court life, and he was free to roam in the
peaceful countryside of his beloved Soochow. He was free
from the pangs of unsatisfied ambition, and from the illu-
sions of youth about his own nature, and that of the world.
Buddhist wisdom did not free him; he remained true to his
Chinese heritage, but in his increasingly profound appreciation of Buddhism he found further corroboration of the
truths that had liberated him.

[31] CCSC 16/16b

CHAPTER EIGHT

"DRIFTWOOD"

KAO CH'I had one source of grief which still gnawed at his contentment after his return to Soochow in 1370, and which in fact had lurked in his mind for many years. It probably was while in Nanking that he wrote the poem "Lying Ill, at Night, Listening to the Neighbor's Boy at His Studies":

> The moon is pale in the sycamores; the sky clear following the rain.
> At my north window I hear the singsong sound.
> How are they to know that in the neighboring house there's a traveller who has no son—
> Hearing this sound, in my illness, drives me to sleeplessness.[1]

Away from home, lonely and ill, Kao Ch'i was depressed by the fear that he would have no son to carry on his name. He then had two little daughters, for a third daughter had been born shortly before his second child died in 1367.[2] He was a fond father, and it undoubtedly was more than the pressing demand of filial duty which made him wish for a son. Once at his friend Yang Chi's house he witnessed a performance before a number of guests by Yang's little son, not yet three years old, reciting a poem of his father's. Kao wrote a poem for Yang:

[1] ccsc 18/12b
[2] ccsc 7/4a, "P'u chih, te erh nü hsiao-hsi," speaks of two daughters in 1369-1370; the poem quoted below thanking the Taoist adept for the painting mentions three daughters. This would date the latter poem before the death of his second daughter in 1367.

I envy you both for your own great abilities, and for
    your handsome son.
At only two years old he can recite his father's poems.
Among all your guests seeing this, who would not share
    your joy?
Only I, reflecting, am made sad by it instead.[3]

Kao Ch'i's friends of course understood this sadness. One
of them, a Taoist adept called Hsüeh-hai, once presented him
with a painting of a Taoist immortal to whom Su Hsün is
said to have prayed for sons, his prayers being answered by
the birth of two sons, the famous poets Su Shih[4] and Su Ch'e.
Kao Ch'i undoubtedly had little faith in the efficacy of the
painting, but he was moved by the thought, and responded
with a poem conveying his gratitude. The poem is long and
full of complicated allusions, but some lines from it bear
translating:

.   .   .   .

Every time I hear the neighbor's sons
On rainy nights, studying the classics and histories,
I get up and sit by the autumn lamplight
Looking at the shadows, sighing long unending sighs.

.   .   .   .

Do you not see, there, my old neighbor
Who has labored so hard at his farming, and has ac-
    cumulated much land?
How bitterly he has struggled to establish his house,
Yet his two sons have thrown everything away, as if it
    were nothing.
What is the use of having bad sons?
I wish for one worthy son,
A link with my ancestors before me
And after me, to carry on my line.

[3] CCSC 18/24a
[4] I.e., Su Tung-po, the famous Sung dynasty personality.

If such result can be worked by this genie, then come
    next year
I must ask you to write a poem for me "On Hanging up
    the Bow."[5]

His Taoist friend, as might have been expected, is revealed
in the last line as a poet; the allusion in the same line is to
the ancient practice of signifying the birth of a son by hanging a bow on the left side of one's gate.

It was not until 1373 that Kao Ch'i finally had the son for
whom he had wished so long. Since the event took place six
or seven years after the gift of the picture, Taoist magic
seems to have been unavailing. He named his son Tsu-shou,
"ancestral gift." His happiness was complete. His elation
shows in the poem and preface for it that he wrote on the
occasion:

"On the Birth of My Son Tsu-Shou"

On the second day of the second month my son Tsu-shou
was born. His mother had had a dream in which an old
woman knelt before her, in a gesture of offering. Then she
conceived, and now has given birth. The prefectual governor,
Wei Kuan, came to offer his congratulations, and hearing
the child cry, greatly marvelled at him. I have already reached
the age of 37 before having this son at last, so how could I
not be overjoyed! Thus I write this poem:

Whether one day he will be stupid or intelligent still
    cannot be known;
But just as he is here before my eyes is enough to bring
    comfort to my advanced age.
To whom should the worthless children in the world
    belong?
Should I expect my son to be a Heaven-sent sage?

[5] CCSC 11/13b-14a

A prophetic dream foretold that he would come, the gift
    of a divine old woman,
And the sound of his crying aroused the amazement of
    the imperial emissary.
Po Lo-t'ien from this moment could have ceased his
    long sighing,
He would now have someone to transmit to posterity
    his "cedar casket poems."[6]

Po Lo-t'ien is of course Po Chü-i, the T'ang poet who, like
Kao Ch'i, sighed for a son. Po never had one, and wrote a
poem charging his daughters' children with the responsibility
for preserving his poems, locked in a chest made from a solid
old cedar tree.

Kao Ch'i's son was foretold in an auspicious dream, and the
governor, Wei Kuan, was startled by the sound of his crying
to proclaim this boy extraordinary. Could such a son have
been other than unusual? The seemingly auspicious associations, however, turned out to be tragic: the son died in early
childhood.[7] Wei Kuan, the governor, and because of him
both Kao Ch'i and Wang Yi, went together to their deaths
before two more years had passed.

Wei Kuan was one of the great men of the early years of
the Ming dynasty. An eminent scholar living in retirement
near Wuchang in the Central Yangtze Valley through the
troubled last years of the Yuan, he was recruited into the
service of the Ming in 1365 when his home region was conquered by the Ming armies. He served well in several administrative posts, and advanced rapidly in rank. In 1368 he became tutor to the heir apparent and other imperial princes,
and also served concurrently in the Board of Rites, where his
scholarship was turned to investigation of the proper form

[6] ccsc 15/9b-10a   [7] However, he outlived his father.

of the ancient rituals. Twice he was sent into newly conquered areas to seek out worthy scholars living in retirement
who might be appointed to the new Ming bureaucracy, and
his recommendations for appointment were almost always
heeded. But his chief interest was in the rites, and this accorded with one of the overwhelming preoccupations of the
early Ming government. In its desire to be proper and ortho-
dox, as well as to define and regulate matters, the early Ming
government spent an inordinate amount of energy investi-
gating and regulating the ritual practices of government. The
Mongols had been lax and deficient in maintaining the
ancient forms and proprieties; both in reaction to Mongol
delinquency and in response to the active, constructive mood
of the national restoration, the Ming established successive
commissions to investigate, to recommend, and to compile
reference books on ritual. Wei Kuan served on several of
these. The Ming founder was apt to be suspicious of those
of his underlings who could use their knowledge of the literary heritage to determine what government should do; this
gave his bureaucrats a power over him which he resented,
yet could not disregard.

Wei Kuan had a further source of personal power, in that
officials recruited by him for appointment might tend to retain a bond of personal loyalty to him, as might also those
recruited in the special Palace Examinations of 1371, at which
Wei had been chief examiner. There is no evidence that Wei
actually attempted to build up anything like a party or faction
under his direction or that he had any interest in such court
politics. But his potentiality for this was not overlooked by
ambitious politicians who were in competition with him for
high place, nor would any such opportunity for personal
power escape the notice of the suspicious emperor. Thus
when Wei Kuan in 1371 offered an inappropriately timed
memorial concerning the sacrificial rites for Confucius, the

court was quick to note his technical error, and the emperor was glad to make an example of him to other ambitious courtiers by demoting him and sending him out to be magistrate of Lung-nan, a small and insignificant county in southern Kiangsi Province. Almost immediately thereafter, however, he was recalled to the court, and again assigned to high office in the Board of Rites.[8]

In 1372 a high official suggested to the throne that Wei's real talents lay in local administration, and that he should be sent to some outlying post for such tasks. In the third month of that year he arrived at Soochow, to be the T'ai-shou, the prefect or governor of the prefecture. It was an important post, since Soochow was the richest prefecture in revenues in the empire and because it had until recently been the capital of a rival government that had been loyally supported by the residents of the region against the Ming conquerors. In the new Ming administrative system, it was placed directly under the central administration, not subordinated to a provincial government. The government needed for this important outpost of local administration a man who could be counted on to watch carefully for signs of lingering anti-Ming feeling and organization, yet one who could bring this richest of agricultural regions with its high level of cultural development, and therefore large numbers of educated men, into wholehearted support of the new dynastic enterprise. A recent prefect, a man who had served only a year, had so oppressed the people in carrying out the government's intentionally punitive exploitation measures that he had aroused dangerous unrest. He had been recalled and punished. Nanking was anxious now to send a man who would be no less active on the government's behalf, but who would command the respect of leading classes in Soochow, and who

[8] The *Ming Shih Kao* states in his biography, ch. 124, p. 12a, that he was recalled before he ever reached Lung-nan, as does the *Veritable Record*, ch. 80, p. 4b.

would gain the affection or at least the acceptance of the whole population. Wei Kuan was in his early sixties, famous for his learning and his integrity, an outsider to the region but also a latecomer to the Ming regime, a man who had been conspicuously both honored and chastened by the fear-inspiring new emperor, and a man who had proved himself a vigorous and devoted administrator. No better man could have been found for this crucial post.

Wei Kuan succeeded almost too well at Soochow. After a year there, in the third month of 1373 he was promoted to a provincial post in Szechwan, but he had so gained the affection of the people of Soochow that they forcefully petitioned the throne to have Wei returned to their prefecture, and their petition was granted.[9] In the third month Wei Kuan was returned to Soochow, having been away at the capital awaiting the imperial decision only a few weeks. He served another year, until the third month of 1374.

It is useful to see what Wei Kuan did in those two years as governor of the prefecture of Soochow to earn himself the confidence of the people there and at the same time to accomplish the purposes of the government in Nanking. Nanking's attitudes toward Soochow were not benevolent. In these early years of his reign the emperor was granting tax relief as a reward to the prefectures around Nanking, for they had sustained his movement during the twelve years in which he slowly developed it from a minor offshoot of the Red Tur-

---

[9] The *Veritable Record*, ch. 80, 3rd month of 1373, under the day *yi-mao*, records this together with a discussion of Wei Kuan's career up to this point. There is no mention of his crime and execution in 1374, or of Kao Ch'i's part in it, at the appropriate point in the *Veritable Record*, so this may explain the appearance of biographical data on Wei at this place. In discussing the reasons for returning Wei Kuan to Soochow, the *Veritable Record* does not mention the petition of the people of Soochow, but records merely: "The Emperor, cognizant of the great size of Soochow Prefecture and the complexity of its administration, felt that no one else could maintain the situation there, hence ordered Wei Kuan to return to that prefecture" (p. 4b).

ban rebellion into a government that could claim to be the
new bearer of the Mandate to rule the world. At the same
time he granted tax relief to the drought-stricken and war-
ravaged areas of the Huai, in which he himself had grown up,
and to areas farther north that had suffered Mongol rule to
the end. But the Southeast triangle was infamously rich. In
the mid-1360's the Ming founder had spoken contemptuously
of Chang Shih-ch'eng, saying that his wealth in the rich
prefectures south of the Yangtze and east of Lake T'ai would
in fact be his undoing; Chang relied on an abundance of
money, and failed to develop a disciplined organization.
Moreover, Chang had favored the wealthy classes, and they
in turn had tended to support him. The stubborn resistance
of Chang's rebel princedom, and the final long siege of Soochow that had tied up the major Ming armies and generals
for a year, in the Ming founder's eyes represented a pernicious
collusion of degenerate gentry with a dissolute leader who had
proved unexpectedly dangerous. Soochow bore the resentment of the entire Ming movement for the irritating delay in
their final push to victory.

But even more than that, Soochow was the antithesis of the
Ming movement in many ways. The Ming founder was a
crude and uneducated peasant from the poorest of the regions just north of the river, while Soochow was the elegant
metropolis south of the river in which the learned of the mid-
fourteenth century had congregated in order to preserve the
refinements of their cultured way of life in trying times, above
all against the threat of rabble rule like that of the Red
Turbans. The emperor's inferiority complex was roused to
reactions of violent hostility by Soochow, the symbol of
superiority in all the things in which he was most obviously
deficient. Therefore he had devised punishments for Soochow. He had banished tens of thousands of the gentry there
to his own home region, to let them taste something of the

hardship of his youth. And when he found that Chang Shih-ch'eng had burned his tax records at the last, to prevent their aiding the new government in administering the region, the emperor had ordered that taxes be collected according to the scale of tenant rents, at twice or more the rate in comparable regions, thereby punishing Soochow and four other prefectures of the region with the highest taxes in all of Chinese history. The revenues from Soochow alone, a single prefecture, were greater than those from many entire provinces.[10]

Yet despite these measures stemming from the emperor's desire to punish and to intimidate, measures which objectively seen were also politically very shrewd, the emperor was not prepared to make war on the values of his civilization, even though it was the hated Soochow which exemplified them so markedly. Chu Yuan-chang, the Ming founder, was in many ways a wise emperor, if a violent tyrant; he was a far-seeing man, even though he frequently gave way to petty recrimination and to violent passions; and in later years he may have become mentally unbalanced. He was far too complicated a person to be summed up in a phrase or to be superficially psychoanalyzed. As he moved up the social scale from illiterate peasant to semi-educated and experienced emperor, he accepted completely the values of his civilization and, in his way, cherished goals in common with his scholar-officials. He wanted the same things for China that the scholars wanted, with the single difference that he wanted to protect his position and pass it on safely to his sons and grandsons, if not for "ten-thousand times ten-thousand years," as court ritual stated it, at least for the foreseeable generations and centuries.

[10] However, the throne took note of bad crop conditions and temporarily eased tax quotas in the winter and spring of 1373-1374 in Soochow and surrounding prefectures, and in the 5th month of 1374 ordered a review and decrease of some tax schedules there. See *Veritable Record*, ch. 89, under day *kuei-ssu*, p. 4a. These temporary measures probably reflected a brief local economic crisis, but they did not basically alter the pattern of punitive taxation.

And he clearly understood that rulership in China meant a sharing of power with the broad open class which had the economic means to educate itself. Wei Kuan's task in Soochow was to bring in the revenues, but also to bring in the people of the former rival princedom, and to make them feel that this new dynasty mediated for all men universally with the cosmic order, that it promised men the continuation of their revered ways, and that it offered to men of ability and ambition the agency for working out meaningful careers. Chu Yuan-chang, despot though he was, understood and accepted these matters as aspects of the responsibilities upon himself. Wei Kuan, with his much deeper command of the learning which articulated and preserved these concepts, set vigorously to prove in his governorship that the common goals of emperor and state and people of Soochow could be achieved. There were precedents, and there were means, and there were men of ability at hand to help him.

Kao Ch'i had known Wei Kuan in Nanking, and had even served as his subordinate in the history bureau, technically under Wei Kuan's division of government, the Board of Rites. Thus Kao Ch'i was required to refer to Wei as his former chief.[11] Wei was anxious to re-establish the acquaintance. Soon after his arrival in Soochow in 1372 he called on Kao, and although he was more than twenty years his senior, and the highest representative of the government in the region, he treated Kao with such deference and sincere friendship that Kao could not refuse to help him. Wei systematically sought out all the other men who had education and ability that could be turned to the common cause. Wang Hsing was called upon, and won over. So was Wang Yi. Kao Ch'i's old friend Chang Yü, who had been living in Hangchow since the fall of Chang Shih-ch'eng, also was recruited. There were

[11] See "Wei Fu-jen . . . ming" FTC 5/15a-16a

* 213 *

many others. Chou Nan-lao,[12] a descendant of the famous
Northern Sung philosopher Chou Tun-yi, was invited to help
the prefect with scholarly tasks. Scholars, former officials, and
men who commanded the respect of the community were
pressed by Wei Kuan into service as consultants and aids. His
own impressive personality, and the force of his character,
assured his success in this task of recruiting local assistance.

All the tasks Wei Kuan assigned these men were to assist
in the restoration of the forms and the institutions of the old
civilization that had been imperiled by ninety years of Mongol misrule and bandit disorder. The people's customs had
degenerated. They had given up the valued old ways. Public
morality had sagged. The people must be taught again. Their
family customs had been influenced for the worse by crude
Mongol ways. Forms of marriage and burial, rituals for honor-
ing the ancestors, courtesies which should be extended to
family heads and village elders and to the officials representing the new government—all had almost disappeared. The
forms must be re-established, and examples given to the people to follow. Education had deteriorated, for it had not
brought the usual rewards in the disorderly times just passed.
Schools must be re-established; the ritual aspects of school attendance in particular must be reinstituted, to make scholars
aware of the dignity of education and the serious purpose
with which they were to prepare to serve their state and their
civilization. The scholars of the region, men like Kao Ch'i,
had to lend their assistance in studying the old forms and de-
vising suitable ways of reinstituting them, and in lending their
presence and their participation in putting them into practice again. Wei Kuan could appeal to their sense of Confucian
responsibility, could arouse in them a sense of mission, and
offer them the satisfaction of accomplishing something for

[12] Chou's name is given both as Chou Nan and as Chou Nan-lao;
writings of his contemporaries seem to prefer Chou Nan-lao.

the good of their community and of their society. Their awareness of Soochow's glorious tradition as a center of learning and the source of a disproportionately large share of the empire's men of talent and ability in the past gave these men a zeal for their work. After long decades of very disheartening experiences, a sense of community purpose was born again, and the exhilaration of the common effort dispelled the lethargy and the apprehension that had hung like a grey mist over the region. Wei Kuan was a leader of men; he restored the vitality of the region. It was not surprising that the men of Soochow were distressed that he was to be sent away after only one year, and that they petitioned the emperor to return him for the continuation of the able governing that he had launched in that year.

Traditional historians have recorded as one of Wei Kuan's greatest achievements the reinstitution of the ancient Rite of Village Wine Drinking. In the fifth month of 1373 the Board of Rites had proclaimed the proper forms for this ritual, and had ordered offices of government throughout the empire to carry it out under the guidance of its educational officials and in conjunction with the respected elders of each community.[13] Wei Kuan undoubtedly had known from his connections with the Board of Rites prior to his service in Soochow that such a proposal was among the many matters of ritual that the government was studying, and knew that the proclamation was due.[14] It is probable that Soochow was the first prefecture in the nation to reinstate the practice, which had lapsed for at least a century. The proclamation

[13] See *Ming Shih*, ch. 56, p. 9a-11a
[14] The emperor had established a commission in the 8th month of 1369 to compile a *Book of Rites* (*Li Shu*) that would serve as the standard for the dynasty in all ritual matters. It was submitted and accepted one year later, and included a section on the Village Wine Drinking Rite. See *Veritable Record*, ch. 56, 1370, 9th month, p. 17a. However, specific instructions to institute the practice of this rite did not appear until 1373.

provided that twice each year, in the first and tenth months, the leading official of the local government was himself to preside at the main place of observance, with other ceremonies to be conducted in each community, there to be presided over by local representatives of the government, in most cases the village elder or the local citizen responsible for the collection of taxes. In the prefectural or county seats the ceremony was held in the school of Confucian studies, with the director of studies acting as master of ceremonies. In smaller localities it was held in the local schools, with retired officials or other men of learning and position supervising.

The purpose of the ceremony was to honor the old men of the community, who were the guests of honor, and to make a public display of forms of etiquette; a complementary purpose was to instruct the people in the laws which affected them. The reading of the laws, normally an abbreviated version of the penal code, was the first order of business after the officials had arrived and the old men were all seated, ranked according to their age. Then followed a feast, in which the niceties of deferring to others for their seniority in age or accomplishment were carried to great lengths. The official instructions for the ceremony state that the main objective was not to eat and drink, but Ming period writers report that this activity was by no means overlooked. One writer of the time describes the sight of the old greybeards sitting "ranked according to their years, ninety and eighty and seventy, bowing and deferring, greeting and responding ceremoniously all around the circle, offering and returning compliments with deportment, waiting for the reading of the law. There would be a solid wall of observers ringing them about, all of whom would be greatly moved by the scene, their feelings made harmonious thereby. When it was ended, these who were drunk would be aided to walk, and all would sing as they returned home. Old and young alike would be overcome with good feelings, the roadways would be filled with laughter and talk. The scholar gentry of the countryside would record it in commemorative verse."[15] The same writer quotes an early Ming proponent of the rite in an optimistic description of the effects of the ceremony: "If every rural community does it without exception, then the ancient proprieties will not be difficult to reinstate; even more easily can filial piety then be made to flourish and can the people's customs be made more magnanimous."[16] Could such ceremonies really transform a society, teach it to be courteous and orderly, improve morality and refine popular customs? If it is easy for us to be cynical about it, it was equally easy for a Chinese of the fourteenth century, reared in the Confucian tradition, to be sincere about it. Such were the ideal institutions of his world. They were ideals that could be realized, and institutions that appeared to be operative. In the face of the historical facts, it is difficult to say that they were not.

When Wei Kuan conducted the first Village Wine-Drinking Rite in 1373 he did it in the name of the whole prefecture, to serve as a model and inspiration to all localities within the six counties of the prefecture. He therefore went out of his way to invite the oldest and most respected men from all of the counties and towns. The most honored guest was an old man of one hundred and five who had been born under Sung rule, and thus was a living link with the revered dynasty under which such refined practices had last been regularly carried out. After the ceremony, when this old man left to return to his home in K'un-shan, a county seat town lying

---

[15] Yeh Sheng, *Shui-tung jih-chi,* abbreviated version in *Chi Lu Hui Pien,* ch. 141, p. 8b-9a

[16] *Op.cit.,* p. 9b. For a valuable discussion of the Rural Wine-Drinking Ceremony in later times, showing the extent to which it had lost its meaning and function by the nineteenth century and perhaps raising some doubts about the optimistic view of it given here, see K. C. Hsiao, *Rural China,* Seattle, 1960, pp. 208-20.

seventy-two *li* to the east, Wei in humble deference escorted him in person to the suburbs, respectfully bowing to him and taking formal leave of him there. This ceremony became a great occasion in the history of the region. His family later erected a hall in their home which they called the Hall of Generations of Longevity, to mark the noble event. A history written in the late Ming period sums up the results of Wei's promotion of these old rites, saying that "propriety and correct teaching flourished and spread abroad."[17] It also notes, in the next sentence, that Wei's "record in revenue collection was the best in the empire." The conjunction of these two evaluations of Wei Kuan's governorship became standard in all later histories. The two aspects of government were not unrelated, nor does it condemn Wei Kuan as a cynic, or as a tool of ruthless despotism, to point out his awareness of the interrelationships of this kind in his varied activities as governor.

Kao Ch'i in the years of Wei Kuan's governorship had just moved back closer to the city, and was beginning a more lively participation in the activities of his friends and in the life of the prefectural city. Wei Kuan's friendship, and his insistence on Kao's participation in the circle of associates who were to play so important a role in the rebuilding of government in Soochow, could not have been anticipated by Kao Ch'i two years earlier. Then he had fled from Nanking, with dignity and honor, but with revulsion and perhaps with fear in his own mind. Public life was forsworn in that flight. That renunciation cost him much, and forced a re-examination of all his long and dearly cherished conceptions. Negatively, he had found the ability to forswear all those goals which had been unquestioned through the difficult years when they were also unattainable. He had evolved a new conception of himself, and of his role as poet and man, and he

[17] *Ming-shan ts'ang*, "Ch'en-lin-chi," 1, p. 8a, bio. of Wei Kuan.

had in that process discovered that the not-unmixed values of the official career were not a *sine qua non* of the good life. Positively, he now discovered under Wei Kuan's forceful influence that there were important and gratifying responsibilities for him that demanded no compromises with officialdom, that left him still free, but that demanded a fuller realization of himself than was possible in the passive life of the poet-recluse. His lifelong urge to heroic accomplishment was re-emerging. The hero's role was being redefined, but in its new form it still was identifiable with that noble impulse which had spurred him to romantic views of himself in earlier years. Kao Ch'i was a man of action. The negative wisdom of his tradition could never satisfy him for long. Even after Nanking, which had proved to be the most profound blow to his certainties that he had yet experienced, he was still unable to remain in the idealized seclusion of the recluse for more than a year. Cress for breakfast and mallows for dinner, even picked from his own garden, became a dull diet.[18] The will to be active in his world could not be long suppressed. As the *Book of Changes* described the duties of the superior man, even under the image of Decay:

> . . . the superior man stirs up the people
> And strengthens their spirit.[19]

Kao Ch'i was still under compulsions, from his cultural tradition as from his own nature, to be a "superior man." Wei Kuan was showing the way to "strengthen the people's spirit." Kao Ch'i must participate in this heroic activity. The Confucian gentleman, even in voluntary retirement, could aid nobly in setting the world in order again, by striving valiantly to overcome decay. This role was natural to Kao Ch'i as soon as Wei Kuan helped him to recognize it in this new manifes-

[18] See p. 189. [19] See p. 93.

tation of itself. It was inevitable that he would be drawn into it.

Fictitious embroiderings of history concocted later say that Kao Ch'i was distressed by Wei Kuan's attentions, and would have preferred to remain aloof. If that is indeed the case, it is difficult to see why he would remain at hand, and in 1373 move again, this time into the city, if he had found the association unpleasant. He had detached himself in the past, and he certainly possessed the means to do so again if he had wished. These fanciful histories go farther, reporting that he had dreams in which a divine figure appeared to him holding a card bearing a warning in the form of a single character "Wei" or a character signifying the city of Soochow, telling him to avoid these as dangers to his life. These reports can be rejected as typical examples of the romancer's delight in omens and signs. Kao Ch'i gives no hint that he was in any way reluctant to join with Wei Kuan in friendship and in informal participation in his work. We can readily imagine, on the contrary, the satisfaction with which he discovered the correctness of his new role, and the conviction with which he joined in the great work of the new governor.

Kao Ch'i's admiration for Wei is expressed clearly in the three extant pieces of his writing—two essays and one long poem—that refer directly to him. In one of the essays he tells how Wei Kuan, in what must have been long and intimate conversations, had recounted to him the events of his mother's life and of his own youth, and had begged of Kao the favor that he compose a mortuary inscription for her grave, setting forth her noble character. Such a request honored Kao Ch'i, showing as it did the great esteem in which Wei Kuan held him. A man of Wei's stature might have been expected to request this favor from some man of his own generation or older, and of greater reputation and higher position than Kao Ch'i possessed. Kao accepted the commission with con-

ventional humility, but with more than conventional polite-
ness in noting that it was Wei's profound mastery of Confucian learning which has brought him high office under the
new dynasty.[20] Wei recognized Kao's superior qualities, and
Kao sincerely esteemed Wei. The single poem is also an outgrowth of intimate association and long conversations, in
some of which Wei had showed Kao some poems written to
him by an eminent poet-scholar named Lü Ssu-ch'eng almost
twenty years earlier.[21] Lü had served in the provincial government at Wuchang in Wei's native province of Hu-kuang in
the mid-1350's, when Wei was living in scholarly seclusion.
Thus they had come to know each other and had exchanged
poems. Lü was famous at the time for his integrity and courage. His poems in his own handwriting became treasured
souvenirs to Wei Kuan, who must have showed them to Kao
Ch'i with greatest pride, relating to his understanding friend
how he had known the fearless and upright Governor Lü in
the disorderly years of the Yuan dynasty's collapse.

Kao Ch'i's poem implies that Lü also had recognized Wei
Kuan's great qualities, and goes on to praise Wei as a man of
character and vast wisdom, whose rise to eminence under the
Ming is no more than just recognition of his worth. He praises
Wei in particular for his faithfulness in the virtue of friendship. His character, he says, was not defiled by the decaying
late Yuan conditions, and he manifests his high standards,
making others also aware of the nobility of Confucian morality.[22] The other essay written for Wei is a brief colophon
to the poems exchanged by Wei Kuan and Lü Ssu-ch'eng,
and it is in similar vein.[23] Kao Ch'i saw Wei Kuan as a great
man. He accepted him as his mentor in the rediscovery of the
Confucian scholar's high standards and inescapable responsi-

---

[20] FTC 5/15a-16a, "Wei Fu-jen . . . ming"
[21] For Lü's bio. see *Yuan Shih*, ch. 185, p. 1a-6a.
[22] CCSC 4/13a-14a   [23] FTC 4/11b-12a

bilities. This attitude restored some of the joy to Kao Ch'i's life. It gave life more purpose, after he thought he had been compelled to renounce purpose. It satisfied his Confucian conscience, by making his contentment with the present form of his life seem to stem from something more positive than escape.

An essay written at this time shows one form of Kao Ch'i's participation in Wei's work of governing. It is on a time-honored theme, setting forth one of the fundamental principles of Confucian political thought: the supremacy of agriculture over all other pursuits. Wei Kuan faced as one of his most serious problems the rehabilitation of the agricultural economy, not merely because agricultural taxes were the basis of the state's fiscal strength, but even more because agriculture was looked upon as the only productive activity, and as the natural occupation for man, assuring him economic and social security and a wholesome way of life, and keeping him from evil pursuits that detached him from his family and social responsibilities and contributed nothing to the public good. The disorders of the late Yuan period, the struggles among the rival rebellions, and the conquest of the region by the Ming armies had displaced large numbers of peasants. The cities were filled with idlers and troublemakers, and fields lay empty. Kao Ch'i's "Exhortation to Agricultural Pursuits" does not mention Wei Kuan by name, but clearly refers to his efforts to "promote the fundamental," which in Confucian parlance meant agriculture:

"Spring rains have spread their moisture through the earth; the farmers' work is about to commence. The Prefect has gone in person out into the countryside, exhorting all of you people to your duties with the truths of promoting the fundamental and enriching customs and practices. However it has not been his desire to draw widely on past affairs; rather he has chosen to deal with the present situation, expressing his instructions in straightforward fashion. You people must listen to him with respect! For the emperor establishes the laws to protect you people, and the people give of their strength to supply the needs of the emperor. This has been established principle, from antiquity to the present. Our august emperor has excised and done away with violence and disorder, and has established an era of Great Peace. He has gained for you people thereby your escape from the spears and the arrows, and lets you employ your plows and harrows, at peace again in your fields. And further, remembering the difficulties of the farm labors, he himself plows in the borrowed field,[24] and also calls elders from the people into audience at court, to admonish and instruct them. For he fears only that you people will be misdirected and idle, and drift into indolence, and fall into crime. How magnanimous is his virtue! Of late, persons bent on acquiring much land have failed to adhere to this intent, and have in some cases been unrestrained in their encroachment and oppression, causing some of you people to abandon your land. Although such situations arouse one's sympathy, lightly to give up one's fields and home, thereby to lack the wherewithal to nourish one's parents, and to fail to support the commonweal above with taxes,—where must the responsibility for such faults lie? Therefore it is desired that you people should tell these things to each other in your countryside, and send word to those who have gone away to return, and to those who still reside to be at peace. Repair your dikes and sea walls; dredge out your canals and ditches. When your strength is insufficient, help each other. When

[24] The allusion comes from the Mao preface to the ode "Tsai shu" in the section "Chou Sung" of the *Classic of Poetry*, where the term *chi-t'ien* is usually explained as a "borrowed field" in which the ruler symbolically plowed a furrow, symbolizing both his and the state's dependence on the "borrowed" labor of others, and the dignity of agriculture as the foundation of the state. The Ming founder observed this ancient rite from the beginning of his reign.

your tools are lacking, borrow each other's. Each of you, exhort each other to sow and to plant so that you can anticipate the harvests of autumn. Don't sit idly by losing this proper time, thereby to bring regrets upon yourselves later on. Still more important, do not engage in treachery, do not pursue the trivial,[25] do not be addicted to drink and gambling, do not engage in feuds and lawsuits, do not fail to be obedient to your fathers and elder brothers, do nothing which transgresses against your home villages. When each family provides its needs, and each person's wants are adequately met, when the proprieties are carried out and righteousness is maintained, so that we have nothing to blush for even as the region once transformed by T'ai-po,[26]—would that not be good to behold! Although our governor is old, he goes with regularity from place to place to examine local practices and to carry out rewards and punishments. You people must all urge each other to these exertions!"[27]

This earnest exhortation is written in elegant phrases and is full of learned allusions. The peasants to whom it was ostensibly directed could not read it, nor even understand it when it was read to them. Kao Ch'i of course knew that. His service in writing such a piece lay precisely in his being able to reach the elements in the population through whom the desired influence could be made to filter through to each local village. The landlord abuses of late Yuan are specifically referred to, and the new Ming's interest in expunging them was well known. Landlords are warned that abuses of tenancy will not be allowed, and are threatened with exposure and punishment, but quite indirectly. Nominally this message is directed to the simple, hard-working peasants, and its message is to be

25 I.e., commerce.
26 T'ai-po was a virtuous, semi-legendary prince of early Chou who governed the Wu region, exercising a transforming influence upon the region, hence setting a high standard for men of Wu.
27 FTC 5/5b

conveyed to them by the literate upper classes whose numbers include most landlords, but also all officials and scholars,
and who together are asked to supervise the revival of the
spirit and morale of a righteously governed, peaceful, and
prosperous countryside. Kao Ch'i himself was a small landlord of very modest means, with friends and neighbors who
were both richer and poorer than himself. Moreover, he was
a respected man of the community. Backed up by a vigorous
and honest governor, men of his kind could do much to clarify in people's minds the common goals and purposes, and to
create the attitudes prerequisite to good government. No one
could phrase an exhortation of this kind more elegantly or
more effectively; this was participation in government of an
immediate and significant kind. Spontaneously and voluntarily, and no doubt with deep satisfaction, Kao Ch'i threw
himself wholeheartedly into Wei Kuan's work, as friend and
honored associate.

Despite his contentment with his self-imposed role, and
the zest with which he engaged in the new activities, Kao
Ch'i's life did not become one of simple-minded bliss. He was
still a thoughtful poet, a man of moods and deep feelings,
sensitive to all the stimuli of his world, many of which drew
from him sympathy and sorrow, anger and irritation. Philo-
sophically he was convinced that fate circumscribed his life,
not, to be sure, mechanically dictating his daily affairs, but
limiting the range of his activities and the scope of his po-
tentialities for action. He was not destined to be a great
official; fate had confined him to the small but not displeas-
ing role that he now found for himself. His conception of fate
complemented his naturalistic apprehension of his universe
and the forces that ruled it. Look at a floating log, he wrote, a
piece of driftwood borne on an impersonal current that
neither gained nor lost by its presence there, and cared not

at all whether it was tossed up on some sandbar, or carried out into the endless sea, or burned as fuel by some fisherman or woodgatherer, or despoiled by boring insects. "Is this any different from the life of man," he asks, "whose fate is determined by Heaven?" Heaven, in his philosophical terminology, is coterminous with nature.

Continuing his analogy to floating logs drifting uncontrollably on the water, he wrote: "For men stand on this world as thick as the trees in a forest, and there are some who are noble, as kings and great lords, and some who are humble, as servants and slaves. Some are so rich that they have a thousand carriage teams, and some so poor that they cannot satisfy their hunger with a bowl of rice. Also there are persons who in one lifetime start out in adversity and end in prosperity, or who flourish at the beginning but are prostrate at the end. Shifts and changes are unpredictable, lacking reason and order and appearance of regularity. If not Heaven, then what causes it to be so? And though it causes it to be thus, yet it does not do so purposefully! Mixing and stirring like the primordial elements, producing whatever it will, it dispenses to men without telling them why, and men, nonetheless, are unable to do anything about it. Those who in these recent times have become discontented with Heaven and have strained mind and body to bring about their own desires, saddened by their losses and pleased by their gains, and to the end not realizing that their gains and losses were not brought about by themselves,—are they not indeed misled?"

Kao Ch'i had much earlier taken the name "driftwood" for his study, and had a tablet to hang over its door in the calligraphy of his friend from the history bureau in Nanking, the great scholar Sung Lien. This essay was written in 1373 on his move into Soochow from the southern suburb, when he again hung the tablet in his study, causing many of his guests to question its meaning. He concludes the essay, explaining: "That is the reason then why I was moved to thought by the drifting wood and chose it as the name for my study. For have you not observed water, and Heaven?[28] The one races on or comes to stop, forming its eddies and whirlpools according to the configuration of the earth; the other rides the movements of the vapors, and thus is moved about. These two are not even able to control themselves. How much less driftwood! How much less man! It is as if I were a log drifting in the space between Heaven and earth. Its goings and its stoppings, insofar as they are past, are now known. But insofar as they are yet to come, what have I to be sure of? I can simply be content with Heaven, and no more. But seeing that my driftwood self has now come to rest, and fortunately has escaped being burned as fuel or bored by insects, this study, then, can be the place where it sinks to rest. And since I have in this fashion replied to the queries, so I have written this for my study wall, to serve to spur me on also."[29]

This naturalistic, somewhat fatalistic conception of man and the world in which he lives permitted Kao Ch'i contentment with his solution to the basic problem of his role, left room for his Confucian optimism and the need for purposeful striving, and still allowed his moods of melancholy or of happiness. Melancholy, in particular, is the poet's province, and Kao Ch'i knew it well. He wrote many poems, preoccupied with the explanation of melancholy: where it comes from and how to dispel it. One of the best dates from the year following the return from Nanking.

"Where Does My Sadness Come From?"

Where does my sadness come from?
Comes autumn, and suddenly it too appears.

[28] Here, more particularly, the sky.
[29] FTC 1/9b-10b

I want to name it, but don't know what to say.
Engulfing me, it alone knows why.
This anxiety cannot be fear of growing old
Nor can I be desolate because of my humble status.
Since neither is it a sigh that I am poor
I suppose it is just the sadness of the wanderer.
Yet if one says that I long for the day of return
Then no, for I've not left my old home here.
And if one says I am to be despatched far away,
Then no, for I shall not be separated from my loved ones.
At first I compared it to the thickly spreading plants
Which receive the evening dews and do not wither.
Again I compare it with the mists and haze
Which the autumn wind cannot disperse.
It spreads darkly through my mind and my sight,
Quickly it comes, but how painfully slow is its leaving.
I ask you, how long to this day
Since this melancholy overtook me?
In the past I lived by the banks of the Western Stream
And then was happy in the curious forms of hills and
    streams.
Now I've returned to my eastern garden
And again I sigh, for the plants and trees are dying.
I live in idleness, and who cares what I do?
Only sadness is always in attendance with me.
Others in this world find their own joys,
They are not yet tired of games and feasting.
I alone have these care-filled thoughts
Pacing, ill at ease, helpless before it.[30]

That kind of engulfing melancholy and loneliness probably
affected Kao Ch'i less after he moved back closer to friends
and the life of the city in 1371. Later, though he still could
write sad poems, he was able to dispel his melancholy. There

[30] ccsc 4/17a-b

is a lyric poem in the *tz'u* form, written to the tune *Lo-chiang yüeh*, which shows the same awareness of melancholy, but a more satisfying resolution which seems to indicate the contentment of his last years. It is called "Chasing Away Sadness":

> You ask what melancholy is like?
> It is like something which must be swept aside unceasingly,
> Like wildly-spreading rootless filaments.
> It seems that when you would drive cares from your breast, you can never reach the end—
> They infuse themselves into the river clouds, and into the riverside trees.
> With nocturnal rain they are in your mind,
> With the autumn wind they are at your head and feet.
> Always they find the place and pursue you
> Even though gate within gate is closed against them.
> How many separating gates does it take to halt them?
> How difficult to adopt the lightheartedness of the maid of Lu.
> Chiang Yen and Yü Hsin
> Wrote their chill and desolate lines for nothing,
> Yet how they take unfair advantage of the wanderer for whom time drags idly.
> Indeed this mood is hard to shake off.
> You see the moon, and still you are sad,
> You look at the flowers, and yet you remain tormented.
> Only with wine are you at last without cares,
> So if more come, I'll not be afraid
> For that shows one how to chase them away again.[31]

If this song is in a lighthearted mood, with its joking references to the singing maid of Lu, who did not care whether she

[31] KHC 4a

sang sad songs or happy ones, and to the elaborately contrived melancholy poems of the early poets Chiang Yen and
Yü Hsin, it nonetheless shows that Kao Ch'i learned to take
his fits of depression in his stride, and this we see also in a
much more thoughtful poem called "On Drinking Alone."

A white sun sinks over the distant river,
The cold wind stirs the tops of the trees.
Feeling lonely and sad I bar the gate and lie down.
Birds of dusk suddenly have all gone away.
I am overcome with the sadness of one who has long
    been wandering,
Melancholy possesses me like a perilous disease.
I sit up, and call for a beaker of clear wine—
Alone I drink and alone go on to sing.
One cup and my cares are set aside
Another, and I know again the harmony of nature.
A few more, and I'm completely drunk—
Anxieties cast off, and cares now very few.
Thus it was that the wise men of old
Would drink, and give thought to nothing else.
I turn my head to smile at my wife.
After all, what do those cares really matter?[32]

That his wife shared in this contentment, and was an understanding companion when he shed his melancholy in this
fashion is borne out by another poem, called "Directed to
My Wife":

Instead of pursuing a livelihood I pursue only spring
And send word to my "mountain wife" not to scold and
    fuss.
I can let go all restraints, and be drunk on a cup of
    wine—
For it is by Imperial Grace that I can be an idler.[33]

[32] ccsc 6/16b   [33] ccys 13b

His "mountain wife" is a humorous way of referring to a rustic wife: Kao Ch'i's wife was from an elegant and cultured family; thus he could joke in this fashion, sharing the joke with her. The imperial grace permitted Kao Ch'i to be an idler, but no doubt his wife's understanding contributed much more than did the imperial grace to the certainty with which he followed his chosen course in these years. The contentment of his life, not deeply disturbed even by attacks of melancholy or by occasional moods of self-reproach, overflows his late poems.

The best of his last poems is a set of five written on one of the regular visits to the Eastern Cottage, the Village of Tall Trees, where his inherited family property was located, adjacent to his wife's family estates. These sum up so well the mood of his last years that they merit translating in full:

I.

My old village, and that little patch of land
Left to me by my forebears,
Relying on it I can be lazy—
I don't till, yet can sit and wait to be fed.
Frost and dew cover the cold countryside;
This is the season when the harvest is gathered.
I have come to collect my scanty incomes
And to take my rest, here on the eastern slope.
Although the harvest this year is not abundant
Still there's enough to keep me from hunger.
I know that a vast salary from high office carries its own
    difficulties;
If I can just retain this, what more should I demand?

II.

Koo-koo! cries the cock from over the courtyard.
The autumn harvest work has everything a bit out of
    order.

A few scattered elms cast their shade along my doorpath.
The scene grows dim; smoke rises from evening fires.
The man of the fields has a life of hard toil
Yet he spends his days with few cares and anxieties.
Especially with this harvest scene before him,
A measure of wine, and all is contentment.
Thus it is that the followers of Chang Chü and Chieh
  Ni[34]
Tilled their own fields, and would not abandon this.

III.

I'm but a commoner from this eastern slope
Who happened to go away and live in the prefectural
  city.
Returning now to rest again in my farm house
I am suddenly overcome by the mood of the countryside.
I am like a fish who has returned to his own deep pool
Overwhelmed again by the joy of life.
Before leaving again, I go to thank my old host's wife[35]
Next time I come I'll cook my own simple fare.
I am not a tax-collector, come to hasten payment;
When I knock at your gate you need feel no fright.

IV.

My court robes have long been laid aside;
I have the wan look of a thin hermit in the wilds.
I want to keep company with the rustics of the country-
  side,
Share in their pleasures, forgetting distinctions of "wise"
  and "foolish."
Since early morning I've been here at this river's edge
Singing aloud, wandering with slow steps.

[34] Two hermits of antiquity, rebuked by Confucius; see *Analects,*
xviii/6.
[35] His tenant's old wife, who has served as his hostess.

Chang Tu,[4] to report on the activities in Soochow. Chang Tu probably reported in private to the emperor that Wei and his associates were engaged in activities that went far beyond the routine responsibilities of office. Publicly, to document his charges, he reported that Wei Kuan had "raised again a base which had already been obliterated," that is, that he had built again on the foundations that the Ming forces had overcome and destroyed. This way of describing Wei Kuan's act of returning the government of the region to the same location from which Chang Shih-ch'eng had held forth made it sound sinister. Perhaps the zealous Chang Tu was eager to be of conspicuous service to the emperor, or perhaps he sincerely felt that the men of Soochow could not be so enthusiastic about a governor unless there was some seditious plot at work. The emperor would be readily convinced. Was not the restoration of a symbol that righteous Ming conquest had levelled to the dust more than just inappropriate? Was it not evidence of anti-Ming feeling? Was there any place where the possibility of anti-Ming feeling might be stronger than in Soochow?

In a rage, the emperor ordered the immediate arrest and execution of Wei Kuan. Normal procedures often were not followed in the early years of Ming. There was no pretense at investigation or collection of evidence, no automatic stay of execution until the fall review of death sentences and the winter execution of those whose cases had been reviewed unfavorably. When the wrath of the emperor was aroused, he acted swiftly to make an example of his victims. It was important to keep too much self-assurance from developing

[4] Two persons by the name of Chang Tu are known to early Ming history; neither is very important, and biographical data is scanty. Lu Yi, *Ping-yi man-chi*, ed. *Shuo K'u*, ts'e 29, p. 4b, identifies the one who impeached Wei Kuan as a native of Kwangtung Province. No information that sheds light on his motive in impeaching Wei and implicating Kao Ch'i and Wang Yi has been found.

among his spreading officialdom. Wei Kuan was the very model of the cultivated, able, self-assured scholar-bureaucrat. To strike him down suddenly and dramatically would strike terror in the hearts of the whole court and the bureaucracy in the provinces. Intimidation could keep them pliable and obedient. Perhaps this is the way that the unpredictable emperor reasoned, or perhaps he really felt that there was treason afoot in Soochow. The formal charge is all that is preserved; the emperor's own mind at that moment can only be speculated upon. The formal charge implied sedition, and for it Wei Kuan was put to death.

An insubordinate and seditious act, indicating an intent to revive Chang Shih-ch'eng's vanquished movement, also implied cohorts among the old Soochow population. Whether the emperor seriously believed that an underground movement existed, or merely seized upon the incident to intimidate the Soochow community and the whole bureaucracy by the frightening spectacle of swift and merciless counterattack, some Soochow heads were needed to fall along with Wei Kuan's. Kao Ch'i's poem congratulating Wei on the seditious act itself clearly implicated him. Wang Yi's poem about the inkstone found while dredging the river associated with Chang Shih-ch'eng's princely way of life was less direct evidence of implication, but it would serve. Both men were clamped into chains and carted off to Nanking, there to die suddenly and cruelly. Kao Ch'i's sentence was to be cut in half at the waist and thrown in a public square. Before the month was out, death sentences had been executed on all three.

Was there more to Kao Ch'i's inclusion than the mere chance of his having written the congratulatory poem? Informal histories, dating from soon thereafter and proliferating throughout later ages, hint that Kao Ch'i had angered the emperor during the two years he lived at Nanking and held office under him, by a poem that reportedly made sly and impolite references to the emperor himself.[5] This seems unlikely, for there is no reason to believe that the Ming founder would have waited to wreak his revenge, or would have concealed his awareness of the true meaning of the poem, had such an incident really occurred. On the other hand, that the Ming founder could be suspicious of Kao Ch'i personally is entirely reasonable. Both Kao Ch'i and Wang Yi were suspect for their refusal to accept high position and honor from the new dynasty and to serve it in official capacity. Beyond that, Chang Tu could have told the emperor about Kao Ch'i's well-known interest in military history and tactics, his associations with the plotters and schemers of Chang Shih-ch'eng's regime, and his leadership of a circle of heroic-minded bravos a decade earlier. Was not Kao Ch'i the possessor of dangerous expert knowledge and abilities? Was he not himself a frustrated schemer only lately and probably insincerely turned recluse? It could well have been his past which now betrayed him. This was a useful opportunity for the Ming founder to destroy a man who might prove dangerous. It was not long before the emperor was to rid his empire systematically of even those who had assisted his own rise to power, for, now that he had succeeded, the talents needed to plot uprisings and lead armies were no longer useful. It may well be that the thought in the emperor's mind was that here in one person were two of the kinds of

[5] This is suggested in Ku Chieh-kang, tr. by L. C. Goodrich, "A Study of the Literary Inquisition under the Ming," HJAS, Vol. 3, No. 3/4, Dec. 1938, pp. 254-311. Ku repeats a suggestion in Kao Chi's biography in the *Ming Shih* (ch. 285), that the emperor nourished an old resentment stemming from poems written when Kao Ch'i was in Nanking. There is no evidence of any kind for this, and it seems to be a totally unnecessary speculation. Shen Chien-shih in his article "Kao Ch'i," in *Chung-kuo Wen-hsüeh-shih Lun-chi* (T'ai-pei, 1958, vol. 3, pp. 845-852) quotes the poems in question and gives the traditional interpretation, without, however, citing any evidence for this interpretation of them.

enemy he hated and feared—Kao Ch'i probably appeared to him as at once an arrogant and slyly contemptuous literary man, and a potential technical advisor to some future military movement against his new dynasty. Why not get rid of him?

Before another month was out, the emperor reviewed the situation more calmly and decided that he had made a great mistake about Wei Kuan. He discovered that he had murdered one of his most able and devoted servants. He made public admission of his error, and ordered an honorable funeral and burial for him at state expense. His family were recompensed. Imperial princes who had been tutored by him publicly honored his memory. It was one of the very few instances of the Ming founder's ever admitting his error. The implication of this admission was to remove the stain of crime from Kao Ch'i's and Wang Yi's memories also, but the emperor made no public statements on this subject and the matter remained ambiguous and uncertain. Kao's family recovered his corpse and took it home for simple burial. His friends wrote grieved poems mourning his passing. His nephew, some thirty years later, collected his poems and quietly prepared them for publication. In Soochow people remembered him, local histories always mentioning him with pride and quoting his poems about places of local historical interest and scenic beauty. Even the gazetteer prepared and published only five years after his death makes discreet use of his poetry, though it does not dare include a biographical notice. Later compilers of anthologies never failed to include him, usually to praise him as the best of the early Ming poets, and often to mourn his undeserved death.

Kao Ch'i's life, like his body, was severed at its mid-point in violent punishment for crimes admittedly non-existent. His career as a poet, like the literary life of his brilliant circle and his promising generation, was snuffed out meaninglessly.

They all died soon thereafter, many of them as had Kao Ch'i. Hsü Pen, who had found a career as a minor local administrative official, was involved in suspected errors and crimes, and sentenced to die. He starved himself in prison in 1376 while awaiting execution. Chang Yü too had a varied career in the petty bureaucracy, and was forced to commit suicide in 1373, knowing that flight from the angry emperor was impossible. Yang Chi committed some minor infraction for which he was sentenced to punishment by hard labor, and died very quickly from hardship, as was intended. Wang Hsing and his son, because they knew much about military theory, were involved in the famous treason charges against a prominent minister in 1390, and were among the thousands who died with their whole clans. Many others of Kao Ch'i's early friends also ran afoul of the tyrant emperor and died violent deaths before his reign was out in 1398. With them died the genius of early Ming poetry. The dismal years of early Ming terror had begun, to last for three decades, and to stultify the creative promise of the remarkable generation that saw the founding of the dynasty. Even had Kao Ch'i not died at this time and in this fashion, the atmosphere of the new Ming world increasingly would have troubled him, and sorely tried the contentment that he had achieved such a short time ago.

All of his friends wrote poems or essays expressing their grief on hearing of his death. Of them all, Chang Yü wrote the half-dozen most moving poems. He had come back to Soochow in the first year of Wei Kuan's governorship, and like Kao Ch'i was associated with him in that work, thus also with Kao Ch'i to the end. In one of these poems he speaks of sitting up in bed, sleepless through the night, pondering the matter as he observes the moon and the stars in the night sky. Their regular and certain movement, he says, gives one the assurance of Heaven's stability and correctness—until one looks at human affairs, for "In the affairs of men there are great errors; the ways of Heaven are in truth vague and unfathomable." A set of three poems written by Chang Yü on receipt of the word of Kao Ch'i's death best expresses the loss which his friends felt, together with their confidence in his enduring achievement as a poet:

I.

I sit before the lamp holding the volume, as two lines of
    tears flow.
My wife is startled by the sight,—how can she under-
    stand?
My old friend of the days by the river's edge is now dead.
In my desk I search for the poems he sent to me.

II.

When the news first came, I believed and yet I doubted
    it.
Now that he is gone, with whom can one discuss poetry?
His little son and young daughters are still too small to
    understand.
To whom shall his thousand poems in manuscript be en-
    trusted?

III.

What in the end came of his lifelong noble spirit?
Neither the emolument of office, nor land,—he is the
    most to be pitied.[6]
But he can be sure of fame that is imperishable
Like that of the Han lyricists, and the poets of the
    Golden Age of T'ang.[7]

[6] Thinking of the plight of his widow and children.
[7] ccscc, sppy ed., appendix to *ts'e* 6, p. 3b

Thus he expressed Kao Ch'i's friends' faith in a man's noble spirit, and in poetry, nor was their faith unjustified. But Kao Ch'i's death, and eventually theirs as well, were a great loss to poetry and to China. Although it occurred at a time of stirring national revival, when the state was successfully organizing all the energies of the people again for vast constructive purposes, Kao Ch'i's death symbolizes the concurrent destruction of much that was good in the life of his civilization.

CHAPTER TEN

EPILOGUE

LITERARY CRITICISM in the Ming period, although of greatest vitality and of interest as an aspect of the history of Chinese thought, does not help us much in appraising the poets of the time. Particularly after the mid-fifteenth century, the critics were increasingly concerned with the definition of what had made poetry great in the first half of the eighth century, the so-called "Golden Age" of T'ang poetry. As this standard was ever more narrowly defined, by the dominant archaists on the one hand, or ever more hotly denied, by the minority "romanticists" on the other, the achievements of a poet like Kao Ch'i tended to be obscured. For Kao Ch'i enjoyed re-creating the styles of the past, and did so with great skill; hence he was not appreciated by the romanticists, who eschewed all imitative modelling on the past. But Kao Ch'i did not confine himself to imitating rigidly the few masters of the Golden Age, so he was not highly regarded by the archaists. Thus, like most later poets, he fell between two highly artificial and unrealistic standards, and was not accorded the attention that his true stature as a poet warranted. Most Ming and early Ch'ing anthologies reflect one or the other of these views. Although they acknowledge that he was the great poet of his age, they usually prefer to say little about him.

By the eighteenth century these attitudes had largely become outmoded, and Kao Ch'i's poetry, along with that of some of his contemporaries, enjoyed considerable revival of popularity. Chao Yi (1727-1814), distinguished scholar and historian, and one of the fine poets of his own time, wrote perhaps the best appreciation of Kao Ch'i that exists in traditional literary criticism. He notes Kao Ch'i's uncanny skill in re-creating the styles of the greatest poets of the past, including Tu Fu, Han Yü, Po Chü-yi, Li Shang-yin, and Wen T'ing-yün of the T'ang dynasty, and Huang T'ing-chien of the Sung. Above all, he claims, some of the best of Kao Ch'i's poems in the expansive and heroic modes could be put into the collected works of Li Po and pass as poems from the great T'ang master's hand. Chao Yi cites convincing examples for each of these claims. However, this does not mean that Kao Ch'i was merely a clever imitator. Rigid and lifeless imitation became the downfall of later Ming poetry; in contrast, he sees Kao's ability to draw inspiration from the past as evidence of poetic genius in its most creative and scintillating workings. Excerpts from Chao Yi's evaluation of Kao Ch'i as a poet form a fitting epilogue to the account of his life:

"By the last years of the Southern Sung, poetry (shih) had reached the extremes of over-refinement and superficiality. It was because of this that the poets of the Yuan and Ming dynasties turned aside, and modelled themselves on the T'ang. And this represented simply the natural workings of the cyclic, repetitious course of styles. In the late Yuan and early Ming period, Yang Wei-chen was the dominant figure, but in his startling eccentricities he imitated Li Ho, while in bewitching seductiveness he imitated Wen T'ing-yün and Li Shang-yin. Thereby he established his own style, to be sure, but in the end it failed to open a strong and vigorous new course to poetry. Even at that time Wang Yi had already labelled him the "devil of literature,"[1] and it was not likely

[1] Wang Yi's characterization of Yang Wei-chen (1296-1370) has been discussed above, in Chapter Seven. Chao Yi here credits Kao Ch'i with having effected a turning point in the development of poetry, away from the extreme style of Yang Wei-chen to a more substantial course of development represented by his eclectic harking back to the best in

that subsequent poets would take him as their guide and model. Kao Ch'i alone possessed surpassing talent, and he wrote poetry of resonant and brilliant tonality;[2] he modelled himself chiefly upon the poets of T'ang, and yet he produced his own new conceptions. Once he started to write, there came into being a vast and resplendent atmosphere, significant for the literary fortunes of the whole Ming dynasty. Critics generally have called him the premier poet of the beginning of the dynasty, and this is in truth no empty statement. . . ."

After discussing Kao Ch'i's versatility in mastering the styles of all ages, Chao Yi sums up his achievement:

"Thus he was able to model himself on the T'ang and still not be limited by T'ang. Later on, those who took the T'ang as their model, such as Li Meng-yang and Ho Ching-ming,[3] merely accorded with the external appearance of T'ang in copying its prosodic forms; in spirit and principle they fell far short. . . .

"But Kao Ch'i can be compared with a sky half-covered with red sunset clouds, reflecting light on the world below from that day to this, a sight ever fresh and new. This is because his native powers were beyond those of all others. . . .

"What a pity that at the age of only thirty-eight he was suddenly struck down and destroyed. He was thereby pre-

---

various earlier ages. Whether Kao Ch'i effected this change or merely embodied it most successfully for his age is a point that might be argued.

[2] *Yin chieh* or "syllabic tonality" is actually a technical term of prosody, but here it apparently is used in a rather general sense, warranting the translation given. For a more technical discussion of it see: Kuo Shao-yü, "*Lun Chung-kuo wen-hsüeh chung ti yin-chieh wen-t'i*" ("On the problem of syllabic tonality in Chinese literature") in *K'ai-ming shu-tien erh-shih chou-nien chi-nien-wen chi* (anthology commemorating the twentieth anniversary of the K'ai-ming Book Company, Shanghai, 1947).

[3] Li (1472-1529) and Ho (1483-1521) were leaders of the archaistic movement in later Ming poetry.

vented from ranging back and forth through the limits of development, to become one of the supreme masters. And yet, throughout the entire Ming dynasty, there was never another poet who could come up to him."[4]

[4] From Chao Yi, *Ou-pei shih-hua*, ch. 8. The translated portions come from the first item under the heading *"Kao Ch'ing-ch'iu shih."* See Chao's biography by Tu Lien-che in Hummel, *Eminent Men of the Ch'ing Period*, pp. 75-76.

BIBLIOGRAPHICAL NOTE

THROUGHOUT, references to Kao Ch'i's works are to the excellent *Ssu-pu-pei-yao* edition of the Chung-hua Book Company (Shanghai, no date), *Ch'ing-ch'iu shih-chi chu*, in six *ts'e*, which is a carefully edited reprinting of the annotated edition of the eighteenth-century scholar Chin T'an. Chin's good *Chronological Record* (*nien p'u*) of Kao Ch'i and other supplementary materials, such as prefaces to various editions of his works, eulogies, biographical accounts, and the like, are also included there. This edition of Kao Ch'i's works is referred to by the abbreviation CCSCC, and its various subdivisions are referred to as follows: CCSC for the chief compilation of the poetry in eighteen *chüan* (*Ch'ing-ch'iu shih-chi*); CCYS for the supplementary compilation (*Ch'ing-ch'iu yi-shih*); KHC for his short collection of *tz'u* lyrics (*K'ou hsüan chi*); FTC for the prose writings (*Fu tsao chi*).

Specialists in the history of China's fourteenth century will, it is hoped, recognize that the view of early Ming history presented here is neither a stereotyped one, nor one lacking foundation in fact. Wherever the facts are questionable, and at the same time highly relevant to the subject matter of this book, the view presented here has been documented, or at least the source of the facts has been indicated.

The fall of the Yuan and the first decades of the Ming, especially the contending rebellions of the period that are discussed in Chapter One, and that form the background of most of Kao Ch'i's life, constitute one of the most fascinating and at the same time one of the most complex periods in

* 249 *

Chinese history. The author has been for some years engaged in a study of that period, and has drawn on the results of that study in a general way. More specific and detailed documentation of all of the events of the period alluded to in this book would be out of place for two reasons. Most of it would involve things that are "common knowledge" among persons familiar with the history of the period. And, in any event, this history forms only the background, not the subject-matter, of this story.

A list of the sources which the author has found most useful in writing this book is appended here. The list is very selective, including items that the author has had clearly in mind while writing this book, but that in many cases have not been specifically cited. Where the item is included in Wolfgang Franke's *Sources for the History of the Ming Dynasty*, Chengtu, 1948, the Franke number is given in brackets, and further identification and comment are usually omitted.

The Veritable Record of the Reign of the Emperor T'ai-tsu (*T'ai-tsu kao-huang-ti shih-lu*). Compiled 1418. References are to the photolithographic edition, Nanking, 1940; the Princeton Library's late Ming (?) *ms* lacks the chapters relevant to Kao Ch'i's lifetime. [1]

Ming-shan ts'ang, by Ho Ch'iao-yuan. Preface date 1640. [16]

Kuo-ch'ao hsien-cheng-lu, by Chiao Hung. 1594. (Library of Congress microfilm.) [32]

Hsü ts'ang-shu, by Li Chih. 1611. [39]

Ch'i-hsiu lei-kao, by Lang Ying. Mid-sixteenth century. [45]

Huang-ch'ao pen-chi. [61] (Also known as *Ming pen-chi*, by Yü Pen; edition of Wang Ch'ung-wu, Shanghai, 1947.)

Keng-shen wai-shih, by Ch'üan Heng. Ca. 1370. [64]

P'ing Wu lu, by Wu K'uan. Late fifteenth century. Edition *Chi-lu hui-pien*. [65]

P'ing Han lu, by T'ung Ch'eng-hsü. Mid sixteenth century. Edition *Chi-lu hui-pien.* [66]

Ming shih. Compiled by imperial commission, 1679-1739. [257]

Ming-shih chi-shih-pen-mo, by Ku Ying-t'ai. 1658. [259]

Ming shu, by Fu Wei-lin. Mid-seventeenth century. [260]

Ming-shih chi-shih, by Ch'en T'ien. 1897. [272]

Ts'ao-mu-tzu, by Yeh Tzu-ch'i. A collection of philosophical comments and historical notes and sketches by a contemporary of Kao Ch'i.

Cho keng lu, by T'ao Tsung-i. 1366. An invaluable collection of notes and sketches and eyewitness accounts of the events of the end of the Yuan.

Chin-ling fan-ch'a chih, by Ko Yin-liang. Preface dated 1627; reprint, 1936. A large compilation in gazetteer form on the history of Nanking's Buddhist temples, emphasizing the Yuan and Ming periods.

(Hung-wu) Su-chou-fu chih. 1379. (Library of Congress microfilm) Gazetteer of the prefecture of Soochow, compiled and printed five years after Kao Ch'i's death. It is a very rich source for the history of the region.

Ch'ün-hsiung shih-lüeh, by Ch'ien Ch'ien-yi. Mid-seventeenth century. A compilation of historical materials arranged so as to form a narrative account of each of the rebellions of the late Yuan period. (In the *Shih-yüan ts'ung-shu*)

Wu-wang Chang Shih-ch'eng tsai-chi, by Chih Wei-ch'eng et al. 1932. An old-style and rather uncritical chronological record of the Chang Shih-ch'eng rebellion, with several appendices containing biographies and other material. It is a useful if not very thoroughgoing attempt to see the history of the period from a non-Ming point of view.

Chu Yuan-chang chuan, by Wu Han. 1948. A very effective

biography of the founder of the Ming dynasty by a leading modern scholar specializing in the period.

Articles by recent scholars cannot be listed separately. The specialized studies of Wang Ch'ung-wu and Wu Han have been particularly useful, but a full listing of the articles by Chinese, Japanese, and Western scholars would be inappropriate in a volume of this nature.